THE ORIGINAL JESUS

Dr Elmar R. Gruber holds a PhD in psychology. His main work is in the field of consciousness research. A scientific adviser to German television and radio, he is also the author of several books and has had over sixty articles published in major scientific journals. He worked with Holger Kersten as co-author of the controversial bestseller, *The Jesus Conspiracy*.

Holger Kersten studied theology and pedagogics at Freiburg University, Germany. An author specializing in religious history, his previous titles include *The Jesus Conspiracy* (with Elmar R. Gruber) and *Jesus Lived in India*.

By the same authors

The Jesus Conspiracy

By Holger Kersten

Jesus Lived in India

The Original Jesus

THE BUDDHIST SOURCES OF CHRISTIANITY

Elmar R. Gruber and Holger Kersten

ELEMENT

Shaftesbury, Dorset ● Rockport, Massachusetts
Brisbane, Queensland

© Langen Müller, F.A. Herbig Verlagsbuchhandlung GmbH, Munich 1995
English translation © Element Books Limited 1995

First published in Great Britain in 1995 by
Element Books Limited
Shaftesbury, Dorset SP7 8BP

Published in the USA in 1995 by
Element Books, Inc.
PO Box 830, Rockport, MA 01966

Published in Australia in 1995 by
Element Books Limited for
Jacaranda Wiley Limited
33 Park Road, Milton, Brisbane 4064

Reprinted 1995
First paperback edition 1996

Cover design by Max Fairbrother
Designed by Roger Lightfoot
Typeset by Footnote Graphics, Warminster, Wiltshire
Printed and bound in Great Britain by
Biddles Limited, Guildford and King's Lynn

British Library Cataloguing in Publication
data available

Library of Congress Cataloging in Publication Data
Gruber, Elmar, 1955-
(Ur-Jesus. English)
The original Jesus: the Buddhist sources of Christianity /
Elmar R. Gruber and Holger Kersten.
Translation of: Der Ur-Jesus.
Includes bibliographical references and index.
1. Jesus Christ–Buddhist interpretations.
2. Christianity–Origin.
I. Kersten. Holger. II. Title.
BT205.G7413 1995
232.9–dc20 94-41193

ISBN 1–85230–835–4

Contents

Acknowledgements

Many people helped us in the course of our investigations, offering valuable support. We would particularly like to thank Prof. Ahmad Hasan Dani, Prof. Florentino Garcia-Martinez, Prof. Hans-Joachim Klimkeit, Dr Hans Wolfgang Schumann, Dr Günther Schwarz, the Centre Sèvres in Paris, and the manuscript section at Leipzig University library. Thomas Gotterbarm made available his findings on parallels between Christian and Buddhist trinities, as well as new research on the history of vedic Aryans, the Jews of Cochin and the legend of Thomas from his manuscript on cultural traditions and spiritual life in modern India. Special thanks go to Elmar R. Gruber's wife, Dagmar, for her untiring advice and constructive ideas, furthering the manuscript's progress.

Picture Credits

A. H. Dani 26, 27
E. R. Gruber 2–5, 8, 11–16, 21–25, 30, 31, 33–36
H. Kersten 17–20, 32
H. W. Schumann 1, 6, 7, 28
Musée Borély 9, 10
F. Petrie 29

The *Nazarene Institute* has now been established at Freiburg so as to better co-ordinate and more meaningfully activate future research on the historical Jesus and his Buddhist-influenced teachings, and also to make findings accessible to those interested. Readers who would like more information about this can write to the following address:
Die Gesellschaft der Nazarener
c/o Holger Kersten
Postfach 961
79009 Freiburg
Germany

Preface

The churches largely dismiss the interest in Buddhism at present being shown in the West as a modish religious trend onto which supposedly unfulfilled longings are projected. The Church is blind to what profoundly moves spiritual seekers. The truth is that the orientation towards Buddhism reveals discontent with the Christian tradition and makes apparent a feeling that the Buddhist religion is more authentic.

The Jesus mediated to us by the Church is not the true Jesus. That is an artificial construction, assembled from true and false fragments of his biography, from authentic and invalid statements, and based on a great deal of inventiveness on the part of Christian writers. When Christianity maintains that it is based on Jesus, the Jesus involved is merely a literary creation. The real, historical Jesus and his concerns are hidden, like a portrait beneath layers of varnish added by 2000 years of church history. If we remove that varnish carefully, like a restorer, without destroying the precious original, the primary colours gradually become apparent. These colours are different from those the Christian churches have taught us to see.

Janwillem van de Wetering, the Dutch writer who spent a long time in a Japanese monastery, tells how a Zen Buddhist monk read the Sermon on the Mount to his abbot, a man who had not learned to read and write, and had never heard of Christianity. The Zen master was profoundly impressed. After the monk had finished reading, the master remained silent for a long time. At last he said: 'I don't know who wrote that, but whoever it was was either a Buddha or a Bodhisattva. What you read to me is the essence of all I try to impart to the monks here.'

For people who know Buddhism, the condensed version of Jesus's views as primarily presented in the Sermon on the Mount directly calls to mind an inner relationship with the Buddha's teachings. The parallels between Buddhist thought and certain New Testament stories – Jesus's parables and his sayings – are not, however, a new discovery. They attracted the attention of alert scholars as early as the start of the nineteenth century. People did not really know what to think of it, but the correspondences were so striking in many respects that more and more became convinced that Christianity had been directly influenced by Buddhism.

Max Müller, the celebrated German Indologist, showed in his highly scholarly studies how Indian fables and other narratives came to the West, retaining their vitality up to the present day. He also demonstrated Indian influences in the Old Testament, as in the name of the peacock. However, this ardent Christian, driven by missionary zeal, for years categorically excluded any possibility of Christianity having been influenced by India. There are many such cases. They show what prejudices impede research into the origins of Christianity, and demonstrate the degree to which our Christian, Western upbringing obstructs, even nips in the bud, any objective investigation of the person of Jesus, his divine descent and his teaching. Is it impossible to view Jesus as simply a human being and perhaps to expose many accounts in the Gospels as embellishments and fantasy? Is it sacrilege to establish the dependence of crucial Christian teachings on another religion? Throughout his life Max Müller sought in vain for historical channels through which Christianity might have been influenced by India. Towards the end of his days even this obstinate sceptic was left with no alternative but to concede such an influence – but with a number of reservations.

Today the evidence is overwhelming. In John's Gospel, for instance, Buddhist ideas occur in sentence after sentence. It is permeated with these ideas to such an extent that theologian J. Edgar Bruns felt impelled to write an entire book about the subject, entitled *The Christian Buddhism of St John* – an astonishing finding for Christians, and even more astonishing for the Church. Astonishment soon becomes amazement when one encounters direct borrowings. For example, the Buddha said: 'Whosoever sees the Dharma, sees me.' Christ in the Gospel according to John says: 'He that seeth me seeth him that sent me' (John 12:45). The Dharma is the great cosmic law underlying our world, corresponding to the concept of the Word, the Logos, in the Gospel which begins by declaring, 'The Word was God.'

As we have endeavoured to reach the foundations of Buddhist teaching in the New Testament, we inevitably had to ask the crucial question of Jesus: 'And what do you think about religion?'

Our exciting voyage of discovery through the labyrinth of intellectual history reveals that Buddhist elements in the New Testament are not the result of chance. They were first disseminated by Jesus himself, so that it can be provocatively stated: Jesus was not a Christian. He was a Buddhist!

However, allow us to proceed slowly, step by step making the unimaginable conceivable, the incomprehensible understandable. Allow us to peel away the layers of later mythology, theology, poetry and fabricated enhancement from the image of Jesus, seeing what remains of his person and his teachings. Allow us to uncover who the original Jesus was.

Part I

INDIA AND THE WEST

Jesus, the Great Mystery

Hardly any other theme has caused such a stir in the Western world as the person of 'Jesus of Nazareth'; hardly any other theme has led to the writing of so many books, or such animated and passionate discussions. And yet the personality of the historical Jesus is veiled in profound darkness. For a millennium and a half there were only accounts depicting Jesus in accordance with official Church theology, written with the objective of strengthening Christians' faith or inducing other people to turn to Christianity. More recently critical thinkers have appeared in Europe, and in the seventeenth and eighteenth centuries, during the Enlightenment, there appeared the first writings which doubted whether 'Jesus of Nazareth' really existed. Such views mainly derived from France and such anti-Catholic Enlightenment philosophers as Voltaire and Holbach. Later even Goethe entered into this discussion, doubting whether Jesus had actually established the Christian religion. In Goethe's opinion, Jesus's disciples had themselves devised the teachings and attributed them to the Nazarene.

During the nineteenth century the New Testament was subjected to scholarly investigation for the first time. It was the beginning of systematic research into the life of Jesus, with German Protestant theology heading the field. The Protestant church accused the Catholic faith of being a heathen falsification of Christianity, and endeavoured to undermine its viewpoint by seeking proof that Jesus had sought something different from what the Catholic church had made out of his teachings. The elucidation of the historic figure of 'Jesus of Nazareth' was intended to serve as a starting point. In 1835 David Friedrich Strauss published his influential book *The Life of Jesus (Das Leben Jesu)*. Armed with uncompromisingly critical rational views, he bluntly rejected the historical factuality of the Gospels. For Strauss they were nothing but legends and pious stories about the figure of Jesus, inspired by the Old Testament. Such opposition went further at the mid-nineteenth century. Bruno Bauer completely banned the figure of Jesus from historical research, simply declaring that the central figure in the New Testament

3

was a mythical invention. Jesus and Paul were said to be nothing but literary fictions; and Christianity was seen as having been created by a fanatical group which concocted the faith around those two invented figures out of Jewish, Greek, and Roman religious traditions.

The best-known researcher in this sphere, Albert Schweizer, a doctor and theologian, was not discouraged by such judgements. For him carrying out research into the life of Jesus was the most tremendous enterprise that religious awareness ever ventured upon. Today we can scarcely appreciate any longer what intellectual barriers had to be surmounted in undertaking a historical consideration of the life of Jesus. Albert Schweizer viewed research into the life of Jesus as 'a school of veracity for the Church', a painful and aggressive struggle for truth.

Today there are well over 80,000 monographs on Jesus, but their impact in terms of illuminating the historical figure is modest in the extreme. Who was Jesus? When was he born? What did he look like? When was he crucified? When, how, and where did he die? Finding answers to those questions soon turned out to be an insoluble problem. In the books written during the first two centuries AD there is hardly any mention of Jesus as a real human being. The later sources are almost exclusively theological writings, which take for granted a belief in Jesus Christ as the Messiah and Son of God. So truly impartial written testimony is practically non-existent, and scholarship is thus not in a position, even today, to say in which year Jesus was born. At issue are the years between 4 and 7 BC since it is known for certain that Jesus was born while Herod was in power (37–4 BC). Hardly any attention is paid in the canonical Gospels to Jesus's childhood and youth, a phase of life of such importance for the formation of a person's character. Even in the accounts of the brief period of his public impact there is only very sparse biographical information about him. It seems as if he was almost completely unknown to the historians of his time, or at least not worth mentioning. How is it possible that they paid no attention to the amazing miracles and extraordinary events recorded in the Gospels?

Around fifty works by Jesus's contemporary Philo Judaeus (20 BC–50 AD) survive, containing much interesting material about history, philosophy and religion, but nowhere in his writings does he mention Jesus, despite reporting extensively on Pilate. We must wait until the second century before hearing of Jesus from an independent, non-Christian source. In his *Annals* (*c.* 117/119 AD), Tacitus, the Roman historian, tells of the 'superstitious sect' of Christians, deriving their name from a certain Christ said to have been executed under Pontius, Governor during the time of the Emperor Tiberius. That account originated about eighty or ninety years after the cruci-fixion, and is based on stories circulating during the second century. In a letter to the Emperor Trajan dating from 110 AD, Pliny the Younger (62–113 AD) writes about Christians in Bithynia, but makes no mention of the founder of their sect. As Emperor Hadrian's head of chancellery, Suetonius (70–140 AD) had access to the state archives and made use of the documents stored there for registering important events during the reigns of previous Emperors. Of the rule of Claudius (41–54 AD) he reported that the Emperor had driven the Jews out of Rome because they caused trouble under the in-fluence of a certain 'Chrestos'. That at least shows there were already adherents of the Christian religion in Rome around 50 AD.

The Jewish historian Joseph ben Mathias (37–*c.* 100 AD), who became a Roman citizen and adopted the name Flavius Josephus, published his *Jewish Antiquities* around 93 AD as a kind of history of the world from the Creation to the beginning of Emperor Nero's reign, intended to acquaint Gentile readers with the history of his race. He gives a detailed account of politics and society at the time of Jesus, and refers to John the Baptist, Herod and Pilate. When describing the stoning of a man called James, he mentions Jesus 'whom people call Christ' as his brother.

The eighteenth book of the *Antiquities* says: 'At this time there lived Jesus, a wise man – if one can call him a human being. He did mighty deeds, was a teacher of men who joyously accepted truth, and won over many Jews and also Greeks. He was the Christ . . .' However, this celebrated *Testimonium Flavianum* (*The Testimony of Flavius*), which characterizes Jesus as a man of miracles and a successful teacher, was certainly not written by Josephus. There was great interest in Josephus during late antiquity, and Christian theologians needed a precise chron-icler of the times like him to have written something about Jesus. The *Testimonium Flavianum* was thus produced in the third century as a declaration contrary to Josephus's recorded opinions as a Jew. The references to Jesus being Christ and more than human are clear-cut indications of the exceptionally crude work of a Church writer. Josephus could not have produced it since the theologian Origen was convinced that he did not believe Jesus was the Christ.

We are faced here with an example of how the historian's work is made difficult. Writers working for the Christian church first came forward in the first centuries of the new millennium as modifiers and distorters of great works from the past. The few copies of such works first fell into the hands of scholarly theologians, who then disseminated their versions. The significance of the propaganda-serving popularization of an idea was all too well known even at that time. One favoured method was to gain reputable heathen or non-Church authors as posthumous witnesses to the Christian cause. Writings by historians enjoying a high reputation for their accurate descriptions of events were particularly utilized for that purpose. They were eminently suitable as 'neutral' witnesses to the historical truth of a religious message. The replicas produced by eager copyists and sent out all over the world were no longer the originals but rather disguised promotional literature – the equivalent of pamphlets which were much more effective among unbelievers and the inconstant (but for the most part educated) than undisguised propaganda. Modern textual criticism is now gradually revealing the presence of insertions which do not accord with an author's style, period, circumstances or thinking, thus showing them to be misrepresentations by the Church.

Justus of Tiberias, a Jewish writer who was a contemporary of Josephus, lived at Tiberias near Capernaum, where Jesus was often said to have stayed. Justus wrote a history that began with Moses and extended to his own times, but not once did he mention Jesus. From Celsus, an embittered anti-Christian, we learn a few supposed facts, but they are hardly flattering to the 'sublime' Christ. The collection of writings that is the New Testament thus initially remained the only source for historical research.

The New Testament contains four Gospels, named after Matthew, Mark, Luke and John. They constitute an arbitrary selection from a much greater number of writings that were in use among the various early Christian communities before the canon was established. During the early period of the Christian movement the multitude of often contradictory texts was so great that the young Church saw only one way of preserving the faith from splitting up into numerous sects: assembling a canon of writings and destroying rejected apocryphal (hidden) texts. Papias of Hierapolis, who is counted among the Apostolic Fathers, attempted to do that in about 110 AD, but failed because of the resistance of individual communities. The first grouping of Gospels in Syrian or Greek, known as the *Diatesseron* (Greek for 'through four'), which was assembled around 170 AD by Tatian, also failed to achieve general acceptance. However, at the end of the second century Bishop Irenaeus of Lyon succeeded in canonizing the four Gospels which have been accepted ever since by instituting as criterion of authenticity the claim that each of them derived from one of Jesus's disciples. That was a problematic assumption even at the time since it was not – and is still not – possible to ascertain when and how those Gospels came into being. Neither original manuscripts nor early references to such manuscripts existed. Even approximate dating is uncertain. Research into the origins of the Gospel according to Mark indicates a time shortly after 70 AD, some twenty years before Matthew and Luke. The text of John was only produced at the beginning of the second century. Between two and three generations thus passed between the crucifixion of Jesus around the year 30 and the first written accounts of his work.

Three of the Gospels are very similar – Matthew, Mark and Luke – with Matthew and Luke deriving much of their text from Mark. In addition, Matthew and Luke made use of a collection of Jesus's sayings which was not known to Mark. This text is known as the Sayings Source, and will be referred to in detail at a later stage. The authors of the first three Gospels obviously pursued different intentions. The Gospel according to Matthew presents Jesus as the consummation of Mosaic religion and as the Messiah announced by the prophets. Luke is mainly directed towards Greeks and Romans, and depicts Jesus not as a national messiah but rather as saviour of the world. The text of Luke does not comprise a coherent biography either, even though the author incorporates historical events in his account of Jesus's life.

The authors of the Gospels would have had little reliable data at their disposal if they had wanted to produce a clear-cut biography of Jesus. Even the early Christian communities no longer had such material, and the historical figure of Jesus had long since been pushed into the background by Christian concerns.

The Gospel according to John is the most recent of all the canonical accounts of Jesus's life. Early Christian writings first mention its existence around the middle of the second century. A Greek papyrus, discovered by the English historian Grenfell, indicates that it dates from the beginning of the second century. This Gospel builds on the first three, incorporating authentic accounts of Jesus's life in a mystically inclined philosophy. Irenaeus maintains that the author is Jesus's favourite disciple John. However, that can certainly be excluded, since the simple fisherman from Galilee was trained in neither philosophy nor Greek, as was the Gospel's author.

The writings attributed to Paul are older than the Gospels. These constitute the earliest documents relating to Jesus. Paul came from a rich Jewish family and acquired Roman citizenship through his father, allowing a change of his Jewish name from Saul to Paul. He was brought up in the Pharisaic tradition, received a comprehensive education, had a sovereign command of Greek, and was well read in literature and philosophy. When approaching the age of twenty he went to Jerusalem to study theology as the pupil of Gamaliel I. He was a strict believer, narrow-minded and faithful to the law, combating early Christian sects with extreme vehemence. He even applied to the High Priest for special permission to persecute the followers of Jesus beyond Jerusalem's city walls, seeing that as a chance of making a good impression on the Jewish religious hierarchy. However, an experience before the gates of Damascus, handed down in the texts as a manifestation of the Lord, transformed him into a convinced follower of Jesus. Perhaps Paul was simply fascinated by the possibility of becoming the spiritual leader of the religious mass movement then coming into existence.

Modern research has revealed that many of the Epistles later attributed to Paul are forgeries or were patched together from a few genuine fragments. The Epistles to Timothy, Titus and the Hebrews are thought to be entirely spurious, while the authenticity of the Epistles to the Ephesians and the Colossians, and the second letter to the Thessalonians, are much disputed. The religious teaching presented in Paul's Epistles is fundamentally different from what research has recognized as being authentic sayings of Jesus, which will be considered in detail in this book.

What we know as Christianity today is not the teaching contained in these authentic sayings; it is the theology disseminated by Paul and the doctorers of his Epistles – the theology of original sin, God's expiatory death on the cross, and the administration of his body (and thus of redemption) by a hierarchy of priests. With its teachings of the sacrifice of God's first-born and the distribution of his body to the faithful in shared consumption, this theology no longer drew on Jesus's words about love of one's neighbour, but rather from the ideas of ancient Mediterranean and early Semitic tribal cults, which demanded of every father the bloody sacrifice of his first-born.

Theologian Eduard Grimm wrote: 'No matter how deeply this teaching may have become established among Christians, the real Jesus still knew nothing about it.'[1] Wilhelm Nestle, a historian of religion, expresses that as follows: 'Christianity is the religion founded by Paul, which replaces Jesus's Gospel with a Gospel about Jesus'[2] – a religion that should rather be called Paulinism. This Paulinism is a misinterpretation and falsification of Jesus's real teachings – a fact that has also been recognized by modern theological research: 'All the beautiful aspects of Christianity are linked with Jesus, all the unbeautiful with Paul.'[3]

There thus exist only a few unimportant, sparsely commented lines about Jesus – even though the dates of other leading figures from even earlier times are fully available. New Testament scholar Ernst Käsemann thus soberly summarizes the outcome of research into the life of Jesus as follows: 'Only a few words from the Sermon on the Mount, the dispute with Pharisaism, a number of parables, a scattering of other things date back in all probability to the historical Jesus.'[4] The conclusion drawn by Rudolf Bultmann, the important critical theologian, is that a clear-cut picture of Jesus's personality and life can no longer be discerned.

Must we therefore give up all hope of being able to redeem the historical Jesus and his life from the darkness of history? That is not necessary. Recent decades have brought so many new discoveries in the spheres of textual analysis and archaeological findings that we can start to collect together what Käsemann lamented as 'a scattering of other things'. And the few authentic sayings by Jesus and the insights assembled about the sociology of early Jesus movements really do cohere as a clear picture – but a picture that in no way fits in with what the Pauline church has administered as the teachings of Jesus for almost 2000 years now. Anyone who reads the authentic words of Jesus finds nothing about original sign, expiatory death and resurrection, but learns a great deal about love of one's neighbour and implementation of the Kingdom of Heaven. And anyone who knows something about the wisdom of the East will think of a man who proclaimed an astonishingly similar message in the Ganges valley over 500 years before Jesus: Siddhartha Gautama, called the Buddha.

Gautama's Awakening

From ancient times Indian religious thinking was shaped by a highly diverse mythology and a densely populated pantheon of gods. Over the course of time the priestly caste of the brahmins, who in the early days of vedic religion did not have any special authority as priests and mainly sang the ancient hymns, became increasingly influential. They rose to become the upholders of a dark spiritual legacy, nourishing the idea that happiness, progeny, celebrity and wealth could only be attained through the right form of contact with the gods. Such contact could only be established by brahmins with their know-ledge of hymns and the correct procedures for sacrifices. The former worship of trees, mountains and rivers, and the belief in a sacred nature within an endless cycle of coming into being and passing away, were taken over by the sacrificial cult of brahmins who asserted that there was no way to salvation except through their rituals. In the sixth century BC the old tribal groupings fell apart and were succeeded by little princi-palities and republics, with towns coming into being whose populations enjoyed hitherto unknown affluence. Vedic and brahminic ideas about religion were called into question. There was widespread dissatisfaction about the power and control exerted by the brahmin caste.

Such changes led many people to reflect on matters that sound remarkably modern. Did the new urban wealth really make them better off than before? Did the way to happiness truly lie in magic rituals and sacrifices to the gods? Were wisdom and insight really only accessible to people born into the brahmin caste and thus entitled to study the holy vedic scriptures? For most people – especially the lower castes or the mass of the non-caste original population – improvement in their social situation was not to be expected on earth, and the consolations of a future existence and the endless priestly rituals did not provide any real hope either. For centuries seekers of God had thronged the banks of the Ganges, but now their number visibly increased. Seized by an inexplicable agitation, they turned their backs on the brahmins and the temples, moving on so as to seek spiritual liberation for themselves. For most of them, their prospects on earth were not particularly inviting, so they plunged into ascetic practices in order to surmount material existence by learning indifference in the face of suffering. They wanted nothing less than to liberate the spirit, the great inner being shackled in the body. Many believed that the necessary precondition for that was to withdraw completely from worldly life. No human relations should hinder them on their long, thorny way toward spiritual perfection. They determined not to burden themselves with guilt acquired through their actions (*karma*) or, even worse, the killing of living creatures. In solitude, turned away from the world, unconcernedly coping with hunger and thirst, heat and cold, longings and desires, they focused their minds on the objective of surmounting the great illusion people were accustomed to call reality.

Such religious 'drop-outs' were to be encountered throughout the Ganges valley – fatalists, materialists, theists, pantheists. Some practised the arts of concentration (*dharana*), of meditation (*dhyana*) and of absorption (*samadhi*) in order to achieve the magical powers that were supposed to result from such practices: knowledge of earlier lives, penetration of other people's thoughts and ideas, making hunger and thirst vanish, discovery of what lies hidden in the future, making oneself invisible or separating one's consciousness from the body and moving into another, achieving the powers of an elephant, and attaining full knowledge of the world, the order of the cosmos and the wholeness of creation.

Among this colourful crowd of spiritual enthusiasts and earnest seekers was to be found a man of noble origins, Prince Siddhartha Gautama from the kingdom of the Shakya, and hence known as Shakyamuni ('the wise man from the house of the Shakyas'). Like innumerable others he sought answers to humanity's fundamental existential questions in the teachings of the wandering ascetics.

Siddhartha came to Maghada (in today's state of Bihar) from a small tribal kingdom in what is today Nepal. He was the son of King Shuddhodana, whose lineage went back to the legendary King Ikshvaku. When Queen Maya's time had almost come, in accordance with tradition she set off, accompanied in the golden palanquin by her sister, towards her parents' house to give birth there. The Queen was so overwhelmed by the beauty of the blossoming grove of Lumbini near Kapilavastu that she stopped for a short rest. The labour pains suddenly got under way and Maya gave birth whilst clinging to the branches of a tree. That is said to have happened in the year 563 BC.[5]

Maya died soon after giving birth, and her sister Mahaprajapati looked after the young Siddhartha from that time. According to legend, Siddhartha Gautama was brought up amid all the wealth and joys of earthly life, completely shut off from the outer world behind the walls of the palace, since his father had been told that his son would be either a conqueror or a redeemer of the world. Guards were charged with preventing Siddhartha from ever seeing any suffering, so as to preclude his turning to religious questions. He was anointed with sandalwood oil from Benares, clothed in fine muslin, and a servant held a white parasol over him day and night. He had at his disposal a palace for the summer, one for the winter, and one for the rainy season, when he remained inside, entertained by women musicians. He married his cousin Yashodhara Gopa at an early age, and had a harem full of beautiful girls. Not even that made him happy. The abundance of a life without wishes did not bring satisfaction. Instead it reminded Siddhartha daily of the transience of all beauty, pleasures and joys. Legend has it that he successively encountered an old man, a sick person, a corpse, and an ascetic during four excursions from the palace. He then asked himself whether there was anything free from age, illness and death, something unchangeable amid the ragings of existence. On his return from the fourth outing, he learned that Yashodhara had given birth to a son, Rahula, but his decision to turn his back on the world of beautiful being was unshakeable. Not even the bonds of a son held him back. Thus at the age of twenty-nine he left the palace, renouncing all his possessions, his father, wife and son, without saying goodbye. He moved 'from home to homelessness'. This 'going out into the world' (*pabbajja*) became the foundation-stone, the first decision, which all those who later went the way of the Buddha were to follow. He crossed three kingdoms with his charioteer Chandaka until by the river Anavama he cast aside his princely garments, cut his hair and continued on foot in beggar's clothing.

Siddhartha Gautama had become one among many seekers in the countryside along the Ganges. He found a teacher, Arada Kalama, and soon discovered that nothing more was to be learned there. His second master, Udraka Ramaputra, was also unable to retain him for long. Both those ascetic philosophers strove for a formless, thought-free life where Siddhartha Gautama perceived an indication of truth but not its presence. Individual existence was still present there, and thus the possibility of rebirth in a lower form of life with ongoing suffering. Buddha, however, was looking for what would make rebirth and death impossible, and therefore decided in favour of a lonely life of wandering.

He travelled around for a long time in search of truth, a search that took him to many of his age's celebrated teachers, yogis and philosophers, until he and five companions finally reached the hamlet of Uruvela, opposite what is today Bodh Gaya on the bank of the river Nirañjana. For six years he subjected himself to painful mortifications and severe ascetic practices until one day, almost skeletal after long fasting, he remembered a moment in his childhood when he had been happy in self-forgetfulness, completely at one with existence. At that moment he had attained the first stage of mystic contemplation – in the shadow of a rose-apple tree at the palace.

When Sujata, the daughter of the head of a nearby village, offered Siddhartha a bowl of rice as he sat by the river, he accepted it. He had recognized that truth does not lie in self-mortification and asceticism; it is an inner event. Strengthened by this gift, he crossed the river and came to a fig tree. He sat down beneath it, firmly resolved not to get up again until he had experienced truth.

During this time Siddhartha attained the insight that 'happiness is the solitude of the satisfied person who hears and sees the truth. Not doing harm is happiness in this world – self-restraint with regard to other living creatures. Happiness is surmounting passion and desire in the world. Surmounting ego-consciousness is in truth the greatest happiness.'[6]

During the night of a full moon in May at the beginning of the forty-ninth day Siddhartha Gautama 'awoke'. He achieved insight into the essence of things, of existence, of the self, and thus became the Buddha, the Awakened One. In the course of three vigils, Siddhartha acquired memories of previous forms of existence and gained insight into reincarnation as other creatures. He also attained knowledge of the Four Noble Truths and of the destruction of the 'three fundamental evils': sensual pleasures, thirst for existence and thirst for non-existence.

The Buddha sat under the Bodhi tree without moving – in blissful rapture for seven days (Plate 1). Legend tells that during this period he was tempted by Mara, the Evil One, since the period directly following enlightenment pointed the way ahead with regard to the worth or worthlessness of Siddhartha's strivings. The Buddha was obviously initially satisfied with being personally redeemed (*paccekabuddha*). The idea of having to proclaim his insights and work as a teacher was not welcome. However, during that time of reaching decisions, the divine Brahma Sahampati implored him to think of those people open to the proclamation of the truth rather than keeping his understanding to himself. Mara, scenting the danger to himself that would emanate from the dissemination of such teaching, attempted to beguile the sitting Buddha, extolling the rapture the latter could attain if he were to enter upon Nirvana (dissolution of the personal self) without delay. But Buddha arose from his place of enlightenment in order to push open the 'gates of the everlasting for those who wanted to hear', and thus became someone 'fully awoken' (*sammasambuddha*).

From Bodh Gaya the Buddha made his way to the Isipatana deer park near Benares, where he re-encountered the five ascetics who had previously left him because of his abandonment of austerities. With his celebrated and historic Benares Sermon (*dhammacakkappavattanasutta*), leading the five ascetics to become his first disciples, the Buddha 'set in motion the wheel of teaching' (Dharma) – see Plate 2. He began his instructions to the five disciples as follows: 'The two extremes should not, O monks, be indulged in by anyone who has set out upon the path. What are those two extremes? On the one side is abandonment to the delights of sensuous pleasures – low, mean, worldly, debased, and not leading to the goal. On the other is dedication to self-mortification – painful, debased, and not leading to the goal. A middle way has been discovered by the perfected one, without pursuing those extremes, O monks; and that brings about seeing and knowledge, and leads to calm, insight, illumination, and dissolution of the personal self.'[7]

The precondition for pursuing the Middle Way, he continued, is understanding of the Four Noble Truths granted him at Uruvela: the truths of suffering, the arising of suffering, the dissolving of suffering, and the middle way leading to alleviation of suffering. In other words the four truths proclaim:

1. All existence is painful; all joys and pleasures are fleeting, without lasting value.
2. Suffering has a cause whereby each element within our experience comes into being dependent on its predecessor in an ongoing cyclical process.
3. The cause of suffering can be ascertained.
4. Suffering can be eliminated if one follows the way that Shakyamuni called the Noble Eightfold Path.

This Noble Eightfold Path is the core of the Buddha's teaching. The Buddhist's way of life, moral attitudes and religious practices are based on it. The Eightfold Path calls for right understanding, right motives, right speech, right action, right means of livelihood, right endeavour, right attention and right contemplation.

Right understanding entails insight into the Four Noble Truths and the impersonality of existence. Right motives mainly involve renunciation of worldly things and avoidance of harm to living creatures. Right attention is one of Gautama's central concepts, which should permeate the whole of a Buddhist's life rather than just applying to meditative practices: complete awareness (*smriti*) of body, feelings and thoughts.

Before the Buddha, it was widely believed in India that the innermost nature of the human soul, the individual self (*atman*), is identical with the unchangeable nature of the Absolute (*brahman*). Atman and Brahman transcend the categories of space and time, and evade any description. That was the soil on which the Buddha's teaching developed. He did not accept the teaching of the eternal, unchangeable Self, but instead viewed existence as an unending flow of change and suffering. From their beginnings without beginning human beings set out on the wheel of rebirth (*samsara*) without hope of ever being united with an eternal Brahman, whatever that might involve. The Buddha did not offer escape from the changeability of all things, a changeability that cannot be avoided by seeking salvation in a theory of an eternal, unchangeable Self. In fact he denied the true existence of a self as either a person's inner foundation or the universe's outer foundation, instead teaching the non-self (*anatman*).

The Eightfold Path basically comprises the Buddha's entire teaching. In order to be able to understand the essence of Buddhism, one must time and again bring back to mind the demands of that Path. It is a focal point within the Buddha's teaching, just as the Sermon on the Mount constitutes a focus of Jesus's teaching.

The Buddha was thirty-six years old when he first presented the Noble Eightfold Path and the five ascetics became the first members of the *sangha*, the community of monks. For forty-four years he wandered through the Indian landscape as a mendicant monk. During hot summer days he often sought refuge on Vulture's Rock above Rajagriha (today Rajgir), with people pouring in from all sides to hear what he had to say.

Not everyone was accepted into the monastic order. The Buddha only took those he thought had the psychological strength necessary for adhering to the rules. Others who felt attracted to his teachings continued their accustomed lives. They became lay adherents, for whom the demands of the Way were less stringent.

Buddha Shakyamuni's followers came from all levels of society, from people outside the caste system to members of his own warrior caste. Even Prasenajit, the King of Koshala, and Bimbisara, the King of Magadha, and his son Ajatashatru, were among his admirers and followers. During the initial period the interest he aroused among the nobility brought generous donations, guaranteeing the erection of monasteries and the *sangha*'s continued existence. A rich merchant bought Prince Jeta's park near Shravasti where the Awakened One liked staying (Plate 3), and presented it to the Buddha.

On a visit home the Buddha converted his father, his step-mother, his son and his nephews Ananda and Devadatta. Those two played an important albeit contrasting role in his life. While Ananda simply lived the Buddha's teachings out of purity of heart, constantly present to meet the Awakened

One's needs, Devadatta took on the role of the sinister am-
bitious man who sought to take his teacher's life, and split
the community when the Master was not ready to name a
successor.

The Buddha did not write down his teachings. He probably
spoke Magadhi, the regional dialect. His discourses (Sanskrit:
Sutra; Pali: *Sutta*) were presented in a poetic way which often
seems tiring and monotonous to the modern reader. They are
characterized by frequent and protracted repetitions. However,
if one considers that only very few people could read or write
during his lifetime, the value of the right form within a lasting
oral tradition becomes apparent. His speeches were presented
so that they could easily be learned. The founder of Buddhism
charged his followers to spread his teachings everywhere so as
to make them accessible to all suffering creatures. He thus
established the first missionary religion. The success of such
an enterprise was crucially dependent on the establishment of
an oral tradition whose content could be passed on as faithfully
as possible.

Immediately after the Buddha attained Nirvana, the monks
assembled at Rajagriha where Ananda, the favourite pupil,
repeated all of his master's sermons word for word. To his
outstanding memory we owe the coming into being of the
Suttapitaka, the heart of Buddhist teaching. Ashvaghosha's *Life
of the Buddha* describes the coming together of the 500 *arhats*
(holy men) after the Buddha had left this life, and presents
their original knowledge of what their master had actually
taught. They went to the cave of Sattapanni on the northern
slope of Mount Vebhara and agreed that the venerable Ananda
should bear witness to all of the Buddha's sermons from the
first to the last. Initially Ananda was not even to be admitted
to this gathering because he had put the mortal remains of the
Buddha on public show in order to induce a more spiritual
attitude in followers.[8] However, on the evening before the
assembly Ananda made great spiritual efforts and attained
sainthood, ascended the Lion Throne and began to recite the
Buddha's teachings, recreating the place, time and person
speaking. The written versions of all these speeches begin with
the introductory words: 'Thus have I heard . . .' The entire
Suttapitaka was written down in that fashion.

The *Suttapitaka*, *Vinayapitaka*, and *Abhidhammapitaka* together
constitute the Buddhist canon, which became known as the

Pali Canon after the middle Indian dialect in which it was recorded. This extensive canon is known as *Tipitaka* (*Three Baskets*) because the texts, written on unbound palm leaves, were collected in baskets. The most recent parts of this collection were written down in the first century BC. The oldest text is probably the *Vinayapitaka* (*Basket of Discipline*), comprising the rules for the community of monks and nuns. Hermann Oldenberg, a connoisseur of Buddhist documents from Ceylon, even thinks it possible that the core of the book opening the *Vinaya* dates back to Buddha's lifetime. This *Patimokkha*, containing a liturgy for confession and a collection of interdictions, probably came into being during the confessionals the Buddha held with his followers. This text must at the latest have existed in written form soon after the Buddha's death. Experts believe that the *Vinayapitaka* reflects a pure form of the original Buddhism. Some of the oldest teachings presuppose knowledge of the *Patimokkha* regulations.

In Sanskrit the Buddha's teachings are known as Dharma (in Pali as *Dhamma*). This crucial Buddhist idea has various meanings. The Dharma is the Great Order, the cosmic law underlying our world. Then it entails the Buddha's teaching because that proclaims the truth of the cosmic law. It is also the manifestation of all things, the world of the phenomenal, to the extent that is also the unfolding of cosmic law. The believer takes refuge in the Dharma, and those who follow Buddhist meditative practices seek to attain it. In this book we will follow the established practice of usually employing the Sanskrit form of Dharma, only using the Pali *Dhamma* when quoting from a Pali text.

In the centuries after the Buddha ceased to be, the Awakened One's teachings spread across the whole of India and finally reached all of South and East Asia. However, Hinduism, which had initially been forced on the retreat by Buddhism, regained power on the Indian subcontinent, and the brahmins finally gained the upper hand in the centuries-long conflict between them and Buddhist monks. From the eleventh century Islamic armies penetrated India from the west. That was the end for the Awakened One's teachings in his homeland. Buddhism was forced into remote corners of the subcontinent, and the Buddha was thenceforth revered by Hindus as a manifestation of the god Vishnu.

The Buddha was not the only great teacher in Magadha who

set out to replace the old religions, but measured in terms of the current importance of Buddhism he was certainly the most successful. Among the most important of the others at that time were his contemporaries Gosala and Mahavira. Gosala taught salvation through joyous acceptance of a life where everything is predetermined by destiny. His Ajivika order was an influential religious movement, but disappeared during the Middle Ages. Mahavira's Jain community, on the other hand, has survived to the present day with a small number of adherents. Mahavira's life and ideas demonstrate many similarities to tnose of the Buddha. They indicate that that epoch was ready for such insights. Like Gautama, Mahavira was a prince, who at the age of thirty left his palace in order to seek the truth as a wandering ascetic (Plate 11). For twelve years he moved through the north Indian plains until he attained enlightenment beneath a banyan tree, becoming a *jina*, someone who conquers himself. After thirty years of teaching he died, leaving a well-organised community of monks and laity who called themselves Jain, 'adherents of Jinas'.

Gautama and Mahavira lived and exerted an impact at the same time, and both were frequently to be found at Rajagriha, the capital of Magadha. At that time, Rajagriha, one of the sixteen great cities of ancient India, surrounded by hills, was ruled by King Bimbisara, who greatly revered both masters. During the first centuries of our millennium, one of the world's greatest and oldest universities, Nalanda Monastery, arose just a few kilometres away. For seven centuries it was *the* intellectual centre in South Asia with 10,000 students and over 2000 teachers offering courses in medicine, natural science, law and philosophy. A Muslim army from the west, thinking that the red-robed monks were soldiers, burned down the university buildings in 1199. The library where nine million manuscripts were stored is said to have smouldered for half a year. The monks continued teaching there for another fifty years until, after a dispute, some brahmins set fire to the place for a second time.

In the hot, dry, dusty landscape of today's Indian states of Gujurat and Rajasthan, white-clad Jain monks and nuns are still an everyday sight, owning only a begging bowl, a wooden staff and a peacock-feather fly-whisk. They carefully clear their path with the whisk so as not to tread on any insect during their daily wanderings. Many even tie a strip of muslin in front of the mouth so as not to swallow flies when breathing in. For eight months of the year they move from place to place as nomads in search of enlightenment and of liberation from the cycle of an existence of suffering. They spend the rainy season from July to October at one of the many monasteries the Jains established in India for their monks, often resplendent marble buildings testifying to the wealth of this community of faith.

The success of the Buddha and Mahavira owed much to the fact that the religious existence represented by the brahmins had become bogged down in rituals. The new teachings appealed to simple people, even though they might have seemed to be directed towards a privileged class. The basic ideas were socially revolutionary in a country where from time immemorial people had been divided into castes, and the original Dravidian inhabitants had been designated as casteless servants of the new ruling class of conquerors. The new teachings surmounted a social system that for centuries had been strictly organized along caste lines, and must have seemed a challenge to the dominant brahmins and warriors. If the Buddha or Mahavira were followed, the warriors would have to lay down their weapons and devote all their time to making progress on the path towards personal salvation. The ruling class was called on to deny its traditional tasks. In the eyes of the dominant minority such views were dangerously revolutionary. If the ways of salvation marked out by the Buddha and Mahavira had not disseminated such a persuasive spirit of gentleness and reverence, there would certainly have been great opposition from the leading representatives of the Indo-Aryan aristocracy. But the warrior caste of former conquerors gradually succumbed to its own failings. After several centuries of constant feuds and family rivalries it destroyed itself, gradually losing the power of political self-assertion. The masses were also long weary of constant suppression and the struggles between the many small principalities striving to control Maghada, and more than ready for social and spiritual renewal. Into the vacuum of a gradually withering Aryan legacy, in both religious and political terms, these new teachings came like a breath of fresh life.

By nature all people are equal, so taught the Buddha. That equality has to be implemented inwardly by penetrating into its heart, which entails the void, surmounting the wheel of rebirth, and entering upon Nirvana. Buddha's teaching is an answer to being's entanglement in the painful cycle of existence, involving three aspects: life is transient, inessential, and thus accompanied by suffering. Suffering arises out of desire and ignorance. Recognition of those truths marks the beginning of the Buddhist way, which leads to liberation from the pain of existence through attainment of Nirvana.

A process of division into various schools was already under way by the mid-fourth century BC. Some sects claimed to implement Buddha's true teachings, while other theologically inclined groupings sought to integrate the Dharma in some system. An attempt was made at a gathering in Vaishali to reach agreement on unified teachings. At that time it was already apparent that the great diversity of religious views among India's many peoples would not easily be unified. Some misleading teachings were supposedly put into the world by brahmins disguised as Buddhists, annoyed at the fact that royal support had been lost to religious competitors.

Infringements of discipline led to the calling of a special council. A number of monks had accepted gold and silver from lay followers, drunk alcohol and ignored regulations about fasting (*uposatha*). Yasha, a pupil of Ananda's who had made these accusations, organized a gathering of 700 *arhats* at Vaishali. The charges were directed against the monks in that place, who admitted their guilt and split away from the other followers, a schism that ultimately led, during the third council under King Asoka, to a far-reaching dispute between two Buddhist communities, those of the *Sthavira* (Adherents of the Eldest) and the *Mahasanghika* (Adherents of the Great Community). The foundations were laid for separation, 300 years later, into two extensive affiliations: the Hinayana, deriving from the *Sthavira*, and the Mahayana, constituting a natural further development of *Mahasanghika* ideas.

These developments in the fourth century BC show that by that time Buddhism had already become a considerable monastic order with a still larger number of lay followers. The monks and *arhats* followed their founder's ideal, so they set off on prolonged wanderings and developed a culture of proclaiming the Buddha's message. There thus came into being the characteristic manifestation of religion. Wandering monks without a roof over their heads, wrapped in saffron robes and with a begging-bowl in their hand, taught the Buddha's ideas throughout the country. They spoke of the Four Noble Truths and of the Noble Eightfold Path, and proclaimed wisdom, ethics and contemplation, as presented in the Awakened One's sermons. The message thus spread rapidly, and the number of followers increased beyond the frontiers of Maghada.

The most important schools of Buddhism remain Hinayana (Little Vehicle) and Mahayana (Great Vehicle), the two main currents established 400 years after the Buddha's passing. Hinayana Buddhism rejected any metaphysical speculation, saw the world and human suffering as real, and taught that redemption was only possible through living as a monk. Hinayana thus became a religion for an elite where enlightenment was reserved for the few who could afford to renounce worldly and human ties. The original equality of all people, as taught by the Buddha, was lost again. Mahayana democratized the idea of redemption. It offered many possible ways to salvation since Buddha consciousness was after all present, albeit usually unperceived, in every human being. This way developed at the beginning of our millennium at Gandhara, the area between Peshawar and Srinigar along the central reaches of the Indus where India had long been in contact with Western cultures – Babylonians, Persians, Greeks. Mahayana also used to be called Northern Buddhism and Hinayana Southern Buddhism. For the mystics of Mahayana the world of appearances and human suffering were an illusion. The only reality was the transcendent, quality-less primal ground from which all phenomena derive. At the heart of the Mahayana way of redemption was an unlimited feeling of sympathy for all living beings founded on the implementation of compassion and all-embracing love. In Hinayana the emphasis is on personal redemption, whereas the Mahayana Buddhist seeks liberation in order to contribute towards the salvation of others. That attitude is embodied in the idea of the bodhisattva (enlightened being). A bodhisattva is a human being who has followed the Buddhist path to the end, but selflessly renounces final entry into Nirvana. He returns voluntarily to the wheel of rebirth until all beings have gained enlightenment. The quality of compassion, supported by the highest degree of insight and wisdom, determines his actions.

It was predominantly that development of Buddhist teaching which provided occasion for comparisons with Christianity. Everything that Jesus said about the moral renewal of life is to be found in the Buddha's teaching, and everything he did was foreshadowed in Mahayana.

Indian Teachings in the Bible?

Traditionally the East is the place for fantastic stories. Reading Eastern stories, one is hypnotized by their 'baroque' opulence and at times one has the feeling of being in a slower time-zone as, at just the most exciting moment, the narrator begins to describe in leisurely detail all the marvellously beautiful ornamentation of, say, a saddlecloth. Among the most splendid examples of the Eastern narrative tradition are the stories in *A Thousand and One Nights*. In India, narrative mastery is long established; one only has to cast an eye over such great epics as the *Ramayana* or the *Mahabharata*. They are full of wonderful fables and astonishing stories. No other writing can hold a candle to Sanskrit literature in that respect. Among Buddhists fables, fairy tales, anecdotes, adventure stories, and pious legends were very important as instructive narratives which could easily be remembered. Wandering preachers liked to employ such material. Many such tales have been handed down in the *Jatakas*, a collection of legends about the Buddha's earlier existences, perhaps dating back to the fourth century BC. In later centuries, when Buddhism declined in India, brahmins took over Buddhist stories and adapted them for their own purposes. Many of those fables are recorded in two big Sanskrit collections, the *Pañcatantra* ('Book of Five') and the *Hitopadesa* ('Pleasing Teaching'), with the former being viewed as one of the most important works in world literature.[9]

The strangers who sat around the fires in the caravanserais at night will have happily passed the time listening to stories and songs. And many took these stories with them to distant countries, telling them again and again. Enriched with local colour, such stories traversed landscapes and epochs. Their manifestations changed in accordance with local customs and contemporary taste, but they retained their core and their predominantly moral lessons.

Max Müller, the celebrated Indologist, managed to demonstrate that some of the old Indian stories made their way, stage by stage, across Asia Minor, Greece, and Rome to modern Italy, Germany, England and France.[10] He even tracked down transformations of old Indian narratives in La Fontaine's famous fables and in the Grimm Brothers' fairy tales.

The oldest writings in the New Testament were produced towards the end of the first century AD. They only took on their final shape, as we know it today, in the fourth century, after many theologically determined changes. The mighty stream of Eastern stories had moved westwards long before that, and Indian religious ideas were disseminated in Palestine and elsewhere in the West.

At any rate, the Christian church was already aware in the second century of external and internal similarities between Buddhism and the New Testament texts. The result was that the Church did everything possible to deny such correspondences. After all, the church fathers knew that Buddha's religion was much older than the one they attributed to Jesus Christ. In their view, what Jesus proclaimed was not a teaching alongside others, a philosophy, an ideology, or even a religion that could be compared with other religions. It was nothing less than the Word of God, presented by his incarnate son. That established the uniqueness and fundamental incomparability of Jesus's message for all time. Any similarity to other teachings had to be a matter of chance or dependent on Christianity.

Almost 2000 years passed before Christian Europe had any idea of the wealth of the religious views of peoples elsewhere. It was travellers during the Enlightenment who brought the news to the West that Europe was not surrounded by barbarians who could only be saved by Christ's joyous message. For the first time people gained a comprehensive knowledge of Eastern religions and discovered their holy books. Attention was again drawn to their links with Christianity. Defenders of the Christian heritage assumed that correspondences between Buddhism and their own religion involved remnants of a primitive revelation which God also accorded other peoples, whereas the adherents of Buddhism asserted that there exists only one Dharma, a great religious law from which all the cults and religions of other nations can be derived.

In the scientific climate of the Enlightenment the idea of revelation lost its sacrosanct character. New hypotheses were sought and the idea of borrowings was developed. But that was not a new path either. The borrowing of intellectual ideas, and especially of important moral or artistic concepts, was much discussed during classical antiquity. During the time of Ptolemy VI Philometer (*c.* 170–150 BC) there lived in Alexandria, *the* intellectual capital of the age, a scholarly Jew named Aristobulus. He is said to have tried to demonstrate in a book now lost that the philosophy of Aristotle's successors (the Peripatetics) was dependent on Moses and the other Old Testament prophets. Aristobulus's derivation theory became the accepted thing, and even such an intellect as Philo of Alexandria, a contemporary of Jesus, repeated the view that Moses was mankind's true teacher, from whom the Greek philosophers had taken over what was good and true in their ideas. Around 140 BC this theory led to grotesque assertions, with Homer, who had died centuries previously, being supposed to have plundered verses from the Jewish Sybil.

By the time people began to consider the possibility that the New Testament had borrowed Indian ideas, they were better informed about historical connections, and that gave rise to a number of theories concerned with tracking down the origins of alien elements in the New Testament.

One of the first to seek traces of interconnections between India and the West was Frances Wilford, a highly educated Hanoverian who worked for the English in India from 1772. Viewed in terms of today's knowledge, the relationships he assumed and his etymological interpretations seem wild and unfounded. He thus identified Prithu with Noah, derived Deucalion from the Sanskrit term Deva-Cala-Yavana, and spoke of links between a certain Salivahana and Christ. At that time the world of Indian ideas was still little researched, and even for someone knowledgeable it must have been enormously difficult to order the unbelievably rich mythological world of the various Indian religions correctly, or to arrange a breathtaking abundance of manuscripts in terms of age, significance, and influence. Wilford did not get caught up in such considerations but mainly based his work on excerpts from the *Puranas* (*Old Narratives*) supplied by an aged *pandit* (Sanskrit scholar). However, he wrote nothing about the age of those stories or their importance within the spiritual framework of Hinduism.

During that period Western scholars also discovered Sanskrit, the cultivated language of ancient India, and an exciting period in comparative philology got under way. The first Sanskrit texts to become known in Europe were Bhartrihari's *Vairagya-*

Shatakas and *Niti-Shatakas*, published at Leiden in 1651 by Dutch-born Abraham Roger, who had been a Calvinist missionary in India from 1630 to 1647. His book appeared in several languages with the German version (1663) entitled *Offene Tür zu dem Verborgenen Heydenthum (Open Door to Concealed Heathenism)*. In his *Gedanken einiger Brahmanen (Thoughts of some Brahmins)* Johann Gottfried Herder referred to these Sanskrit epigrams, thereby adding them to wisdom literature.

Scholars soon discovered remarkable parallels between the Christian religion and Indian beliefs. Of course, most Western thinkers took as their starting point an unspoken agreement that all religious truth could only come from the Old Testament. Claims began to be made that Brahminism was dependent on the Old Testament. The opposite view first appeared in a work published at London in 1779, deriving many elements in both Old and New Testaments from Brahminism and Buddhism.[11]

The more the world of scholarship found out about the age of Indian manuscripts and the nature of their religious views, the more obvious similarities with Christianity became for many people. The possibility that Christian authors had gathered inspiration from Indian, and particularly Buddhist, writings was discussed ever more publicly. In the nineteenth century, with its initially romantic and later naturalistic enthusiasms, individual researchers, uninfluenced by dogmatic views, began to establish such studies on a scientifically respectable basis.

Of great significance were investigations by Arthur Schopenhauer (1788–1860), the important German philosopher for whom Buddhism with its world-denying undertone provided justification for his pessimistic philosophy. Schopenhauer made no secret of his view that the New Testament had to derive from an Indian, and particularly a Buddhist, source. All the important elements of the New Testament were said to entail amazing correspondences with Indian precursors. The ascetic attitude to life, the ethical system, the pessimistic undertone, and even the idea that divine consciousness incarnates itself in earthly form, were claimed to be characteristically Indian. In addition Schopenhauer maintained that Brahminism, Buddhism and the New Testament were essentially similar.

At the same time as Schopenhauer was writing down his thoughts about India and Christianity, Isaak Jakob Schmidt

(1779–1847), a Russian diplomat, arrived in Sarepta among the Kalmucks of Central Asia. He soon became well versed in Mongolian and Tibetan (both language and literature), and even translated parts of the Bible into the Kalmuck variant of Mongolian. His studies suffered a bitter setback when he lost his valuable collection of manuscripts during a Moscow fire. He nevertheless wrote a very scholarly study that has remained a trail-blazer up to the present day,[12] demonstrating that the Christian and Gnostic concepts that emerged everywhere between Alexandria and Syria at the beginning of the first century AD were closely related to Buddhism. His Buddhist-influenced writings about Schopenhauer also made a considerable contribution towards Western philosophy taking such ideas seriously.

It would be surprising if all the investigations of this theme were comparably thorough and scientifically honest. In fact religious controversies soon muddied any clear view of what could be justly upheld and what was more or less well-packaged propaganda.

Louis Jacolliot, who for a time was a judge in the French colony of Chandernagore near Calcutta, wrote a work about the Indian roots of aspects of the Bible which was soon much talked about. *La Bible dans l'Inde*, published at Paris in 1869, attracted enthusiastic supporters and furious critics, and his theses resulted in a more intensive scholarly discussion of the relationship between Buddhism and Christianity – partly in order to refute his assertions. This development led to the most fruitful phase of investigations in this sphere, from the last two decades of the nineteenth century until the First World War.

Jacolliot had challenged the scholarly world by boldly asserting that biblical authors had made what for Christian believers were shocking borrowings. He thus presented a brahminic creation myth in which Brahma is said to have created Adima and his companion Heva as the first human beings, giving them the island of Sri Lanka as their home. In Sanskrit *adima* means 'the first', a meaning that Adam does not possess in Hebrew. Of course such discoveries, backed by the context, were calculated to convince less-informed readers and to force scholars to check such claims. In fact this account of the creation is to be found in the *Bhavisyat-Purana*. The 1897 Bombay edition of these *puranas* contains the entire beginning of the Old Testament from the first people in paradise to the flood, with Noah appearing as Nyuha. So was Jacolliot right? Were the first pages of the Bible a brahminic survival reshaped to meet Jewish needs? Far from it. Anyone informed about Indian texts knows that *puranas* are an extremely flexible form of litera-ture, which adapt to the times, incorporate alien material and continue prophecies of future events up to the present day. The supposedly old texts – a *Bhavisyat-Purana* is known from around 400 BC – appeared time and again in updated versions over the course of their long history. The 1897 version thus contained depictions of Genghis Khan (1155–1227), Timur (1336–1405), Kabir (sixteenth century), King Akbar (1556–1605), and even the Russian tsar. Similarly, the biblical story of the creation was only incorporated in modern times. The per-petuators of this work should not, however, be accused of literary deception. Borrowings from religious traditions are a trade mark of this literary genre, recurring time and again.[13]

Jacolliot, who devoted his spare time to studying Sanskrit and Hindu holy books, made the mistake of taking too many of his ideas from conversations with brahmins. These crafty interlocutors served up the craziest of inventions for the gulli-ble Jacolliot. The Frenchman thus quotes passages from the Vedas which are not to be found in any Veda, and he garnishes his exciting discoveries with etymological analyses of Sanskrit words which are either not Sanskrit or mean something com-pletely different from what he thinks.

Uncritical enthusiasm for such insights led to the publication of works which made incredible claims. Around the turn of the century, T. J. Plange's provocatively entitled *Christ – An Indian?* (*Christus – ein Inder?*) claimed that the most important charac-teristics of the ancient Egyptian, Persian, Greek, Roman, Jew-ish and Germanic civilizations derived from India, and that even Moses had been initiated in Egypt into the secrets of Indian teachings.

On the other hand, Jacolliot provided a reason for setting up level-headed research into the problem. One of the most im-portant forerunners was Rudolf Seydel (1835–1892), Professor of Philosophy at Leipzig University, who made a name for himself with an outstanding presentation and evaluation of Schopenhauer's work. In two highly scholarly studies[14] he succeeded in showing that the Gospels are full of borrowings from Buddhist texts. This meticulous work led Seydel to con-clude that a text he characterized as a Christian working of a Buddhist gospel must have served as the basis of the writings of the New Testament. That would mean that even before the Christian Gospels were written down a Buddhist text was in circulation in Syria and Palestine, which was then adapted by followers of Jesus to accord with their views.

That was a challenge for the scholarly world. Seydel's findings could not simply be dismissed, like the work of Jacolliot and his epigones. For many otherwise rational scholars, calling into question Christianity's basic convictions was sacrilege. It was as if Seydel had crossed a boundary that had to remain sacrosanct for a Christian researcher. For instance, Indologist Leopold von Schroeder, who had no problems with demonstrating that Pythagoras had gained all his knowledge from India, simply did not want to accept that Christianity had been influenced by Buddhism, and dismissed Seydel's theories as 'bordering on madness'. Such opinions demonstrate how difficult it is to overcome religious prejudices. They reflect the degree of uncertainty aroused by facts which shake the longest-established forms of self-understanding within Western culture. Fortunately a number of scholars decided to devote further attention to the theses of a researcher whose views were to be taken seriously. Many had to accept Seydel's findings, although the importance of individual borrowings was differently assessed. Among the most important and trail-blazing works were books by G.A. van den Bergh van Eysinga, Richard Garbe, and Hilko Wiardo Schomerus.[15] The comparative material assembled by Albert J. Edmunds, an American scholar, is a real treasure trove.[16] Without clarifying the question of dependences, he simply selected texts from the great wealth of Buddhist writings and compared them with passages from the New Testament. He left to other scholars the analysis of the frequently amazing correspondences.

The Great Upheaval

Before starting to assess how Buddhist material was taken over, we need to undertake a journey into the past. This will be an exciting voyage of discovery through the great cultures of ancient civilizations in search of interconnections and exchanges of ideas and views of life, in search of answers to the question of whether distant peoples knew of one another so long ago and were able to adopt unfamiliar viewpoints. After all, many sea routes to distant continents were still unknown a few centuries ago, and long journeys were seen as dangerous adventures. How difficult contacts across great distances must have been in epochs whose technologies were far less developed.

In the period from 800 to 200 BC there occurred a unique breach in intellectual history. The famous German philosopher Karl Jaspers speaks of a 'historical mystery'. We can discern comparable, related developments that took place, independently of one another, in three areas.[17] Jaspers calls this epoch the Axis Time. In different parts of the earth the Axis Time gave rise to great personalities and ideas, decisively shaping the centuries that followed, right up to the present day: the Buddha, Confucius, Lao-Tse, Plato, Socrates, Zarathustra, Elijah, Jeremiah, etc. They had in common a capacity to comprehend the world and existence rationally, coming to the conclusion that everything falls into two fundamental spheres, into subject and object, spirit and matter, mind and body; and that the true self yearns for release from the horror of unfulfilled being-in-the-world. 'It is the *real human being*, bound and veiled in the body, shackled by drives, only darkly aware of itself, that longs for liberation and redemption, and can already attain them in this world . . .'[18]

The idea that human evolution is reflected in the evolution of human consciousness is an exciting thesis. With regard to the development of religions and cultural achievements in the time before history, it offers an indispensable means of throwing light on mysterious events. How did it happen that identical forms of belief emerged in different parts of the world at about the same time – for instance, in the tenth millennium before Christ, with the cult of the Great Mother, accompanied by comparable social and political upheavals where agriculture and forms of urban settlement replaced the previous hunting and gathering – even though no links existed between the different peoples involved? The answer can only lie in the fact that the process of natural evolution does not just occur on the biological level but also on the level of the human intellect and spirit, where evolution of human consciousness occurs in clearly distinguishable phases. If a new level of development has been attained, that receives expression in various forms: religious systems, social organization, art, architecture – in short, in the achievements that constitute civilization and culture.

Although Jaspers was not concerned with a step-by-step process of evolution, he was of the opinion that such a completely new spiritual leap must have been the reason for the unfolding of the Axis Time, since that can be dated much more precisely than considerably earlier parallels among developing high cultures.

There is certainly some truth in Jaspers's view, but one must ask to what extent the increased correlation involved in the Axis Time may be the outcome of changed international relations. No one would attribute the fact that nowadays, say, fashion trends spread like wildfire all over the globe to some mysterious, simultaneous, independent manifestation. Our modern information culture makes possible enormously rapid global exchanges. And that process began to get under way thousands of years ago. The Axis Time occurred during a formative epoch, with unprecedented connections between distant peoples and unusual mobility. This mobility was by no means just external; it also involved intellectual flexibility. Of course we should not prematurely conclude that similar discoveries in the West, the Middle East, Persia, India and China were all the outcome of exported traditions. However, we should also not leave out of account the fact that the new mobility – perceptible as human unrest on a global scale – constitutes the flip-side of the evolution of human consciousness. Both developments were interdependent. The human mind unfolded *because* peoples left their tribal areas and moved into new environments, got to know unfamiliar races, customs, attitudes, plants and animals, and experienced the expanse of the world. On the other hand, the great migrations were simultaneously the outcome of an upheaval within a human consciousness no longer satisfied with traditional ways and demanding fresh challenges and new horizons.

Important movements of peoples took place at a time when the Great Upheaval (as we would like to call this intellectual and physical process) was already under way. We will show that it can already be seen in the third millennium BC when the first important trading relations were established by land and sea between distant peoples, with the result that significant high cultures were established, above all along mighty rivers: the Nile, Euphrates and Tigris, and Indus. Only in the second half of the second millennium was this international linkage disrupted. From northern and central Asia huge masses of

people streamed into more fertile and mineral-rich areas, settling everywhere in southern Eurasia. These invaders intermingled with or destroyed existing high cultures. Around the
end of the second and beginning of the first millennium these
newcomers became sedentary and trading relations were
gradually resumed. The closer we come to times when contacts
between peoples became closer and more regular, the more
difficult it becomes to penetrate the history of ideas. We encounter correspondences that are so striking and unusual that
they can no longer be adequately explained in terms of Jaspers's
understanding of the Axis Time as a historical mystery. International interweaving proceeded at an even greater pace. It
seemed as if the Great Upheaval was only just getting going.

Even at the start of the Axis Time, peoples from Greece to
China were involved in an amazing range of exchanges, considering the technology available at that time. Goods from
southern China were delivered to Egyptian merchants; religious ideas and philosophical concepts reached the most
remote areas, becoming sources for new traditions.

It is thus much more problematic to view the leap in consciousness marked by the Axis Time merely in terms of a
mysterious synchronistic impact, as opposed to considering it
against the background of the material and spiritual effects of
the Great Upheaval. The decisive factor is that the philosophical and spiritual systems devised by the most outstanding
representatives of the Axis Time constitute an intellectual expression of that Great Upheaval. They speak to us, as Jaspers
said, of a profound yearning for liberation and redemption, a
longing for the spiritual home that was lost amid earthly self-
forgetfulness. This shared longing for the re-establishment of
an original state of affairs in the true spiritual home was the
unmistakable outcome of the physical and spiritual changes to
which peoples were exposed. Homelands were left behind and
became mythologically transmuted into lost 'paradises' and
vanished 'golden ages'. From that period of human history,
individual aspects of moral principles, ways of regaining lost
wholeness and multiple borrowings were integrated into local
systems by intercommunication.

One of the first questions we have to answer involves the
kind of contact that existed between India and the Mediterranean in pre-Christian times. Only if we manage to produce
a clear picture can we track down the sources of Buddhist-

Christian parallels. Our investigation of East-West contacts during that period will therefore always be accompanied by the question whether Indian religious ideas could have got as far as Palestine, the area where Jesus was at work and Christianity came into being, and how such ideas might have been transmitted.

A superficial look at history leaves an impression of great power blocs which led a more or less isolated existence, largely separated by what were then thought to be immeasurable distances. Only occasional border disputes and courageous incursions deep into enemy territory broke through that relative remoteness. Extensive trading was only pursued with kingdoms close at hand. However, if we endeavour to uncover the network of international relations during the centuries before our millennium began, many connections become apparent despite the lack of sources at our disposal.

The Dawn of High Cultures

Let us travel back 5000 years. At that time the first centres of high culture were flourishing along great rivers: Egyptian culture on the Nile, Babylonian in the Land of the Two Rivers, and the Indus civilization on the river of the same name, which today crosses Pakistan from north to south.

What was known as the Amri culture was already fully developed along the Indus at the end of the fourth millennium BC. It was followed by the important Harappa culture, which was at its height from the mid-third to the mid-second millennium. At that time the Indus cultures extended into the upper Land of the Five Rivers (Punjab), stretching over 1000 miles from Rupar in the Simla mountains to Sutkagen Dor in the south-west. The Kathiawar peninsula constituted the southern border. Those are astonishing dimensions. The Indus civilization was thus about twice as large in land area as the ancient Egyptian kingdom, and around four times as big as the empire of Sumer and Accad. As early as the fourth millennium the inhabitants of the Indus civilization practised agriculture, yoked bulls to two-wheeled carts, used elephants as beasts of burden, and tamed horses.

The Harappa culture is among humanity's oldest civilizations, and it attained an unusually high degree of development. It is remarkable for high-quality pottery, complex town planning, carefully designed houses with bathing facilities and sanitation, and, above all, for an abundance of seals with characteristic emblems and a developed script (Plate 15). These seals indicate without the least doubt that intellectual and religious life flourished during the Harappa period. The essential characteristics of this civilization were very similar to what was to be found in the Sumerian, Egyptian, and Babylonian cultures.

After Harappa there was an obvious decline. Only simple grey or dark pottery existed in the Jhukar culture, and the few seals that have been discovered completely lack inscriptions.

The three high cultures in Egypt, Mesopotamia and the Punjab expressed themselves in different styles of art, architecture, state structures, writing and languages. These forms are so characteristic that it is possible to distinguish at first sight between Egyptian hieroglyphs and Assyrian cuneiform inscriptions. And yet they sometimes demonstrate astonishing similarities, such as the pyramid and the ziggurat, mythological motifs, etc. Harappa depictions discovered during excavations in Pakistan are thus reminiscent of the celebrated Gilgamesh epic from Sumer. The degree to which individual civilizations were aware at this early stage of the existence of other important high cultures can only occasionally be ascertained. For us the interesting question is: when were extensive contacts established between the realm of Indian culture and the West, and what kind of relationship did that involve? Historians have often raised that question, especially since cultural correspondences obviously exist between the Indus valley cultures and Mesopotamia, indicating contacts at an early date. Radhakrishnan, the important religious historian and philosopher, even came to the conclusion with regard to the Indus valley civilization that 'this culture is linked with that of Sumer, which transformed itself into Babylonian culture, thereby establishing a tradition that Europe has inherited'.[19]

Let us consider the most revealing evidence which points towards the link whereby the Asiatic cradle of civilization influenced the origins and development of Western culture. Such testimony is to be found in the seals used to stamp their goods by inhabitants of the Land of the Two Rivers and of the Indus valley. In autumn 1923 archaeologists excavating Kish near the

Euphrates found a seal which was obviously not manufactured
in that area. It turned out to come from the Indus valley, and
was dated by the archaeologists to at least 2000 BC.[20] How did
this Indian seal end up in Mesopotamia, an area more than
1200 miles away by land, and what was the significance of this
token of a remote culture being left in the Land of the Two
Rivers? This find was highly significant since it emphasized
that cultural correspondences do not have to arise independently, but can also be the outcome of reciprocal stimulation.

Of course a single seal by no means explains far-reaching
similarities comprising entire ways of life. Fortunately this discovery was followed by others. Archaeologists were soon reporting several similar finds at Lagash in southern Babylon,
Umma, Tell Asmar, Agrab, Ur, and Susa. At Ur they found a
seal dating from pre-Sargonid times (before 2500 BC), which is
a local imitation of an Indus seal. Several of these seals have
typical Indus inscriptions, including the frequently found fish
symbol or a male figure with extended, thread-like limbs and
rays emanating from the head – also a characteristic motif for
seals from Mohenjaro and other excavation sites in the Indus
valley. Such a strange long figure is not otherwise to be found
on Babylonian seals. It is certainly Indian or the outcome of
Indian influence.

A dig at Ur in 1926 produced part of a brick and a small
stoneware beaker bearing characters largely identical to Indus
inscriptions. The astrological character of some seals is also
striking, including the image of a water-carrier with two stars
and a scorpion over his shoulder. The scorpion was a character
in Indus valley inscriptions. The zodiac seals discovered in the
Land of the Two Rivers also include elliptical forms, pointed at
extremities, which were of importance in the Indus valley too.
A square seal-mould containing no fewer than ten typical
Indus characters turned up at Umma.[21]

Perhaps these finds indicate that there were early borrowings in the sphere of astrology. Mesopotamia is usually viewed
as the cradle of astrology, but after such discoveries of seals
with astrological symbolism related to the Indus valley, it is
quite possible that the basic elements in what was later to be
the celebrated Babylonian astrology derive from the Harappa
culture.

Some seals are comparable in material and form but not in
images and characters. Mesopotamian seals have thus been

found made from grey soapstone with a creamy surface. The reverse side is raised, dome-like, with a diagonal loop embellished with three vertical stripes and four rings with centre points, forming the corners of what is virtually a square. Such seals are absolutely characteristic of the Indus valley.

The oldest Indian seals found in Mesopotamia date from the time of Ur's third dynasty (2047–1939 BC). A number of other objects including pearl necklaces, terracotta statues and dice, probably also originating in the Indus valley, were found alongside the seals.[22] Such finds certainly demonstrate unambiguously that regular trading contacts between the two cultures existed before the Isin-Larsa-Babylon period (around 2000 BC) at a time when the Harappa and Mohenjaro civilizations, which produced such seals, were flourishing (the first half of the third millennium).

The fact that scarcely any objects from Asia Minor have been found in the Indus valley constitutes a problem with regard to a more accurate assessment of exchanges between the two areas. A number of Mesopotamian, Egyptian and Cretan artefacts may have been uncovered, but they do not match the quantities of Indus seals along the Euphrates.[23] Perhaps this may indicate that the inhabitants of the Indus valley were the more active traders, who did not shun long journeys, and that early cultural exchanges were specifically due to their industriousness.[24]

So how should exchanges between these two cultures be viewed? More recent excavations in the vast areas between Mesopotamia and the Punjab offer a framework of explanation for both these early links between the two cultures and the development of the first urban civilizations. The importance of the Elamites in this rise of civilizations was long underestimated. Their area of settlement lay north-east of the confluence of the Euphrates and the Tigris, in what is today Iran. Elamite culture was thought to be greatly influenced by Babylon, and the Elamites' place in history mainly involved Babylonian attacks on their territory. Archaeological discoveries have now shown that a proto-Elamite culture flourished in the fourth millennium BC, 200–400 years before the oldest Indus valley culture, the Amri culture, in centres only 600 miles away from the later high civilization of Harappa.[25] The main proto-Elamite finds have been in south-eastern Iran and Baluchistan. At Tepe Yahya, for instance, there came to light an astonishingly highly developed culture (between 4500 and 3300 BC), remarkable for the processing and export of the mineral resources with which the region was unusually blessed. Among the many products of the Elamite highlands were wood, lead, copper, tin, silver, alabaster, diorite, obsidian and horses. In comparison Mesopotamia was relatively poor in minerals and natural resources, so that its development depended on goods from Elam. That explains the constant attempts during later times (from Sargon around 2300 BC) to conquer Elam and incorporate it in the Babylonian empire. Conquest was never achieved, however. The demand for goods from Elam also gave rise to extremely interesting social and political developments, leading to a flourishing urban civilization in Mesopotamia.

Proto-Elamite culture also seems to have exerted a direct influence on the rise of the Harappa civilization. Previously archaeologists and early historians had only been able to register with astonishment the explosive evolution of Harappa culture. Proto-Elamite finds now explain why, after many centuries of stagnation, a high form of civilization could suddenly – and for long inexplicably – come into being. It was fertilized by exchanges with the inhabitants of Baluchistan, centred on Tepe Yahya, Bampur, Shar-i-Sokta, Tal-i-Iblis and Shahdad. The increasing number of key settlements further east towards the Indus area, such as Kulli, Amri, Kot Diji, Mundigak and Shah-i-Tump, were the result of the requirements of reciprocal trade, leading ultimately to the highly developed Harappa culture.

We now also understand why relatively little evidence of trade between Mesopotamia and the Indus valley has been found. The overland trade routes inevitably led through proto-Elamite – and later Elamite – territory. The Elamites never allowed control of such wealthy commercial centres to be wrested from them, so that exchanges of goods seldom involved direct contact between the two cultures but were instead mediated through these middlemen. Strangely, no harbours have been found on Elamite territory. The Elamites obviously restricted themselves to trading by land, and this tipped the scales in early intercultural relations in south-western Asia. It forced inhabitants of the Indus valley to establish a sea route through the Persian Gulf so as to open up a direct way to their trading partners along the Euphrates and the Tigris. That sea route must have become known during the second millennium BC at the latest.[26] Trade with Mesopotamia first took place by way of the passes of the Hindu Kush, but the new phase of east–west interaction by sea must have followed fairly soon afterwards. We know today that adherents of the Indus valley culture used ships similar to those of the Sumerians for crossing the sea.[27] The remains (including a shipyard) of a large 4000-year-old harbour town have been excavated at Lothal on the Gulf of Cambhay, north of Bombay. From harbours like that the towns of the Harappa culture maintained trading relations with areas as far away as the Mediterranean, as is indicated by ships' anchors (similar to Syrian and Cypriot anchors of the time) discovered off the Gujarat coast.

The Babylonian attacks on Elamite territory must also have led to campaigns further afield – as far as Bactria (in the north of modern Afghanistan) and the Indus valley. A bas-relief showing prisoners with a Bactrian camel, an elephant and a rhinoceros has been found in an Assyrian building near Birs Nimrud. A memory of that – albeit mythologically embellished – was preserved centuries later by Ktesias, who told of expeditions by Nino, the legendary founder of Nineveh, to Bactria, and by Semiramis, an Assyrian goddess, to India. Semiramis is said to have established the town of Kophen or Archosia whose ruins have been found at Kandahar (Afghanistan), and probably derive from an Assyrian ruler.

The mysteries surrounding the origins of ancient cultures in and between the modern states of Iraq and Pakistan are gradually being elucidated, and we are starting to recognize that over 5000 years ago the people there did not shrink from travelling huge distances in order to enter into contact with other societies.

Important contacts between India and a high culture to the West – immeasurably far away for those times – certainly existed over 4000 years ago. The adoption of images and inscriptions on seals indicates that such links did not merely serve commercial interests. These seals are of much more far-reaching cultural significance, relating to mythical and religious concepts and – through the characters – to means of intellectual expression. However, the extent of such intellectual and spiritual exchanges can only be fragmentarily reconstructed today, and it is to be assumed that these early relations were not continuously developed but petered out with the decline of empires, dynasties and entire cultures, only to be taken up again in later times.

Around the middle of the second millennium BC the old Harappa culture vanished when towns in the Indus valley were abandoned. One of the rivers that irrigated the area dried up, leaving behind the desert of present-day Rajasthan. At the same time vedic Aryans swept in from the west, reaching the Indian subcontinent in several waves and bringing an entirely new culture, religiosity and way of life, including Sanskrit,[28] the language in which the ancient sacred texts of the Vedas and the epic *Ramayana* and *Mahabharata* are written.

During the same period the Kassites, Hurrians, and Hittites, whose languages were closely related to those of the Indo-Aryans, invaded the Middle East. The Hurrians conquered northern Mesopotamia, eastern Asia Minor, Syria and Palestine. An end was put to the first Babylonian dynasty by the Kassites, a people that migrated from the mountains of Iran. The Hittites ruled in Anatolia from around 1650 to 1200 BC. The Aramaic tribes also migrated during the second millennium, the time of the Great Upheaval, like other tribes in the Middle East: the Ammonites, Moabites, and Edomites. The tribes that formed the Israel of that time most probably came from the middle Euphrates area. Joshua's acquisition of land by war, as described in the Old Testament, in reality entailed this prolonged process of peaceful migration (around the fourteenth to the twelfth century BC).

One outcome of these extended migrations is that we have scarcely any information about east–west contacts during the period from the downfall of the third dynasty in Ur (1939 BC) until the start of the first millennium BC. This was a time of upheavals resulting from the great movements of peoples. Of course the lack of evidence of cultural links, in the form of archaeological finds, does not mean that such relations were non-existent. There was an interruption at the level of high civilizations, but the spread of different, predominantly Indo-Germanic tribal groupings also led to the dissemination of autonomous culture and religious ideas to remote areas.

The sociologist Alfred Weber put forward a thesis about the uniformity within the Eurasian bloc which was established as far as Iran and India through incursions by chariot peoples towards the end of the third millennium, followed by eques-trian tribes from Central Asia around 1200 BC. In his opinion, the horse, hitherto unknown in those countries, led to an experience of the world's immensity, resulting in the conquest of the old high cultures. The interconnections within this unified bloc have given rise to bold speculation. Astonishing similarities between depictions on Indus valley seals and representations on Celtic objects have led to the assumption that a pre-Indo-Germanic culture even extended from Gaul to India. A frequently deployed example involves the correspondence between the horned Celtic god Cernunnos, sitting in the Buddha position, depicted on the Gundestrup cauldron (*c.* second to first century BC) and what is known as the proto-Shiva on a Harappa seal from the Indus valley (*c.* 2000 BC). There are great similarities: a male, horned figure in the ascetic's lotus position with a striped robe and surrounded by animals (Plates 13 and 14). In the wake of work by Celtologist J. Vendryes, this Cernunnos figure is seen as having been taken over from the Pashupati of Indian mythology, the Lord of the Animals said to be shown on the Mohenjodaro seal.[29]

Numerous analogies and correspondences with India are also to be found in the Celtic and Celto-Iberian religion, which was familiar with the idea of reincarnation, a vegetarian diet, the tree cult and the swastika, a symbol that is found even today on the door-posts of Basque farmhouses. In the Musée Borély at Marseille there are two sitting stone figures, presumably cult idols, dated as originating in the second century BC. They were found at nearby Roquepertuse near small caves chiselled into the smooth rock-face. Although these figures are headless and believed by scholars to be Celto-Iberian gods, yet they are astonishingly similar to early Buddhist works of art, to bodhisattva sculptures characteristically sitting in the lotus position, with the brahminic cord over the shoulder and bangles around the neck and upper arms as insignia of worthiness (Plates 9 and 10). The positioning of the arms and hands is also reminiscent of the *mudras* (gestures) in statues of the Buddha. One hand points towards the earth (*bhumisparsa-mudra*) attesting to the truth of the teaching, while the other is in front of the breast in a gesture of encouragement (*abhayamudra*). A Buddha's head from the same period has even been found in a Celto-Iberian burial chamber in the south of France.[30]

It is speculated that at an early stage of the Amri culture (fourth millennium BC) a unified population group, to which the Sumerians belonged, had spread over a large part of Asia Minor. Some Indian researchers even believe that there never was an Aryan invasion and the Indus valley culture was already Aryan. The Saraswati, extolled in the Aryan Vedas as the country's most holy river, which during the Harappa period irrigated what is today the Thar desert and flowed into the Persian Gulf east of the Indus, dried up long before the Aryans – and thus the Vedas – are said to have reached India.

Perhaps the boldest hypothesis on the geographical spread of Indus valley cultures was put forward by scholars in the 1930s. It sought to demonstrate that the still undeciphered written characters used by inhabitants of the Indus region were closely related to those to be found in the distant Easter Islands.[31]

The Aryan tribes that moved into India after the decline of the Indus valley culture were originally semi-nomadic and only later became sedentary. They brought the vedic religion, a form of belief focused on the here and now, stressing pleasure and cultic practices, with Indra as the most popular god. Linguistic scholars believe that the Aryans came from the steppes of Russia, but recently a number of researchers have concluded that these tribes originally lived in Anatolia and northern Iran. In the course of almost a thousand years vedic expansion extended its sphere of influence ever further eastwards, as one of their texts proclaims: 'People move from the West to the East, gaining land' (*Kathakam* 26:2).

The cuneiform contractual documents relating to the Hittite kings of Mittani, found at Boghazköi in Asia Minor and dated at around 1400 BC, preserve a unique echo of spiritual exchanges within just a few centuries. They contain invocations of the Gods Mi-it-ra, Ur-w-na, Indar and Na-sa-at-ti-ia, all deities worshipped under the same names (Mitra, Varuna, Indra, and the Nasatyas) in ancient India.[32] In fact the mythology, religious traditions and social arrangements of the vedic Aryans are comparable with those of the Iranians, even the Greeks, and later the Romans, Celts, Germans and Slavs. The ancient Persians, whose language differed little from Sanskrit, also called themselves Aryans ('noble'). The *Avesta*, the holy scripture of ancient Iran, is in part almost identical with the *Rig-Veda*, the oldest Indian text. The Indian god-king Rama is to be found there, as well as *soma*, the divine potion (*haoma* in ancient Iranian) and the holy river Saraswati (Haraquati).

After working through astronomical references in ancient Aryan religious writings, two Indian astronomers came to some instructive conclusions. Professor R. Kochar believes that the *Ramayana* came into existence around 1500 BC in modern Afghanistan. His calculations also show that the even older *Vedanga Jyotisha* was written in Babylon. However, Dr B.G. Siddharth from Hyderabad attributes the *Avesta* and *Ramayana* to the seemingly inconceivable date of 7000 BC. In his opinion, the *Rig-Veda* even originated a thousand years earlier in Anatolia. Such dating may be more realistic than at first appears. A team of researchers from Heidelberg University has found the remains of a highly developed urban culture, dating from the seventh millennium BC, at Nevali Cori in Turkey. The sculptures discovered there include the life-size depiction of a man displaying all the characteristics of a priest from the time of the *Rig-Veda*.[33]

Peacocks, Gold and Precious Woods: Solomon's Expeditions to India

While Indo-Germanic tribes were settling Anatolia, Persia and India, the Jews entered history for the first time (around 1400 BC). In letters from Tellel-Amarna we read that Hebrew nomads had infiltrated Palestine, which was under Egyptian rule. At that time the Jews were a barbaric nomadic people with only rudimentary social forms. The tribes that sought refuge in Egypt were most probably still largely subjected to slavery. It was the unusually charismatic leadership of Moses that induced his people to renounce polytheism and delivered them from oppression. The early books in the Old Testament preserve very clear echoes of cultures which dominated the Jews in the course of their history. J.H. Breasted, the celebrated Egyptologist, maintains that the law elucidated in Deuteronomy, the fifth book in the Old Testament, is basically a simplified version of Hammurabic laws, while the proverbs of Solomon and many psalms are based on ancient Egyptian literature.

The ethnic relationships and trade routes prevalent in early history will probably long remain an area of assumptions and hypotheses. Nevertheless those connections must have been far-reaching. In the fifteenth century BC the Egyptians even came into possession of goods from the Far East, which reached the Land of the Nile either by way of the Sumerians or through the earliest Phoenician expeditions. In Egyptian graves from the Eighteenth Dynasty (ending in 1476 BC), archaeologists have found Chinese porcelain vases. The Egyptians also used Indian indigo for dyeing, and Indian muslin was sometimes employed for their mummies.[34]

In the centuries that followed, when ascertainable points of contact between India and the West became ever clearer, the ancient Jewish sphere of culture for the first time entered upon exchanges with the East. From the reign of King David (around 1000 BC) to the times of the prophet Isaiah (*c.* 740–690 BC), there flourished Palestine's modest but very important trade with Ophir, that mysterious place which could be viewed as the proverbial Eldorado. Gold, sandalwood, precious stones, ivory, apes and peacocks were transported by the ships of Hiram and Solomon from Ophir and its twin town Tarshish.[35] For centuries historians and interpreters of the Bible racked their brains about where this legendary Ophir could be. It was attributed to many areas – to Arabia, Africa, Asia, and even Peru. But what was the true destination of these ships charged with assembling valuable goods for Solomon's court?

Let us take a look at the facts. Solomon had good reason for assuring himself of active Phoenician support. However his expeditions may be viewed, no one disputes that the Phoenicians were masters at that time of both the Mediterranean and seas further to the east. They were *the* traders. No other people so boldly ventured onto the world's waters. No other people counted so many expert mariners among their ranks, who would even have dared sail around Africa. Characteristically, the Phoenicians had no land on which they settled, but rather a network of shipping facilities and numerous far-flung outposts at places across the known world. Solomon's representative for the voyages to Ophir was Hiram, from the Phoenician city of Tyre. He was an exceptionally expert seaman, unlike the people from the Red Sea tribes.

Ophir must have been unimaginably far away since journeys took not less than three years.[36] Expeditions set off from the harbour of Egeon-Gober (Ezjon-Geber) near Elath on the shores of the sea of reeds in the land of the Edomites, a people already conquered by David because of the caravan route to the Red

Sea and under Solomon dependent on Israel.[37] From there the
journey went through the Red Sea towards the south-east. But
what was the destination? We gain a clue about the geographical location of Ophir and Tarshish from the exceptionally valuable goods, apart from gold, for which sailors ventured upon
such uncertain and arduous enterprises: almug trees, peacocks
and apes. All these trading goods were indigenous to India.
Apes could also be procured elsewhere and it is uncertain
whether almug trees of the quality desired by Solomon were
available in other places too; but peacocks were only to be
found in India. However, the evidence that all three were
fetched from India is provided by the Hebrew designations
used in the Bible, which are direct derivations of Indian words.
Almug trees are the aromatic red Indian sandalwood (Sanskrit
valgu); peacocks (Hebrew *thukkiyim*) are *tokei* or *togai* in Tamil,
and *sikhin* in Sanskrit; *koph*, the Hebrew word for ape, is *kapi*
in Sanskrit; and ivory is *shen habbim* in Hebrew and *ab* in
Tamil.[38] It is also independently known that peacocks were
exported from India at the time when the Old Testament books
of Chronicles and Kings were put together. Their designation
reveals too that other trading goods mentioned in the Old
Testament obviously came from India. The aromatic resin derived from aloes (*ahalim* in Hebrew – Proverbs 7:17, Song of
Solomon 4:14) is derived from the Sanskrit word *agaru*.

Although the names of trading goods derive from Dravidian
(Tamil) words, that does not necessarily signify that Ophir
must be sought in southern India, where Dravidian tribes
lived. The sandalwood and peacocks could have been procured
from Dravidian dealers elsewhere in India while keeping their
original names. There are many indications that Hiram's ships
sailed to a port in the north-west of India, in the area where
the Indus entered the sea. Two well-known researchers into
antiquity, Christian Lassen and Sir Alexander Cunningham,
identified Ophir with the ancient Aberia, the Abhira of Sanskrit
geographers, which is the name given to the area of the Indus
delta.[39]

We should not imagine that Hiram, who sailed to Ophir for
Solomon, was the first mariner to make his way to this legendary land. As early as the second millennium BC, constant Assyrian
attacks forced the Phoenicians to expand their Mediterranean
trade and to seek new seas on whose shores they established
colonies. Long before David and Solomon they had agreements

with the Edomites, permitting them to use Edomite harbours on the Red Sea. The passage to Ophir was not unknown to them, and they obviously travelled part of the way along the established sea route used for trading between Mesopotamia and the Indus valley cultures.

The time devoted to such enterprises was very worth while, since the Phoenicians, despite apparently already knowing the monsoon winds, did not go directly to the Indian subcontinent. As a nation of traders they knew how to do business at all the ports along their way. Moreover they would have spent a considerable time at Ophir and Tarshish, since the rare goods they sought had to be fetched from far away. On setting out from home Hiram's ships sailed along the coast to Yemen, steered by way of Cape Guardafui to the island of Socotra, and from Aden took a course north-eastwards along the Arabian seaboard. At the Straits of Hormuz they first went to the Bahrain islands and then proceeded eastwards towards Ophir and Tarshish. A stay at Bahrain made good sense for Hiram since two of the islands, Tylos (Assyrian: Dilmun or Tilmun) and Aradus, are thought to have been the oldest Phoenician settlements in the Persian Gulf. Archaeological excavations on the islands confirm that they were crucial centres for sea trade between the Harappa culture and Mesopotamia as early as the third millennium BC.[40] The Bahrain islands thus remained an important centre for exchanges of goods between East and West. Accadian texts spoke of the Alik Tilmun, who traded between Ur and Tilmun. Ivory, precious woods, cotton, pearls and copper came from distant lands (Makkan and Meluhha). Archaeological finds, texts and commercial records from the reign of Ibbi-Sin at the end of Ur's third dynasty (1963–1939 BC) clearly show that Makkan and Meluhha were identical with the coastal region of eastern Baluchistan and the area around the Indus estuary. The Phoenicians eventually took over Tylos and Aradus as ideal bases for their trading expeditions to the eastern seas.

Hiram's objective Ophir was the very area that was once called Makkan/Meluhha and visited from Tilmun. The Sumerians had already followed the same route in acquiring a much-coveted kind of wood and the highly popular 'multicoloured bird from Meluhha' – the peacock – the very goods that Hiram was charged with procuring for Solomon's court.

The expeditions to Ophir constitute a clear indication of what may be the oldest east–west sea trade of any significance over very great distances. It is quite possible that Indians themselves participated in the voyages to Ophir, since sea journeys on big ships are mentioned in old vedic texts such as the *Rig-Veda* (twelfth to tenth century BC).

The *sind* (or *sindu*) and *misu* wood the Assyrian king Sennacherib (704–681 BC) used for columns and doors in his palaces was imported from Makkan. The word *sindu* is not to be found in old Babylonian and Sumerian texts. *Sindh* is the Indo-Aryan designation for the river Indus and the landscape through which it flows. From Iran, where displacement transformed the word into *hind*, the name reached Greece, where the inhabitants of the area where the word originated were called Hindus, the term still used for their religious allegiance. Sind wood was certainly felled along the Indus where there were exceptionally rich and excellent supplies, as we know from later reports written during Alexander's India campaign. Also much in demand in Mesopotamia was the resin from *Ferula galbaniflua*, which was highly reputed for its healing powers. This plant was indigenous to eastern Iran and Afghanistan, and had to be fetched from there.

In 689 BC Sennacherib devastated Babylon in one of many punitive Assyrian expeditions against revolts in the south of the country. After the Medes from Persia succeeded in inflicting a major defeat on the Assyrians (625 BC), the Semitic nomadic tribe of Chaldeans strove for dominance of Mesopotamia. Under the leadership of Nebuchadnezzar (604–562 BC) their kingdom was extended as far as Egypt. The Chaldeans then became of great importance for sea trade with India. There is much evidence of great activity by sea between the two countries from the seventh century BC onwards.[41] Sea trade was obviously dominated by the Dravidians during that epoch, although Aryans were also involved. In writings produced around 300 BC – the *Dharmasutras* by Baudhayana and Gautama – we read of long sea voyages being forbidden to orthodox brahmins, with infringements punished by loss of caste status, but we do not have to conclude that Aryan brahmins held aloof from adventures on distant seas. In the Baudhayana *Dharmasutra* it is conceded that the northern Aryans paid little heed to these proscriptions.

From Agatharchides of Knidos (second century BC) we learn that Indians travelled from the Indus estuary to the land of the

Sabaeans, to Dvipa sukhatra, the name Indians gave to the island of Socotra off Cape Guardafui. *Sukhatara* means 'very happy'. Later that epithet was applied to the whole of southern Arabia, known as Arabia Felix, 'fortunate Arabia'. The fact that Indians had trading settlements in the land of the Sabaeans is indicated by a place in Arabia bearing the Sanskrit name Nagara ('town'). Indians were also to be found on the East African coast at that time, and even on China's shores. They acted as intermediaries in the busy trade by sea which linked Babylon and China. Deutero-Isaiah mentions the Sin as a people that visited Babylon (Isaiah 49:12), which must mean the Chinese, whom Indians called K'îna. Links between China and Babylon necessarily involved India. It has even been suggested that astrology and magic reached China from a Chaldean source, intermingled with Indian ideas, by way of traders on the Erythraean Sea after 665 BC. The fact that rulers in the Land of the Two Rivers were well informed about treasures from distant India, and did not want to do without such splendour in their courts, is demonstrated by the beams of Indian cedar which Nebuchadnezzar employed in his palace at Birs Nimrud. At Ur the neo-Babylonian Temple of the Moon was roofed with Indian teak.

Solomon's peacocks are again encountered in this later trade with Babylon. An early Buddhist narrative, the *Baveru-Jataka*, confirms the export of peacocks by Indian merchants to the land of Baveru (Babylon). It is said that in an earlier existence as a peacock the Buddha ended up in Baveru. The popular tale underlying the *Baveru-Jataka* must be very ancient. We know that peacocks were imported into Babylon long before the sixth century BC. The annals of Tiglath-Pileser III, King of Assyria from 745 to 727 BC, reveal that tribute included 'birds of the heavens with purple and blue wings' – certainly Indian peacocks.

The intensity and cultural significance of connections between Mesopotamia and India by way of the Persian Gulf during the Assyrian and Chaldean epochs is demonstrated by the Indian adoption of written characters. The oldest forms of North Semitic script are found in Brahmi characters, which were introduced between 890 and 750 BC by Indian merchants from Mesopotamia.[42] This form of writing was initially exclusively employed in administration and trade. Only around 250 BC did Brahmi spread across the whole of India after important changes and additions had been made, producing an

incomparably precise alphabet. The start of Achaimenidic
dominance in Iran under Achaimenes (705–675 BC) was accompanied by the establishment of Aramaic as the official language
throughout the country. The proto-Aramaic alphabet arose in
the Indus area and led – by the third millennium at the latest
– to the development in this part of India of Karoshthi script,
which like Aramaic ran from right to left. However Karoshthi
remained a regional script, whereas the Brahmi alphabet became the basis for today's Indian alphabets, headed by
Devanagari. The Indian merchants who brought North Semitic
characters to their homeland also introduced Semitic legends.
Some are already to be found in the *Brahmanas* (eighth–seventh
century BC), the oldest vedic writings. There we encounter the
story of the Babylonian flood (*Stapatha-Brahmana*), which seems
to have got to India by way of the same stable maritime
relations.

So there can be no doubt that after centuries of sea trade with
Mesopotamia Indians had permanent settlements in the Babylon
of the sixth century BC. Babylon was, as Berosus, a Chaldean
priest of Baal (third century BC), wrote in his celebrated chronicle,
a city where very many foreigners lived. That was not just
chance. The city, previously known mainly for its temples,
quickly became one of the world's largest commercial centres.
Nebuchadnezzar had had it rebuilt and splendidly adorned,
making it into an unparalleled wonder.

During preceding centuries relations between the people of
the Land of the Two Rivers and the Jews were more political
than economic. In the mid-ninth century the revived Assyrian
empire launched an attack against Palestine and Syria. Shal-
maneser III (859–824 BC), who already imported Indian
elephants, briefly threatened Israel and Judea, but in the eighth
century both states flourished again with various Aramaic
tribes struggling for precedence. Under Tiglath-Pileser III,
Israel and Judea were conquered by the Assyrians and condemned to vassalage.

When the Chaldeans ruled in the Land of the Two Rivers,
there occurred an event which not only made biblical history
but also decisively influenced the transformation of Jewish
religious ideas. In 587 BC Nebuchadnezzar captured Jerusalem,
and many Jews were deported to Babylon for fifty years of
captivity (586–536 BC). That corresponded to two generations
in terms of the life expectancy of that time. At any rate most

of the Jews who returned from exile to Palestine had been born in another country. They had become acquainted with Babylonian lifestyles and had grown up in a flourishing metropolis, open to the world, where there was a great mixture of peoples. Despite all separatist attempts by the Children of Israel to keep foreign influences at a distance, they were subject to their conquerors' command and thus constantly exposed to the peculiarities of the alien cultures. A lack of contact with Indian migrants and traders would have been much more astonishing than its occurrence. It would perhaps have been even more amazing if the Israelites had not passed on the tales, stories and legends from India and other parts of Asia that went the rounds on the streets of Babylon as in all Oriental cities. Zarathustrian teachings from Iran, which were listened to sympathetically by Jews in opposition to the Babylonians and in the hope of liberation by the Iranians, became part of the exiles' treasury of legends.

It can in fact be demonstrated that from this time onwards Indian, Persian and Babylonian elements multiplied in Jewish writings and turned up in cultural and religious life. Consider Chapters 40–55 of the Book of Isaiah, which are attributed to a Deutero-Isaiah. They were written in Babylonian exile. The author known as Deutero-Isaiah came from Mesopotamia, and his texts were influenced by Zarathustrian ideas. Part of what is known as the Trito-Isaiah (Isaiah 6:17) even describes a Persian ceremony. Strikingly, only after the period of exile did the idea of a redeemer become a key element in Jewish eschatological[43] belief – the redeemer that Zarathustra had prophesied, whose appearance would be accompanied by the Last Days with a great battle and victory over the powers of darkness.

Not all Jews returned to Palestine. Some even remained in the Land of the Two Rivers, or moved further east into Persian territory or even to southern India, trading with their home country. Constant exchange with the East also guaranteed an unbroken communication of ideas to Canaan. For instance, the apocalypse described in the Book of Daniel is simply an adaptation of the Persian apocalypse with minor alterations.[44] The late Jewish fourth Book of Ezra talks of the separation of families on the Day of Judgement – a typically Iranian motif.

The Jews owed their liberation from captivity to King Cyrus (550–530 BC) of the Persian Achaemenidian dynasty. In a mighty expansive thrust he conquered the Medes and Lydia, captured Babylon in 538 BC, and thereby established the Persian Empire. Under the leadership of Darius I Hystaspes (519–484 BC) that great empire soon extended from the Mediterranean to the Indus. Driven by the centuries-long hatred that separated Babylonians and Persians, he did everything to eradicate Babylon's glory once and for all. At the start of the fifth century Darius had dams constructed to block access to the Euphrates and Tigris. These crucial channels for sea trade were quickly obstructed and withered away. Faced with that emergency, Chaldean merchants sought other harbours so as to keep their business going. They established a colony at Gerrha, far down the Gulf, where they pursued even more active trade with India.[45] It was probably the Semitic tribe of the Nabataeans which settled in Gerrha alongside the Phoenicians, and there is no reason to assume that Indian merchants in Babylon did not follow their example. It is uncertain when Gerrha was established, but it must have been after the Persians conquered Babylon. Not all foreigners left Mesopotamia's fertile river valleys. Many gladly remained in Babylon's tolerant atmosphere, open to the world, thus establishing one of the oldest multicultural societies, whose influence extended westwards to the Middle East and eastwards to India and China. We know that more than a hundred years after Darius II (423–404 BC) had liberated the Jews from Babylonian captivity, many nations crowded together in lower Mesopotamia. Even permanent garrisons of foreigners from Armenia, India, Afghanistan, Asia Minor and Arabia found a new home there.[46] However, Babylon's star had long been in decline. By the time of Strabo (63 BC–26 AD) Babylon had become an unimportant city with a great past.

The Persian campaigns did not just destroy Babylon; they even reached Egypt. In those times of political and economic upheaval, merchants from Yemen took advantage of the situation and became the main traders in the Erythraean Sea. The lion's share of business with India and equatorial Africa fell into the hands of businessmen from Mouza, Aden and Kane. In the Red Sea at that time navigation was controlled by a vanished people whose remnants Theodore Bent discovered in Mashonaland (in the heart of Zimbabwe) and close to the Red Sea. At a later date the Mouza traders gained control over Azania (modern Somalia), and the Sabaeans established settlements in India. When the Greeks arrived, they found Sabaean fortresses and factories on India's western coast.[47]

In the fifth century trade with India entered upon a new dimension. We know that from the fact that at this time certain Asian goods became known in Greece under their Indian names. Rice, one of India's main exports, was a widespread source of nourishment during the age of Sophocles (496–406 BC). The Greek term for rice is identical to the Tamil *arisi*. Aristophanes often mentions peacocks. Peacocks and Indian sandalwood were – as has already been shown – known in Palestine under their Tamil names. Around 430 BC peacocks and rice are mentioned in Greek texts without any further explanation being thought necessary. They must have been widely disseminated in Greece by 470 or 460 at the latest to be thought generally known in the Athens of thirty years later. Self-evident acquaintance with Indian goods is of great importance since it occurs in the epoch immediately after the Buddha's death, enabling us to pose the provocative question: did initial knowledge of the Dharma reach Athens along with established trade with distant India?

The Indian Philosophy of Pythagoras

We have spoken of trading relations and important cultural exchanges between India and Western peoples up to the fifth century. Despite the paucity of records to date, far-reaching connections and surprising borrowings can be ascertained. If we ask to what extent these contacts influenced intellectual and spiritual life in the most important Mediterranean culture of the time, that of the Greeks, we come to an amazing conclusion. Viewed from the standpoint of Greek philosophy, the Indian connection exerted a considerably more significant impact than all the trading links would indicate.

Even among the Ionian nature philosophers there are important ideas that seem extremely Indian, with the result that already in antiquity it was said that Thales, Empedocles, Anaxagoras, Democritus, Pythagoras, and others had visited the East in order to pursue their philosophical studies. At a later date, some similarities to the Upanishads are to be found in Plato (427–347 BC), who upheld the idea of the transmigration of souls.

Thales of Miletus (c. 650–560 BC) believed that all existence

derived from water. The India of vedic times was dominated
by the mythological idea of the primal water out of which the
entire world emerged. Anaximander of Miletus (610–540 BC)
saw the basis of all things as involving an eternal, infinite, and
indeterminate primal substance from which specific matter
arises and to which it returns. Samkhya teachings in India
speak analagously of *prakriti*, the primal matter from which all
scattered matter derives and to which all that is reverts. The
Samkhya doctrine, a sober, rational, almost scientific system,
was a further philosophical development of ancient Indian,
pre-vedic views from which Buddhism, Jainism and Yoga also
drew. Its basic elements are to be found in the *Maitrayani* and
Shvetashvatara Upanishads.

Heraclitus (*c.* 550–480 BC) gave celebrated expression in one
of his obscure aphorisms to unceasing change and transformation in the world of appearances: 'Everything is in flux.' The
Samkhya teaching of constant destruction and renewal of the
world could hardly be summed up more concisely.

Xenophanes (570–475 BC), founder of the Eleatic school,
based his work on profound doubts about popular religions.
The views of his Indian contemporary Gautama the Buddha
derived from a similar process of thought. Both were extremely
dissatisfied with the prevalent popular form of belief, and
reached similar conclusions through reflection alone. With
Xenophanes this led to the insight that there could only be one
God, who stood above all gods and men. He was said to consist
of just an eye and a mind, effortlessly dominating everything
by way of his spiritual insight. With the Buddha that understanding took another form. He declared himself to be 'the
highest among gods and men, who has attained the highest
wisdom and possesses an all-seeing eye (*samanta chaksu*)'.[48]

In fact the Eleatic teachings are basically the same as those
of the pre-Buddhist Upanishads. Indologist Richard Garbe has
pointed to the striking fact that both systems put forward
amazingly similar claims about the One Truth.[49] Indian echoes
are clearer still in Parmenides (*c.* 515–445 BC), who declared the
entire sensuously experienceable world to be an illusion. Whatsoever exists in dispersion and multiplicity, subject to change,
is only appearance. Only the infinite, the indestructible and the
omnipresent possesses reality. In its essential aspects that view
accorded completely with the Upanishads and the philosophy
of Vedanta derived from them, and is among the oldest surviv-

ing Indian ideas. The key statement in Democritus's metaphysics (*c.* 460–370 BC) – 'From nothing will come nothing. Nothing that is can be destroyed' – is to be found almost word for word in the Samkhya.

Another parallel is apparent in the special significance both the Upanishads and a number of Greek philosophers assign to the investigation of one's own being. Yoga was developed so as to create practices that would make possible such systematic research into the self with the objective of achieving spiritual insights. In the West self-investigation became a moral obligation. Both Thales and Socrates (470–339 BC) are said to have urged, 'Know thyself', and Heraclitus responded to the Ionian research into nature: 'I am researching into myself.'

Those correspondences cannot easily be derived from the mysterious impact of the Axis Time. If we contemplate the teachings and life of Pythagoras (*c.* 570–480 BC), it becomes all the more difficult to attribute them to a mysterious simultaneity, without any knowledge of Indian ideas.

In a very impressive study, Indologist Leopold von Schroeder has demonstrated Pythagoras's many relations with the Indian world.[50] One of Pythagoras's views immediately attracts attention, as his identification as it were: the teaching of the transmigration of souls. The idea of reincarnation was completely unfamiliar in Greece before Pythagoras, and most writers, following Herodotus, have sought the origin of that idea in Egypt. Hekateus of Abdera maintained that Pythagoras had brought a *hieros logos* ('holy book') back from Egypt. Two centuries after Pythagoras, when Alexander the Great reached the Indus, he thought he was standing by the sources of the Nile in Upper Egypt. It could be that Hekateus's account is based on a similar misunderstanding, resulting from the age's lack of geographical knowledge. Pythagoras's teaching about reincarnation certainly did not come from Egypt, since the idea of transmigration of souls was also unknown there. In antiquity, however, Egypt was viewed as a mysterious land of great erudition. People were inclined to seek the origin of all unexplained ideas in Egypt. The concept of the reincarnation of the soul in other forms and living beings was only to be found in India from early times, playing an important part in everyday religious life. Leopold von Schroeder thus concludes: 'Pythagoras can only have taken over this teaching from Indians.'[51]

Already during antiquity stories then in circulation maintained

that Pythagoras had visited Eastern countries. Alexander Polyhistor (first century AD) wrote of Pythagoras having discussions
with Indian brahmins, who taught him their insights into the
essence of mind and body. The exceptionally scholarly
Clement of Alexandria (*c.* 150–214 AD) spoke of long-
established stories about Pythagoras having travelled to India
and being instructed by wise brahmins there.[52]

The Samkhya Indian philosophy and the Buddha's religion,
both of which came into being at precisely Pythagoras's time,
emphasize redemption from the cycle of rebirths. They view
the soul as being trapped in the body. Only through a process
of recognition of this state of affairs can the soul be liberated
from its body and spared having to return to the suffering of a
bodily existence. Strikingly, Pythagoras similarly believed that
the soul is bound to a body, buried there, *as a punishment*. He
too viewed the body as a prison. In his *Admonitions Concerning
Embodiment of the Soul, Banished to the Earth*, Empedocles (*c.* 500–
430 BC), who owed many of his views to Parmenides and
Pythagoras, even spoke of the 'alien garment of the body'. For
Empedocles the soul was put into a body once again because
of an accumulation of guilt. After death, however, a decision
was taken about whether it should be absorbed in the cosmos,
deserved Tartarus, or was destined for a renewed passage
through human and animal bodies. Empedocles linked the
teaching of the transmigration of souls with a theory of
development. According to that, nothing could come into
being that did not previously exist, and nothing that existed
could pass away. That too is very similar to the characteristic
Samkhya idea of the uncreated and infinite reality of creation
(*sat-karya-vada*).

In India the form of re-embodiment was similarly dependent
on previous behaviour (*karma*). In brahminic thought the soul
that has lived well may be granted a life in heaven or – remarkably – a blissful existence on the moon. Amazingly, Pythagoreans also knew that view, and for them the moon was the
home of the blessed.

Like the Buddha, Pythagoras was also able to remember
previous existences. He maintained that he was once Euphor-
bos, then Pyrander, and another time the son of Hermes. It
was said to be Hermes who granted him such memories of all
his former lives.

If the idea of reincarnation was all that was to be found in

Pythagoras, that might be seen as an intriguing separate development. However, this unconventional philosopher's thinking reveals a number of special features that could only have originated in India. He laid down that his followers should be vegetarians. He not only rejected the eating of meat but also repudiated beans. Why on earth did he impose this completely inexplicable ban on the eating of beans? In India eating meat was not generally forbidden, but during the brahminic period vegetarianism was increasingly taken up. In the *Maitrayani-Samhita*, after the *Kathakam* one of the oldest *Yajurveda* texts (*c.* tenth century BC), we find the following regulation for people making sacrifices: 'He should not eat any beans; beans are not sufficiently pure' (I, 4:10). In the *Kathakam* too the eating of beans is expressly forbidden, and the *Taittiriya-Samhita* designates beans as being unsuitable for sacrifices because they are cultically impure. This parallel is so unusual and odd that even a level-headed researcher like Leopold von Schroeder views it as being more than just coincidence.[53]

The Pythagorean School disseminated the teaching of the five elements, which were comprehended as being originally related to the five regular bodies. For Pythagoreans the fifth element was ether, which encompassed the other four. Pythagoras seems to have taken over the doctrine of the five elements from India, where it was widespread. It was systematically presented in Kapila's Samkhya philosophy, which was also taken up by the Buddha, who is said to have added consciousness as a sixth element.

Nor is that all. Alongside the transmigration of souls, the ban on eating beans, and the teachings about the five elements, the following astonishing correspondences with Indian ideas are to be found in the Pythagorean system:

1. the distinction between heaven, earth, and space
2. the view that heaven is populated by gods, earth by human beings, and air by demons
3. the distinction between an immortal, spiritual organ of knowledge and a material organ that disintegrates with the body
4. the distinction between the coarse material body and a subtle etheric sheath of souls
5. the lack of a concept of God, as in Samkhya, which was ultimately an atheistic view of the world

Pythagoras was known for both his un-Greek views and also for the esoteric community he established around himself, where secret teachings were transmitted orally. In fact the religio-philosophical group was very similar in character to the communities of Indian monks that were increasingly set up at that time. Numbers played an important part in the Pythagorean fraternity. Mystical qualities were attributed to them. That is why everyone remembers Pythagoras's name in conjunction with mathematics lessons as Pythagoras's theorem.[54] Does that involve one of Pythagoras's most profound discoveries? Far from it. Moritz Cantor, the famous mathematician, has graphically demonstrated that Pythagoras's theorem and irrational magnitudes in mathematics originated in India.[55] Cantor may not have indicated Pythagoras's dependence on India, but he clearly showed that the Vedas possessed detailed drawings enabling priests to calculate the orientation of altars, where right angles had to be accurate. This procedure, concluded Cantor, was correct, and only possible through knowledge of Pythagoras's theorem. The Shulvasutras reveal that centuries before Pythagoras vedic priests knew 'his' theorem, explaining it (according to Cantor) as Pythagoras himself was likely to have done rather than in Euclidean fashion. The theorem played a major part in ancient Indian geometry rather than just being an incidental priestly achievement.

Finally, we would like to draw attention to a remarkable correspondence. The term *sãmkhya* differs only in the length of the two vowels from *samkhyã* from which it is derived, and which means 'number'. A Samkhya is thus, like a Pythagorean, a 'philosopher of numbers'.

Since the Pythagorean system has so many unusual elements in common with Indian ideas (in particular Samkhya teachings), it can only be concluded that Pythagoras was in contact with India. It is not possible to determine whether he gained his knowledge from a travelling brahmin or whether he himself was in India. The latter is more probable and would accord with his restless personality, constantly in search of knowledge and testing out new frontiers. Leopold von Schroeder presumed that Pythagoras could not satisfy his craving for knowledge at home so he set off on long journeys to seek insights among unfamiliar peoples. Richly laden with Indian wisdom, he returned to the Western world, transplanting 'buds of learning whose far-reaching importance for Greek culture, and thus for Western culture as a whole, was only fully acknowledged many centuries later.'[56]

Alexander at the Indus

The great conquerors also sought the wisdom of remote peoples. They were certainly not just concerned with seizing riches and subjugating nations. A degree of scientific interest and delight in discovery also underlay some of their campaigns. The mighty Achaemenid prince Darius I Hystaspes, who conquered and destroyed Babylon, was thus not satisfied with integrating areas around the Indus into his empire. He wanted to find out more about this unfamiliar world which was now part of his sphere of influence. For that purpose in around 520 BC an expedition under Skylax of Karyanda was sent from the Gandhara region to explore the Indus estuary. Skylax travelled down the Indus and continued around the Arabian coast to Suez. The expedition took thirty months, as the ships had to be constructed on the spot. Unfortunately Skylax's exceptionally important account of this voyage has been lost. We only know about his experiences through Herodotus of Halicarnassus (c. 490–425 BC), the 'father of history', and some of the knowledge he gained about India is also preserved in Aristotle (on the status of kings), Athenaios (soils and flora), and Philostratos (mythical peoples).

A description of the earth by a contemporary of Skylax's, Hekataios of Miletus, was for centuries of decisive importance in geographical and ethnographic knowledge. Hekaitos was a much-travelled, politically active historian who produced a genealogical tree of rulers' families and a kind of comprehensive travel guide. He also reported on the Gand(h)arai or Gand(h)arioi, the inhabitants of Gandhara.

Later Greece received detailed news about India from Ktesias, a man from Knidos in Caria, who for seventeen years was personal physician at the court of King Artaxerxes II Mnemon (404–358 BC). After his return he wrote two books, *Indica* and *Persica*, which contained very interesting and precise observations about body care, clothing, trade and flora in the upper Indus valley – alongside the fantastic ethnography, characteristic of antiquity, of tribes on the fringes of the known world (for instance, people with dogs' heads).[57] Close relations existed between India and Persia at the time of Artaxerxes. The old land routes were still intact, and the Persian Achaemenids controlled the region up to the Punjab. Gandhara was mentioned in the first inscriptions concerned with Darius I Hystaspes, and Western influence can be demonstrated in many aspects of life there at that time. The lower Indus area was among the Persian satrapies. Herodotus reports on the high level of tribute India had to pay its conqueror, Darius I.

During the last two centuries of Achaemenidic dominance, there were frequent exchanges and regular traffic between the different cultures. The empire's sphere of influence extended over enormous areas. India, Egypt, Syria, Asia Minor and Mesopotamia were all united in the Iranian imperium. Contact between the many different tribal groupings inevitably led to numerous culturally significant encounters. Under Xerxes (486–465 BC) a contingent of Indian troops participated in the attack on Greece through the pass of Thermopylae and in the sacking of Athens, while Darius III (336–331 BC) threw Indian warriors against Alexander's raging army.

Knowledge of India attained a completely new dimension with Alexander the Great's celebrated – and for its leader ultimately so tragic – campaign during the years 327–324 BC. Many details have been handed down to us in accounts of the fighting used by Flavius Arrianos (c. 95–175 AD), Curtius Rufus (first century AD), and Diodorus Siculus (first century AD). The Indian campaign was intended to secure mastery of the world for the mighty Macedonian army, which had triumphed over Darius III, the powerful Persian king. Alexander set out to gain possession of the last known patches of territory for his immeasurable empire. He wanted nothing less than to reach the eastern and southern limits of the inhabited world (*oikumene*). He thus reached the middle Indus, the area the ancient geographers in his homeland had described.

In 327 Alexander secured the link to the West by way of a chain of garrison towns, and at the end of the year moved from Bactria into Indian territory. His diplomatic skill enabled him to make rapid progress without having to fight. As early as spring 327 he crossed the Hindu Kush with 120,000 foot-soldiers and 15,000 cavalrymen. At the beginning of 326 his army had reached the Indus.

The region's ruler took Alexander's advance as a favourable opportunity for both safeguarding his cultural monuments and getting rid of disliked neighbours. The old Indian idea was that the kingdom close at hand was the natural enemy while the kingdom further away was the natural ally. Ambhi, the master of Taxila, hoped that submissiveness would be rewarded by his being granted neighbouring territories. He sent ambassadors to Alexander proclaiming voluntary submission. The city's valuable buildings thus avoided destruction in war.

Before Alexander could make a triumphal entry into Taxila, he first had to cross the Swat valley, which was controlled by the wild mountain tribes of the Asvakas, for whom the only acceptable alternatives were victory or death. If one remembers the determination and persistence of the mountain peoples during Soviet occupation of Afghanistan and up to the present day, one can get some idea of the test Alexander had to undergo in this region. At that time his star was still in the ascendant. He mastered that hurdle, and as soon as he had crossed the Indus moved further eastwards against Poros, supported by 5,000 of the King of Taxila's warriors. Alexander deployed cunning in defeating Poros's considerably larger army. The Greek force stormed further, over the rivers Chenab and Ravi (Greek: Hydraotes) as far as the Beas (Greek: Hyphasis) and into the area between today's northern Indian towns of Amritsar and Jullundur. Alexander was only concerned about reaching the end of the inhabited world, and he thought that had been achieved in these furthest satrapies of the Persian empire while simultaneously believing that he had got as far as the source of the Nile. In the Indus and the Hydaspes the Greeks found crocodiles, and in another river, the Akesines, lotus blossoms; crocodiles and lotuses were only familiar from the Nile. This reveals the lack of information available in Alexander's times for establishing one's situation and understanding global geography.

When inhabitants of that area told Alexander of a people which owned huge herds of elephants and dwelt in an immeasurably large area of land to the east, and also spoke of a river that flowed in the same direction,[58] he knew that he had not reached either the source tributaries of the Nile or the eastern limits of the *oikumene*. Nothing stopped Alexander. He wanted to push onwards. But his Macedonian troops were weary after long years of war. They mutinied and finally forced their leader to turn back. In autumn 325 Alexander left Indian territory, reached Susa in Persia after twenty months, and died at Babylon a year later.

Alexander and his troops headed homeward by land. He left behind Nearchos, an experienced mariner who, like Skylax two centuries previously, was supposed to return by travelling down the Indus and then by sea. However, a westward journey by ship was not desirable at that time since the south-western monsoon was blowing. Alexander had discovered that the ocean in that locality could be crossed before the Pleiades vanished, i.e. from the start of winter until the solstice. Nearchos was intended to wait until the wind changed in order to travel with the favourable north-east wind prevalent from November. Nevertheless, he had to set sail as early as the beginning of September since he was under attack by Indians. He launched his ships near Xylenopolis ('wood town') on the southern reaches of the Indus. The town's name indicates the wealth of wood that used to be exported from the Indus valley. Nearchos first landed on the sandy island of Krokala. In his celebrated *Naturalis Historia*, Pliny the Elder (23–79 AD) provides an impressive description of the discovery of the sea routes to India, beginning with Nearchos. From June to September, says Pliny, the Indus estuary could be reached from Cape Syagrum in Arabia by way of the *favonius* wind, known as *hippalis* (the south-west monsoon).

The fact that Alexander's India campaign is not mentioned in any old Indian sources is not surprising since he obviously largely succeeded in taking territory without any fighting (except against Poros). Scarcely any changes resulted for the local populations, since Indian rulers remained in office. Persian satraps were merely replaced by Greek governors. However, even long before Alexander, Indian records contained the names Yavana or Yona as designations for Greeks and Greece. The terms derived from the Hellenic area of Ionia, and constitute an infallible sign of early Indian awareness of Greece.[59]

After Alexander the world along the Indus was no longer as it used to be. He had numerous towns established and a number of garrisons remained. Peithon, one of his governors, ruled the lower Indus area, and Philippos was in Taxila. For a decade the political situation was unclear, with Greeks and locals disputing power. The territory of the Seleucids, who inherited a great part of Alexander's empire, extended from the Aegean to

Arachosia and the Indus. On the fringes of those areas arose small Greek principalities which for over two centuries fostered intensive intercultural clashes in the Punjab area. Those princes' coins convey an impression of the cultural intermingling involved. The inscriptions are usually in two languages, Greek and Karoshthi. Alexander was by no means just interested in acquisition of land. His retinue included writers whose skills revealed them to be intellectuals, men with a lively interest in the morals, customs and religions of distant countries.

After 317 tranquillity returned to the Indus. The Indian king Chandragupta Maurya, founder of the celebrated Maurya dynasty, conquered the area and incorporated it in his empire. In a battle near Taxila he defeated Seleucus I Nicator (358–281 BC), the successor to Alexander's kingdom between the Euphrates, Persia and the Medes. Seleucus was aware of the difficulties involved in trying to win back, let alone holding onto, this frontier area, so he concluded an alliance with Chandragupta. The outcome inaugurated a new phase of Indian relations with the West. Regular political contacts were initiated whereby Megasthenes, an envoy from Seleucus, was sent to the Indian court at Pataliputra (modern Patna) around 300 BC. Greek-Indian relations were thus upheld and intensified. There was also a private and friendly exchange of letters between Antiochus I (280–261 BC) and Bindusara (298–274 BC), Chandragupta's successor on the Maurya throne.[60] Bindusara asked the Greek king to procure for him sweet wine, dried figs and an eloquent Sophist. The Indian ruler wanted to find out about Greek philosophy. After Antiochos had informed his Indian correspondent that Sophists could not be bought in his country, Deimachos was sent as the Greek envoy.

Despite all the cruelty of the Maurya way of governing, they were rulers who embodied the spirit of their country: the wish for comprehensive wisdom and a need for cultivated philosophical and religious conversation. The ambassadors at Indian courts from the Maurya period onwards were thus not primarily politicians but well-educated men who certainly observed customs and thought in the host country with great curiosity.

It was 160 years since the death of the Buddha when Alexander started to withdraw from the Land of the Five Rivers, leaving behind his garrisons. The Buddhist community had taken shape in two councils – one immediately after the Buddha's death (*c.* 480 BC), or to be more accurate after the great 'extinction' (*mahaparinirvana*), and the second around 380 BC, and the Master's teachings had been preserved and spread. During that long period the Awakened One's message both reached the various parts of the kingdom (around Magadha and Videha on the lower reaches of the Ganges), and also increasingly spread in the Punjab, Maharashtra and Sri Lanka. The monks following the wandering life the Buddha had shown them, and moved along the great rivers to the mountainous regions and to the old cultural area of the Indus and its tributaries.

The Greeks following Alexander encountered Buddhists in the region around Taxila and in the Swat valley. The Indian ascetics Alexander met in Gandhara, called *sarmanai* or *samanaioi* by his informants, sat under holy fig-trees.[61] Those must have been *shramanas*, a term applied to Bhuddist monks living from begging. It cannot have included orthodox brahmins, especially since *shramana* is only used in connection with ascetic wandering monks. In addition, only among Buddhists was the fig-tree held in such high cultic repute since it was under a similar tree that the Buddha achieved enlightenment. The Greeks called one of those ascetics Kalanos since he used to greet them with the word *kalyanam* ('hail'). Kalanos incinerated himself on a funeral pyre in front of Alexander's army.

It is to Megasthenes, the Seleucid envoy to Chandragupta's court, that we owe the most detailed description of Indian life at that time. Among other things he reported on the supremacy of the brahmins, and it is also in his accounts that we read about the Buddhist *sarmanas*. As we have said, Chandragupta was the founder of the glorious dynasty of Maurya kings. Around 320 BC he seized power at Magadha, the ancient political centre on the eastern Ganges, by overthrowing the usurping clan of the Nandas. He succeeded in incorporating the Punjab into his kingdom in the north-west, and also added territory in the areas of what are today Afghanistan and Baluchistan. Chandragupta, primarily abetted by his cunning chief minister Kautilya, brought a spirit of unemotional *realpolitik* into this first extensive Indian empire. He organized an incredibly efficient government with a carefully graded hierarchy of officials whose competence impressed Magasthenes. Within a short time the state had attained high standards, as is shown by the *Arthashastra*, the age's famous primer of state, most probably written by Kautilya himself. The detailed description of absolutist royal power and the rational arguments on behalf of expanding and upholding that power have provoked comparisons with Machiavelli's *Il Principe*. The *Arthashastra* characteristically defines the art of governing as *dandaniti*, the science of punishment. The first Maurya kings interpreted that literally. Their epoch was exceptionally cruel. Bindusara, Chandragupta's son, even had the honorary title of *Amitraghata*, the Slaughterer of Enemies.

Magadha had of course long been the centre of new religions. Mahavira had been there 200 years previously, preaching his message of extreme asceticism and reverence for life. The highly revered and often-visited places where Buddha Shakyamuni had spoken were close to the new capital Pataliputra: Bodh Gaya where he achieved enlightenment; Isipatana (modern Sarnath) where he first publicly proclaimed his teachings; Kusinara (modern Kasia) where he achieved Nirvana; Rajagriha, Magadha's former capital and the site of the first council; and finally Vaishali (modern Basarh), the scene of the second Buddhist council.

One sign of the new self-assurance displayed by this first Maurya king was his flirtation with these non-brahminic religious systems. Chandragupta is said to have renounced his throne in despair at his powerlessness after prolonged famine in the kingdom and spent the last twelve years of his life as a Jain monk – a sign of the truly new age that began with the Maurya dynasty, with unity in the empire and an ongoing attempt at intellectual and religious renewal through Buddhism and Jainism.

The first big breakthrough for Buddhism came with Asoka (in fact Asokavardhana), the third ruler on the Maurya throne. He liked being called Priyadarshin, the Loving One, or Devanampriya, Beloved of God. From 272 to 232 BC, Asoka unified almost all of India under his rule. Unlike his grandfather Chandragupta it was not repentance at the end of a long life as a ruthless pursuer of power that led him to Buddhist ideals; at an early age he recognized the splendour of the ideas guiding the wise man from the Shakya family. He devoted all his energies to spreading the Buddha's teachings – and not just among his subjects. He also wanted neighbouring states and all peoples in what was then the known earth, no matter how distant, to hear the Buddha's joyous message, as the Master had enjoined his pupils.

Asoka's life should not, however, be romanticized. He was

not a man of peace from the start and thus predestined to accept the Awakened One's teachings, comprehending them as salvation for his subjects and the whole of humanity. Asoka was a divided character. His cruel streak is by no means the grotesque invention of historians. As a young man he was sent by his father Bindusara with a great army against Taxila. His mission was to subjugate the notoriously rebellious tribes in the north-west of the kingdom. As they had done with Alexander, the clever people of Gandhara offered no resistance and thus preserved their beautiful city from destruction. The triumphal entry into Taxila gave Asoka a taste for power, which his upbringing had taught him to enjoy. His most urgent wish was to seize his father's throne and do away with his life. The King, however, was well aware of the power-game and banished his son to the remote region of Uggajini as deputy governor. When Taxila rebelled again shortly before Bindusara's death, the monarch sent another son, Susima, to whom he had promised the succession. Asoka immediately took advantage of this situation, hurried to Pataliputra, and seized the throne once his father had died. His first great deed as the new Maurya king must have made him seem a true offshoot of this dynasty to his subjects. Apart from Tishia, who had been born to the same mother as himself, he had all his brothers killed, including Susima who tried to resist. In the fourth year of his reign Asoka had himself crowned at Pataliputra. In the same year he renounced the brahminic faith and became a Buddhist.

Asoka's Mission: The Buddha's Teaching Conquers the World

There are various legends about Asoka's turn to Buddhism. One says that he was persuaded to adopt the new faith by Nigrodha, the son of his oldest brother Sumanas, whom he had murdered when seizing the throne. Another maintains that his conversion was sparked off by a Buddhist monk who displayed complete serenity when put to torture.

The real trigger for his turn to the religion of the Awakened One, however, was in all probability a terrible campaign against the Kalinga kingdom in what is today Orissa. Asoka had many of his deeds, orders and thoughts recorded on rocks and pillars, and in the celebrated Thirteenth Rock Edict he noted with pedantic accuracy the cruel success of this military mission: 150,000 people were deported, 100,000 killed, and many more died as a result of the war. By then Asoka was sick of the scrounging brahmins at his court who, spoiled by his father, exploited his generosity and supported the Maurya's Machiavellian policy. Asoka had already been investigating other teachings, and these, like the Jain and Buddhist doctrines, abhored the use of violence against human beings and even other living creatures. Asoka was shocked by his own cruelty and did not flinch from saying so to his subjects in the same rock edict: 'After Kalinga had been annexed, the Beloved of God was very seriously preoccupied with the *Dhamma*, loved the *Dhamma*, and taught the *Dhamma*. The Beloved of God felt remorse for the conquest of Kalinga since when a hitherto un-vanquished land is overrun, the murdering, death and deport-ation of people is exceptionally distressing for the Beloved of God and weighs heavily on his soul.'

That inscription can certainly be numbered among the most impressive and moving in human history. Such repentance and return to morality and rightful behaviour by a merciless ruler facing up to his own deeds are unparalleled. Neverthe-less, it may justly be asked whether Asoka's rule really was transformed into noble actions based on Buddhist ethics, cen-tring on an unconditional respect for all life. There is no indica-tion of any reparations for the injustice done, nor that Kalinga regained its independence and the deportees returned home. Religious striving, moral behaviour and political action obviously remained segregated in the thinking of this exceptional ruler. No matter how morally superior the King's edicts may seem to us, they reflect a love of self. Asoka certainly tried to establish a new world order based on Buddhism in his kingdom. He struggled to achieve this goal, and it was probably primarily a struggle with himself. Conquest through the Dharma, he wrote towards the end of the Thirteenth Edict, is true conquest. From that time onwards he devoted his entire life to bringing about the conquest of his old self by the Dharma. Perhaps he made such great efforts to spread the Buddha's teachings everywhere because he himself had great difficulty in submitting his own life to them. The burden of long-established structures of domi-nance was too great.

The statement at the end of the Thirteenth Edict also indicates the age of Buddhist texts that are often only available to us in versions dating from around the first centuries BC and AD. We have to presuppose much older versions or a very accurate oral tradition since in his reference to *dharmavijaya* (moral conquest – conquest through the Dharma) Asoka is obviously playing with a passage from the *Dhammapada* which says: 'If a man should conquer in battle a thousand times a thousand, and another man should conquer himself, the latter would be the greater victory. Conquering oneself is truly better than victory over another being' (8:4–5).

In the Kalinga kingdom Asoka issued edicts that were intended for his officials. The first begins with a beautiful declaration: 'All human beings are my children' – an echo of words attributed to the Buddha. 'What I wish for my children – that they may share in well-being and good fortune both in this life and in lives to come – I also wish for all people.' He also had rock inscriptions established all over the country, proclaiming his policy of Dharma. He extolled the gentleness of the new teaching, affirmed the protection of all beings, and advocated the furtherance of human well-being and virtue. He exhorted his people to pursue goodness and compassion, generosity and gentleness, obedience and respect. He also called on his successors to observe the Dharma as the best guideline.

Archaeologists have continued to discover new Asoka edicts to the present day. The many languages and characters in which they are written, and the multitude of locations in which they are found, from India's most easterly areas to Afghanistan in the west, provide impressive testimony to Asoka's dedication.

On the Girnar rock in the Gujurat peninsula Asoka reported on the implementation of the Buddhist message of compassion with its central duty of avoiding harm to any living creatures (*ahimsa*). At his court he almost completely eliminated meat-eating, and in the Second and Fifth Rock Edicts he laid down that certain species of animals were no longer to be killed or castrated.

> Avoid any sacrifices or otherwise doing anything that could injure animals . . . Be magnanimous to friends . . . Do not get involved in quarrels and disputes . . . Attempt to be of a pure heart, modest, and honest . . . Do not only think of your good aspects; remember your faults and try to correct them.[62]

If one did not know that those words are taken from various rock edicts by Asoka, they could easily be thought to come from a wise teacher in another age and another country – Jesus.

Asoka also endeavoured to make provision for medical help for both humans and animals. He ordered the cultivation of healing plants brought in from distant lands. Some 84,000 stupas and innumerable Buddhist monasteries are also said to have been built at his instigation. He had the caves of Barabar dug out of the wild, fissured hills near Bodh Gaya – simple, unadorned monastic cells, which have become well known through the film of E.M. Forster's novel *A Passage to India*. Asoka was not satisfied with that either. In the seventeenth year of his reign a grand council of Buddhists was held in Maghada under his patronage, and the most important outcome, in terms of world history, was the implementation of the Buddha's call for extensive missionary activity.

Asoka was not an isolated ruler within a small, unknown, Oriental state. He ruled over a globally significant empire in an epoch when international diplomatic contacts were already a matter of course. At the court of Bindusara and later Asoka, Dionysios was the representative of Ptolemy II Philadelphus, the Greek ruler of Egypt. Against the background of such stable international contacts, Asoka arranged for Buddhist missionaries to be sent beyond his national boundaries to the courts of friendly rulers across the world so that they might preach the Dharma.

In the Thirteenth Rock Edict, Asoka named the kings to whom he had sent his missionaries: Amtiyoka – Antiochus II Theos (261–246 BC), the King of Syria; Turamaya – Ptolemy II Philadelphus of Egypt (285–247 BC); Amtekina or Amtikini – Antigonus Gonatas of Macedonia (276–239 BC); Maga – Magas of Cyrene (*c.* 300–250 BC); and Alikasu(m)dara, who is either Alexander of Epirus (272–255 BC) or Alexander of Corinth (252–244 BC). In the Second Rock Edict only Antiochus is mentioned, and the other princes are designated his *samantas* (neighbouring rulers). So there is no doubt that Asoka sent Buddhist missionaries to the courts of Greek rulers.[63] One inscription refers to the sending of missionaries on no fewer than 256 occasions. In the Fifth Edict their task is precisely defined: 'They are concerned with the adherents of all sects, and their task is to establish this religion, pursuing its progress as well as the utility and well-being of the faithful. They are concerned with the Yavanas [Greeks], the Kambojas, the Gandharas ... and the other border peoples, warriors, brahmins, the rich, and the poor ...'

Asoka's missionary activities were implemented at a time when political and economic relations between India and Western peoples had stabilized. We have mentioned permanent Indian settlements in the Land of the Two Rivers and along the Arabian coast; and there is increasingly frequent information about flourishing ports which from year to year sent ever more ships to the West – from the Coromandel to the Malabar coasts and up to the Indus estuary. Asoka was alive in the epoch following the Axis Time, when intellectual exchange was enormously intensified through both the expansion of trade and the conquest of established cultures. New elements were thus constantly superimposed on old traditions. The outcome was the birth of those characteristic mixed religions which appeared throughout the Middle East as far as Iran, as a sign of what was known as Hellenism.

The term 'Hellenism' was coined by J.G. Droysen, an important historian, to designate the period after Alexander the Great until the end of the Ptolemies (323–30 BC), the 300 years leading from Greek culture up to Christianity. Hellenistic culture extended to Carthage and Rome in the West, and to Parthia and India in the East. The post-Alexander rulers of the first generation, the Diadochs, were soon caught up in petty wars so that sovereign territorial states arose under the Macedonian dynasties of the Ptolemies, Seleucids and Antigonids. From 280 BC the Attalids also reigned, constituting the 'Greek kings' in Bactria and India after the end of the third century BC. Greek lifestyles spread everywhere within the Hellenistic sphere of influence, offering self-awareness as the main vehicle of culture. The idea of the *polis* experienced a renaissance thanks to the many towns established by Alexander the Great and Seleucus I. The *polis* was the self-administered city-state, a community of inhabitants with established political rights and duties. After Alexander's India campaign, Greek philosophy strikingly turned to religion, with theological systematization becoming ever more prominent. Contact with the East had by then certainly left profound traces, and Western intellectuals were prepared to avidly soak up wisdom from the East. Droysen thus characterizes this epoch as the 'unification of Eastern and Western traditions under the power of Hellenistic education'.[64] This period of history is called Hellenism because Greek ideas extended over the whole of what then constituted the world of culture. It was characterized by a strong tendency towards religious syncretism – the intermingling of various religions or individual elements, but often without inner unity. This Hellenistic syncretism was in fact characterized by an openness towards the East. The Euro-Asian world of culture chose to take up Eastern ideas, thereby preparing the way for the Jewish diaspora and the redemptive religions dating from the Roman period. The moment for a Buddhist mission could not have been better chosen. The upholders of Hellenistic culture were virtually waiting to be fertilized by exotic ideas from the East so as to create a ferment from which new concepts of the world could be formed.

During the period of Maurya domination, Taxila in Gandhara had become a great international city. At the same time Alexandria in the Nile delta flourished as the centre of Hellenistic scholarship. After Alexander founded Alexandria in 331 BC, the city became Egypt's Greek capital. Throngs of Greek colonists came to the new metropolis, comprising a colourful mixture of peoples, together with Egyptians, Jews, Arabs, Iranians and Indians. Alexandria became the Ptolemies' capital. The city owed its historical and cultural importance largely to the generous support it gave to scholars in all spheres, who were able to devote all their attention to the pursuit of their studies. For them Ptolemy I Soter (305–285 BC) followed the advice of Demetrios of Phaleron and established the Museion, based on the model established by the ancient School of Philosophy. This centre for scholars was linked with the royal palace, underlining the kings' involvement in the progress of the sciences. Many artists and scholars lived and worked in the Museion, where they could study philosophy, philology, literature and theology in complete freedom. From the very beginning, important philological studies on textual criticism, editing, and exegesis were pursued, and the Museion library soon possessed the unimaginable total of 500,000 papyrus scrolls. One of humanity's worst ever cultural catastrophes occurred in 47 BC when most of those unique manuscripts succumbed to fire during the war with Caesar. Ptolemy II Philadelphus, under whom Alexandria most flourished, founded a second, smaller library in the Serapeion. It was to this far-sighted and open-minded ruler that Asoka sent his missionaries, while other delegates travelled by land to King Antiochus of Syria.

During the period when Asoka's Buddhists moved westwards, Eratosthenes, the Greek geographer, depicted the outline of India, the location of Sri Lanka, the Ganges delta and the direction of the monsoon winds. In a resplendent procession through the streets of Alexandria around 270 BC, Ptolemy II presented Indian women, parrots and peacocks, and his grandson Ptolemy IV (221–203 BC) travelled in a luxurious Nile ship embellished with Indian jewels. Great interest in innovations and the simultaneous wish to spread intellectual life across the world as the crown of cultural achievements led to a rapid boom in international trade and travel. That in turn resulted in Greek science becoming known in India within just a few years so that Indian scholars borrowed the technical terms used in Alexandria for their own astronomical tracts.[65]

The Ptolemies devoted particular attention to trade with India. The intensity of their concern with the East is shown in plans for building a canal from the Nile to the Red Sea. That project was never implemented, but Ptolemy II Philadelphus established the important harbour town of Berenike on the Red Sea in southern Egypt. In the first century BC a Greek merchant settled there, and in his *Periplus Maris Erythraei* he provides precise information about trade routes, the goods transported, the length of voyages, the number of ships and much else besides.[66] From that work and many other geographical accounts from the Hellenistic period we are well informed about Indian links with the West, particularly with Alexandria – and thus with the Jewish sphere that interests us.

The Indian ships mainly came from Zizerus, Mangalore and Nelkunda on the Malabar coast, and even from Balita (modern Calicut) in the far south of India's west coast. They sailed to Mouza in Arabia, and then on through the Red Sea to Berenike. From there the Indian goods were taken by camel across the Theban desert to Koptos, shipped down the Nile to Juliopolis, and finally reached Alexandria. Alexandrian merchants mainly used the same route. Sometimes they chose to go from Myoshormos in southern Egypt to the Arabian harbour of Leuke Kome and onward to Muziris in southern India. The Muziris he mentions is not today's Cranganore on the west coast but the Muziris on the east coast close to the Kaveri estuary.

Strabo, the famous geographer, provides an interesting account of the importance of trade during the Hellenistic period. Aelius Gallus, who was Prefect in Egypt around 24 BC and travelled the trade routes to the Red Sea, told him that no fewer than 200 ships sailed to India from the port of Myoshormos alone. That route must have been used for a long time, promising assured and lucrative trade.

There were three ways of steering for the various Indian harbours: along Arabia by way of Karmania and Gedrosia to the Indo-Scythian coast and on to Barugaza (Broach) on the river Nammadios (Narmada); from Cape Guardafui or from the harbour town of Kane (west of Suagros) to the southern Arabian coast (modern Ras Fartak), and using the monsoon winds to cross the ocean to Muziris and Nelkunda.

The mouth of the Indus continued to be a favoured destination. There lay the port of Barbarikon through which the important trading town of Minnagara had dealings by sea. The *Periplus* mentions a large and diverse variety of Indian trading goods. Those ranged from harem girls, slaves, horses, Indian butter, an immense number of plants, medical herbs, smoked products, metal articles, jewels and clothing. Chinese goods – mainly furs, cotton and silk thread from Thinai – were transported by way of Bactria and the markets of Dimurike and Karpasus to the ports of Barbarikon and Barugaza. Products from inside India such as indigo, fine Bengali muslin, rice and the much-extolled aromatic root kostus were trans-shipped at Barbarikon. Beams of wood, sugar-cane honey and sesame went to Arabia from Barugaza. Further south, at Muziris and Nelkunda, dealers procured ivory, coral, pearls, crimson and tortoises.

Up to the third century BC Yemen seems to have been the central market for Indian goods. For a long time such trade was in the hands of the Semitic Sabaeans, who probably owed their proverbial wealth to the market. During the Ptolemaic epoch the Sabaeans and their large fleets dominated the exchange of goods. At the beginning of the second century the island of Socotra became the central trading place for the route to India. It was there that dealers from Palestine acquired a large number of expensive spices, some of which came from the Coromandel and Malabar coasts.[68]

The busiest Indian harbour was Barugaza. From there roads ran to Baithana and Tagara in the southern Indian hills, both centres of trade. In earlier times Shurparaka, south of the Narmada, was a favoured port for sea trade.

From Taprobane (Sri Lanka) the Arabs imported cinnamon, and from India kasia (or kassia).[69] Taprobane was long considered another world. According to Pliny, troglodytes, the original inhabitants who lived in caves, transported the cinnamon across the seas and sought to find wives in Ethiopia. They then returned with glass and ornaments, such as have been excavated by archaeologists in southern India. The Singhalese also actively participated in sea trade. Pliny writes of them travelling, without navigating by the stars, by catamarans, which could be loaded with 300 amphorae (around 75 tons). For ascertaining the presence of land they used pilot birds, a method which is also confirmed in Buddhist writings. The Tamils of the Coromandel coast were excellent seamen. They possessed armed fleets, which they sent to Sri Lanka, Indochina and Indonesia. It is thus probable that southern Indians and Singhalese travelled to Arabia at an early date.

The Hellenistic epoch resulted in political upheavals in India. Euthydemos seized control of the Greek Bactrian kingdom which had gained independence from the Seleucids. His son Demetrius (*c.* 200 BC) succeeded in conquering a number of provinces in northern India. Finally Greek Bactrians attacked India, occupied the Punjab, and penetrated as far as Magadha before being driven out by the Scythians and Parthians from Iran. From the time when Mithridates I was ruling (around 150 BC) and the final defeat of the Greek Bactrian kingdom, the regions comprising Iran and large parts of the Near East came under Parthian influence. Various Parthian rulers controlled an area that included Syria/Palestine and India. Around 150 BC a certain Apollodotos established what was known as the Greek-Indian kingdom. The most outstanding among his successors was Menandros or Milinda, who probably reigned at Sagala (Lahore) around 100 BC, and attained a place of honour in Buddhist history. A series of dialogues between someone known as Nagensa and King Menandros is recorded in the *Milindapanha*, which many scholars believe to be one of the most important works in world literature. Menandros the Greek is depicted there as a lawful heir to the Sophists' dialectical tradition, a typical scion of Greek scholarship. In his free moments he loved to conduct religious disputes, teasing illustrious teachers with his clever questions. He finally succumbed

to Nagasena's outstanding skill in the presentation of the
Dharma, and, convinced by the excellence and truth of the
teachings, became a Buddhist. This work is an exceptional
presentation of Buddhism. Rhys Davids, an important researcher into Buddhism, even goes so far as to say that the
Milindapanha is not just a masterpiece of Indian prose but also
the best text of this kind ever written.

On coins depicting King Menandros there are frequently
Buddhist symbols such as the eight-spoked wheel of the law,
known from comparable depictions on Buddhist monuments
in Sanchi and Bodh Gaya. Other coins display as a Greek
epithet, the literal translation of the Indian word *dharmika*, a
believer in the good law (an orthodox Buddhist). News of the
glorious holiness of King Menandros reached as far as Greece.

Under the protection of Menandros Buddhism spread from
Gandhara further to the west and north, where it was also
accepted by the Central Asian nomads who increasingly settled
in Bactria. Around 80–60 BC Alexander Polyhistor wrote of
Bactrian priests whom he called *samanaioi*, showing them to be
Buddhist monks. The great Parthian empire extended in the
west to Syria and in the east to India. The old land routes from
Gandhara to the Mediterranean coast passed through its territories around the turn of the millennium.

By this time trading was no longer a matter of chance; it was
established in stable institutions. The *Pax Romana* under Augustus (27 BC–14 AD) led to the checking of Arab pirates, and
very much supported exchanges of goods between India and
the West. Around the turn of the millennium the Romans
owned their own warehouses or trading posts in southern
Indian coastal towns with citizens there as permanent resi-
dents.[70] A Tamil poem from Kaveripatnam on the Coromandel
coast plays with the reputation Mediterranean traders had in
southern India. Low-value Roman coins, minted in India, were
discovered there. Arikamedu, near today's Pondicherry on the
south-eastern coast, was a centre of Roman trade with India
(Plate 15). It is possible that there was still a Buddhist community
there in Roman times since researchers assume that Arikamedu
is derived from Arugamedu, 'the hill of Arugan'. *Arugan* is the
Tamil version of *arhat*, the word used to designate Buddhist
holy men.[71] Excavations at Arikamedu and Virapatnam have
uncovered many objects from the Mediterranean. The origins
of some of them can be discerned from the makers' marks,

indicating, for instance, amphorae and pottery from Arezzo in Tuscany. Roman merchants were not only active in Arikamedu. Large amounts of Roman coins, particularly from the early imperial period (Augustus to Nero), have been uncovered in southern India. In Akkenapali, archaeologists recently dug up over a thousand Roman gold and silver coins.[72]

We also hear of an Indian delegation reaching Rome at the time of Augustus. This included a Buddhist called Zarmanochegas. That Hellenized name has been interpreted in various ways. Some assume it is derived from the Indian Shramanacharya, Master of the Mendicant Monks. Another translation interprets the ending 'chegas' as *shakya*, which would make the word mean something like 'Monk of the Shakya' or 'Adherent of Shakyamuni'. Zarmanochegas was thus viewed as being a self-depiction as a Buddhist mendicant monk rather than a personal name. He was certainly a master within his metier. The foreign ascetic, naked and annointed with aromatic plants, mounted a funeral pyre in Athens and set fire to himself – as Kalanos had previously done before Alexander's army (Plate 22). The Buddhist monk must have made a great impression since his ashes were placed beneath a long-celebrated monument. Even a century later, when Plutarch was writing, people called it the Indian's grave, and it bore an inscription referring to the event.

The port of Muzuris in south-western India was an important Roman settlement at that time. Here, as in nearby Cochin, there was a big Jewish colony, which has survived to the present day (Plate 23). The Jews of Cochin belong to two tribes, known even today as 'white' and 'black' Jews. The latter date their arrival in Kerala to the year 587 BC. Legend has it that they are the descendants of the Jews dragged off to Babylon by King Nebuchadnezzar, and American researchers have in fact recognized ancient Babylonian influences in the music of Cochin's Jews. According to another legend, Solomon's trading ships brought their forefathers to India. The 'white' Jews believe that their ancestors fled here in 135 AD after the Romans destroyed Jerusalem. These Jews are probably the descendants of an Alexandrian trading colony. When the Roman Emperor Caracalla perpetrated a bloodbath at Alexandria in 215 AD, their way home was cut off and they remained in distant India.

Christianity also reached southern India at that time by way of Muziris and other harbours on the Malabar coast. The oldest sure evidence dates from 180 AD when Pantainos of Alexandria found an Aramaic copy of the Gospel according to St Matthew during a missionary trip to Kerala. However, southern Indian Christians believe that Christianity reached their country immediately after the crucifixion of Jesus. The Portuguese who landed on the Malabar coast in the sixteenth century were surprised to find both synagogues and many churches whose priests maintained that the Gospel had been brought to India by the apostle who had touched the wounds of the arisen Christ. 'Doubting Thomas' is said to have reached Muziris in 52 AD.

There are various legends about how Thomas got to India. The apocryphal *Acts of Thomas*, written around 225 AD at Edessa in Syrian Mesopotamia, reports that after the ascension the apostles drew lots to decide in which country each of them should preach the Gospel. India fell to Thomas. At that time Habban, an Indian merchant, was in Syria. He had been sent from Gandhara by Gondophares (19–49 AD) to seek an architect for the construction of a new city. Jesus appeared to Habban and without further ado sold him Thomas as a carpenter. As Habban's slave, Thomas reached King Gondophares's court at Taxila, which with its important university was then Buddhism's intellectual centre. Keralan legend says that Thomas came by ship to Muziris where he was greeted by a flute-playing Jewish girl. He baptized brahmins and Jewish merchants, founded seven churches and then moved on to the east coast. Twenty years after his arrival in southern India he succumbed to the plotting of envious brahmin priests. A representative of the King killed him on a hill near Madras.

It is possible that the apostle really did sail on from northern India to Kerala. The early Christian communities in Persia, which claimed Thomas as their founder, indicate that the apostle first reached India by land. The Grecian-Buddhist art style developed in north-western India during that period, and there was a constant influx of artists and craftsmen from Asia Minor and Egypt. There is much evidence to show that Jesus himself, after surviving the crucifixion, took the land route to India.[73] While Thomas preached the Gospel in the south of the subcontinent, Jesus remained in the north-west, where he ultimately died. Tradition has it that the grave of the prophet Yuz-Asaf at Srinagar, the capital of Kashmir, is indeed Jesus's grave.

In the fourth century AD Syrian Christians arrived in southern India by sea. They had been persecuted in their homeland by the Roman church because they did not want to recognize the supremacy of the Pope. An initial group reached Muziris in 345. They found the grave of the apostle Thomas near today's Madras and erected a church there. When the Portuguese discovered this shrine in 1523, Christians, Hindus and Muslims were still venerating the apostle's finger-bone and the tip of the lance with which he was supposedly killed (Plate 20).

Part II

JESUS – THE BUDDHIST

Buddha and Jesus: Infancy Parallels

India had been linked with the West for many centuries. Long before Jesus came onto the stage of history we find Indian gods, stories, myths, entire philosophical systems and religious customs in the West. We even find Buddhist monks on the shores of the Mediterranean, and in areas close to Palestine it was considered highly modern to discuss Indian teachings.

The authors who were later to work on the texts of the Gospels were caught up in that exchange of ideas. We have seen that as early as the time of Solomon the Jews had contacts with India, which received isolated expression in the Old Testament. After the Babylonian captivity Jewish communities remained in the Land of the Two Rivers, Persia and even southern India. From that time there were direct intellectual and spiritual links between the Children of Israel and the East. All the preconditions existed for borrowings from Buddhism in the writing of the Gospels. We will show how the world of Buddhist ideas played an important part in the Hellenistically tinged literature of the time, and it would have been surprising if the authors of the New Testament had not also made use of that source. What is astonishing is the frequency of their resort to Buddhism. They were obviously of the opinion that Jesus's teachings had much in common with those of Buddhism, and sometimes they could not decide whether a story came from Jesus or Gautama. This astonishing inner relationship between the two great masters, Jesus and the Buddha, has time and again attracted the attention of alert intellects over the course of history.

But where did these similarities in their teachings come from? Are they mainly literary alignments established by the writers of the Gospels or independently developed products of a comparable spiritual direction, or had Jesus already known of Buddhism, with the result that the creators of the New Testament were oriented towards India?

When we start to look for Buddhist material in the New Testament, we do not have to ask ourselves how much of the

Buddhist texts is embellishment, editorial addition, philosophical interpretation and theological modification. That would be necessary if we were seeking the authentic Siddhartha Gautama, the historical person of the Buddha and *his* original words. For the comparison with Buddhism, we can take Buddhist writings as they have come down to us, including all the changes and additions over the years. After all, the authors of the Gospels and apocryphal Christian texts could also have encountered those writings in such a form. So too could the early adherents of the Jesus community, and Jesus himself might well have come into contact with the Dharma.

Of the enormous number of writings produced by Buddhism we will limit ourselves to those that were produced before Christianity came into being and before the public appearance of Jesus, only emphasizing the age of texts and oral traditions when that is necessary to understand a context.

Research into the Indian sources of Christianity, which produced so many amazing discoveries around 1900 mainly thanks to Seydel's work, almost came to a standstill after the 1920s. The reaction of the Catholic church, which wanted to hush up an unwelcome theme, may have played a part in that. Henri de Lubac, the celebrated religious historian and theologian at the Lyon-La Fourvière Jesuit faculty, who expressed a cautious acceptance of the idea of borrowings from Buddhism in Christian literature, was reprimanded, censored and condemned to silence by the Vatican. Only after the Second Vatican Council (1962–5), when such rigidity towards other religions was alleviated and the interreligious dialogue was sought with Buddhism, was attention again directed towards this issue, which had long been officially pushed on one side. New archaeological discoveries and improved philological methods have in the meantime extended the possibilities of analysis. The most recent work on this theme thus makes convincingly clear that the beginnings of Christianity were dependent on Buddhism, only leaving open the question of how the content of a foreign religion was taken over on such a scale and adapted to other needs. Such work includes the book by Roy C. Amore[1] (to which we shall return) and the recently published and very impressive study by the literary scholar Zacharias P. Thundy.[2]

Thundy demonstrates that stories about the childhood and adolescence of Jesus correspond in many details with those about the Buddha. Arthur Lillie, a civil servant for the British in

India at the end of the nineteenth century, expressed his amazement at the similarities between the life stories of the Buddha and Jesus as follows: 'It seems to me that the biographies of Jesus and the Buddha throw constant light the one on the other.'[3] Thundy now convincingly shows that the basic Buddhist texts and traditions are older than comparable Christian writings, and that borrowings in the overwhelming majority of cases were by the West from the East rather than vice versa. He comes to the conclusion that the sources of stories about Jesus's childhood mainly lie outside the Jewish tradition, and that this foreign influence existed from the start of writing down the Gospels.

Deploying modern methods of literary research such as the deconstruction of texts, he documents the fact that a great number of individual sources from other cultures served as a basis for the Christian narrative. He identifies the structural assembly of the Gospels with their 'obscurity, abruptness, fault lines and suggestive influence of the unexpressed sources'[4] as being the work of different authors at different times. The Gospels were thus by no means written by the single authors we know under the names of Matthew, Mark, Luke and John. They were produced by many authors as compilations of oral and written sub-texts subjected to editorial reworkings and considerable revision. Against the background of Hellenistic syncretism, many stories imported from India flowed into the Gospel texts and apocryphal literature. That is particulary true of the narratives about Jesus's childhood.

Jesus's biographers knew next to nothing about that part of his life, so they had to improvise. Subject to the theological dictate that Jesus should be portrayed as the Son of God and Redeemer, they mainly made use of mythical narratives appropriate for the presentation of the early years of a divine child. The texts of the Mahayana schools, making the human being Siddhartha Gautama into a god, turned out to provide suitable models. Thundy stresses the Christian authors' literary activities, and sees no reason for borrowings from specifically Buddhist works other than the fact that these stories were accessible in the Alexandria, Syria and Palestine of that time, offering ideal templates.

That finding is certainly consistent. We merely doubt that the availability of suitable stories was the only reason for echoes of Buddhist writings, ideas and teachings to appear in so many places in the New Testament. We shall show that there were other, and much more surprising, reasons for the selection of Buddhist material. Those both present a fresh picture of the coming into existence of the Christian Gospels, and also reveal Christian origins that throw completely new light on Jesus the man, his life and his teaching. However, let us first consider the dependence of literary aspects of Christian teaching on the Indian, and specifically Buddhist, legacy.

Borrowings in the narratives of Jesus's childhood are so numerous that, following Thundy[5], we can only touch on them in passing. They start with the idea of the pre-existence of the founder of each of the two religions. Mahayana Buddhists revived the ancient Indian view that gods come down to earth from time to time in human or animal form. Indians call such an incarnation of an *avatar*. Just as the Buddha is said to have spent time in the Tushita heaven before descending to earth, the Gospel according to St John speaks in its very first sentences of Jesus being an incarnation of the Word, which is identical with God. Later, according to this Gospel, Jesus himself maintains: 'Before Abraham was, I am' (John 8:58).

The genealogical trees of Gautama and Jesus both point to royal origins. The presentation of extended genealogical descent with which Matthew begins his Gospel is remarkably paralleled in a Buddhist text where the Buddha's origins are similarly narrated.[6] Even immaculate conception and virgin birth are foreshadowed in Buddhism. On a night when the moon was full, Maya, the wife of King Suddhodana, had a strange dream. A white elephant with six tusks and a lotus blossom in its trunk descended from heaven and slipped into her womb. Thus, according to the legend, did Buddha consciously and willingly enter Maya's body. The idea that virgin birth accorded with moral and spiritual purity, with the absence of sin, was thus already present in Buddhism.

The significance of an elephant was not comprehensible to readers in the West, so the way in which the white elephant was transformed into a white dove in a Christian apocryphal text is of particular interest. In the Story of Hannah Mary's conception is described in astonishingly similar fashion to that of the Buddha. In a dream-vision Mary sees a white dove descending from heaven and entering her body. The white dove was taken over by writers of the Gospels as a symbol of the Holy Spirit, and the Ebionite Gospel says that after Jesus's baptism the Holy Ghost in the form of a dove entered his body so as to show that Jesus had through baptism been as it were conceived a second time as Son of God. We are all aware of the long theological discussions, so impenetrable to common sense, about the nature of Mary's virginity – the immaculate conception and her virgin state before, during, and after giving birth. Such remarkable concern with detail does not appear in the Gospels; this is the fruit of later theological nit-picking. It is, however, obvious that this part of the Gospel story is also drawn from the Buddhist tradition. Maya's virgin state is treated in great detail in Buddhist texts, which endeavour to demonstrate that even after the Buddha's birth his mother was 'undefiled'.

We know the story of Joseph's perplexity about his wife-to-be being pregnant before they had come together (Matthew 1:18), and how an angel informed him about the background to the pregnancy, an announcement which he unhesitatingly accepted. All those elements are similarly present in the story of Gautama's birth. King Shuddhodana was also informed by angels (*devas*) about the 'Noble Bodhisattva's' miraculous conception. Both Shuddhodana and Joseph are presented as pious, upright men.

Also of interest is the fact that the circumstances surrounding Jesus's birth accord to an astonishing extent with myths from the Hindu cult of Krishna. Mary gave birth to her child as she and Joseph were travelling to another town to pay taxes there, and so too did Yashoda deliver Krishna when journeying with her husband for a similar purpose. Like Jesus, Krishna was born in a manger among shepherds, and both of them escaped the infanticide ordered by a tyrant and were taken into exile. There are indications that the depiction of Christ as the good shepherd and proclaimer (in John's Gospel) of a religion of love also derives from a Hindu tradition involving a shepherd god.

During Gautama's conception and birth a great light shone over everything in the world. Christian nativity stories also tell of wondrous manifestations of light. The light of the Lord fills the shepherds with fear (Luke 2:8), and in another version a blinding light shone into the cave[7] where Mary was, and this was then replaced by the infant Jesus (Proto-Gospel of James 14:10–12). Nor should we forget Matthew's well-known version of the Magi from the East who saw Jesus's star (Matthew 2:2).

Thundy draws attention to a detail that at first seems unworthy of attention.[8] A Buddhist legend reports that the newly born child was wound in swaddling clothes. Matthew does not mention that minor detail, but Luke and an apocryphal text known as Pseudo-Matthew do. It might be assumed that infants were usually treated in that way, so that this does not involve any borrowing from a foreign text. However, Thundy believes that precisely this inconsequential detail is worthy of attention. Why should Luke and Pseudo-Matthew have mentioned such a commonplace if they had not copied it from another source? As far as Pseudo-Matthew is concerned, it is very probable the author frequently copied extracts from narratives of the Buddha's childhood, so it is very likely that the detail of Jesus in the swaddling clothes was also based on an Indian legend. In Pseudo-Matthew there are a large number of clear-cut, very specific borrowings from Buddhist writings. Those include wild animals becoming tame at the sight of the holy child, the trees whose branches bent low through the boy's magic powers, a fountain of water bubbling out of nothingness, and temple images of other gods which crash to the ground and disintegrate before the youngster. There can be no doubt that they all come from identical tales in the *Lalitavistara* and other biographies of the Buddha.

A curious parallel exists to the seven steps that Siddhartha Gautama is said to have taken immediately after his birth. They are an essential component in the legend of the Buddha child because the number seven is of great symbolic importance in Buddhism. Paul Mus has shown that Gautama's seven steps are linked with his capacity for levitation.[9] Buddha's 'floating' steps are paralleled in an apocryphal story about Jesus's childhood. The Proto-Gospel of James (6:1) describes how the child grows and suddenly takes precisely seven steps. The mother is delighted and exclaims: 'Praise be to the Lord, My God! Thou dost not need to walk on this earth when I take thee to the Temple of the Lord.' There is an obvious inner link between these two versions of the story about seven steps with the associated ability to rise above the earth in more than a metaphorical sense.

Thundy reports on a number of other astonishing parallels in these stories of childhood, suggesting that future research should devote much greater attention to Indian sources so as to clarify the textual history of the Gospels. Some sections of the New Testament have already been studied in greater detail, and their dependence on Buddhist material was clearly demonstrated. We shall present some of those findings in order to show how far-reaching Buddhism's influence is on parts of the New Testament that the Christian has learned to view as characteristic aspects of his or her religion. Those include Jesus's presentation in the Temple and the appearance of Simeon.

The Wise Man and the Chosen Child: Asita and Simeon

Many attentive investigators of Christian and Buddhist writings have noticed the existence of an inner connection between the glorification of the young Siddhartha Gautama by an aged seer and the story of Simeon in the temple (Luke 2:25–35). In a vision Asita saw how gods on Mount Meru were full of joy, dancing and singing, and he asked them the reason for such jubilation. Their answer was: 'The Buddha-to-be, the best and matchless jewel, is born for the weal and welfare in the world of men, in the town of the Shakyas, in the region of Lumbini. Therefore we are joyful and exceedingly glad.' Asita set off for the house of King Shuddhodana where he took the newly born son, the future Buddha, in his arms, recognized the thirty-two signs characterizing a great man, and began to cry. Concerned bystanders asked whether something terrible would happen to the boy. Then Asita explained that this prince would set in motion the Wheel of Teaching because of his compassion for people's suffering. This Incomparable One would establish a widespread religion, but he, Asita, was too old to experience it. He was crying because he would die before the Buddha could proclaim his teaching.

The story of Asita the seer is to be found in many biographies of the Buddha both from the time after Christ and in one of the oldest Pali texts, the *Suttanipata Nalakasutta*, which originated at least a century before the new millennium got under way. Nevertheless, people have often argued that it is not necessary to assume dependence. The old man of declining years, symbolizing former times, paying tribute to the child in whom a new age begins, is said to be an archetypal image which is not restricted to a single culture but can arise independently anywhere where heroes are mythically elevated in literature. Certainly an archetypal element as foundation for the two stories is not to be excluded. They follow the examples set by the legends of heroes in all times and cultures.[10] Details of the narrative as presented in Luke show, however, that the mythic embellishment of the image of Jesus was based on borrowings from the Buddhist tradition.

According to Luke, Jesus was brought to Jerusalem for presentation in the Temple forty days after his birth. In that city lived a pious old man named Simeon who had learned from the Holy Ghost that he would not die before he had seen the Lord's Anointed. In the Temple Simeon took the infant Jesus in his arms and knew that he would die at peace, having experienced the birth of the Saviour.

The correspondences between the Buddhist and the biblical narrative are striking.[11] Both involve old men who have devoted their lives to religion and have been told by heavenly beings of a child that will become a bringer of salvation. Both take the child in their arms and prophesy their own death before this infant has grown up. Inspiration from the Holy Ghost leads Simeon to identify the child as a 'Messiah sent by the Lord'. Asita is taught in a vision from the gods to recognize the 'coming Buddha'. Conspicuously, and going beyond any archetypal explanation, the chosen boy is in both stories extolled by angelic hymns – an idiosyncrasy that leads even such a sceptical Indologist as Richard Garbe to say that this remarkable concurrence is 'beyond chance'. He is also surprised that so many characteristic elements have remained in the Christian transformation of the Buddhist original.[12]

The fact that the presentation of a child in the Temple was by no means a Jewish custom is another striking indication of the interdependence of these narratives. The Mosaic law merely envisaged purification for the mother, where neither the father nor the child were to be present. In India, however, it was usual for a newly born infant to be brought to the temple as a mark of respect to the gods. The *Lalitavistara* thus tells how Gautama was taken by his parents to the temple. It looks as if Luke attempted to depict the presentation as a Jewish custom so as to justify the incorporation of the Asita legend and the visit to the Temple with the firstborn. He thus adapted the Indian original to Hebrew customs. If the imposed Jewish elements are put aside, there remain elements which were at the centre of the Buddhist legend about Asita. Luke's dependence on the Indian story can even be established in a verbal parallel. Asita's vision is depicted as a visit to the Tushita heaven, the very heaven in which the Buddha lived before his incarnation as Siddhartha Gautama. This stay in heaven by a perfect ascetic is to be viewed as a kind of out-of-body experience, and so Asita reached Shuddhodana's house spiritually, as it were 'through the air'. Luke also has Simeon led to the temple by the Holy Spirit (*en to pneumati*).[13]

Moreover the author of the Gospel according to Luke also likes breaking the flow of events with hymn-like canticles or addresses, which are always similar in character and tone. He shares that with Buddhist sutras, which are time and again relieved by *gathas*, rhythmic insertion of a metrical nature.

In Luke the presentation of Jesus in the Temple is followed (2:41–52) by an account of the twelve-year-old Jesus vanishing while in Jerusalem for the Passover. His parents finally find him in the Temple, astonishing teachers with his views. For that there is also a Buddhist parallel in the *Lalitavistara* where the little Prince Siddhartha is lost during an outing with friends. His father finally finds him sitting under a tree, sunk in religious contemplation. This tree miraculously throws a shadow as if the sun were at its zenith, when it is in fact close to setting. Moved by that sign, the father bows down to his son. In both narratives the son is lost and is found again implementing religious practices.

Even without Buddhist influences, we would expect a legend like that of the twelve-year-old Jesus discussing with teachers in the Temple. The archetypal model of the saint includes his manifestation as *puer senex* – the 'old youth' or the 'wise child'. One need only open a book of mythology teeming with gods who were miraculously clever children to see how quickly such myths form around important figures. One pious legend, developed about the Buddha at a later date, tells of his having been a teacher of the laws even within his mother's womb, and of his having proclaimed the purpose of his human incarnation immediately after birth.

Another parallel is to be found in the glorification of the Lord's mother. On his return from journeys outside the palace, a girl extolled Gautama's beauty and majesty in the following words: 'Truly blessed is the mother, truly blessed is the father, truly blessed is the wife that has such a husband as this.' Siddartha Buddha became very thoughtful on hearing those words since they contained an untranslatable play on words. The word *nibutta* (blessed) can also be interpreted as 'surrender' and 'dissolution', which drew Gautama's attention to the related *Nibbana* (Nirvana). Against the backdrop of the experienced misery of this world, this song makes him comprehend that true blessedness cannot be found outside Nirvana.

That is immediately reminiscent of the unrelated words of a woman (Luke 11:27–28) inserted when Jesus is talking about driving out unclean spirits. This too involves glorification of the mother. The response here takes the form of more profound religious thoughts. In both cases the circumstances and the beatitude involved are astonishingly similar. Matthew and Mark do not mention this episode, and their narrative continues without interruption. Luke's unexplained insertion of this incident in an unrelated course of events indicates that the glorification was a previously existing fragment of text whose place was uncertain. Its strangeness can be explained by the fact that it was of Buddhist origin.

The Teaching About Rebirth

In considering the teachings of Pythagoras we saw that his view of reincarnation came from India. Despite all the purges, that idea of rebirth is also preserved in various places in the New Testament, and it even seems as if this un-Christian concept was taught by Jesus himself. How is that possible? Did Jesus derive his attitude towards reincarnation from an Indian source, like Pythagoras half a millennium before him?

To do justice to ideas about reincarnation in biblical writings, tracking down their sources and traditions, would necessitate a separate book. What is certain is that the idea of reincarnation is among humanity's oldest. From the religions of Stone Age hunters it entered into shamanism,[14] reappeared in the cult of the Great Mother among pastoral peoples, and then later in the mystery religions of the Near East. In India belief in rebirth took on an autonomous development in earliest times, and was constantly a central focus in religion. We have seen that Pythagoras derived the concept from India. In Hellenistic times with the accompanying opening to ideas from the East, Indian views on rebirth became known in Palestine. They must have mainly spread from Alexandria where such teachings were eagerly discussed. There was a renaissance of interest in Pythagoras at that time too, so interest in reincarnation was nothing unusual among Hellenistic intellectuals.

One can therefore say that the idea of rebirth and the trans-migration of souls was rooted in Jewish popular sentiment in that age. That can be demonstrated in a number of declarations in the New Testament. Just think of the disciples' question to Jesus about the man who was blind from birth, asking whether the man himself had sinned, or his parents, that he was born unseeing (John 9:2). The assumption that the man himself could have sinned of course presupposes that the sin was committed in a previous life and also incorporates the Indian idea of *karma*. *Karma* signifies 'deed/action', and the Indian concept of rebirth puts particular emphasis on the fruits of actions, whereby good and bad actions affect their originators in both this and future lifetimes. That is why the Buddha put attentiveness at the centre of his teaching of the Eightfold Path: attentiveness to our deeds, but above all to our thoughts and our words, which precede deeds.

What we find in the New Testament as a self-evident belief in rebirth was by no means familiar to the Jews of earlier times. Hellenistic philosophy had disseminated that view within its sphere of influence. The concept of rebirth (*gilgul*) only became established in Jewish circles around the start of our millennium. Talmudists started from the assumption that God had created only a specific number of Jewish souls, which were constantly reborn. For punishment they returned in animals' bodies. According to that view, a human has to live through a prolonged transmigration of souls (*gilgul-neschama*) until re-demption (*tikkun* – 'right order, harmony') is attained. The idea that redemption only occurs when the goal of earthly develop-ment is achieved indicates Indian and Buddhist origins. These Jewish teachings first arose during the Hellenistic period.

Ideas about reincarnation certainly occupied an important

place in Jesus's views on life. That can signify two possibilities: either Jesus was a Hellenistic wisdom teacher who adopted the concept of rebirth as a philosophical approach, or he derived the idea from Indian sources. The way in which the teaching about rebirth is integrated in his message and made a fundamental component in his own understanding of redemption makes the assumption of Indian roots seem very plausible. Only in India did reincarnation enjoy similar acceptance, and only in India was it linked with moral teaching akin to what Jesus disseminated in Palestine. That is why Jesus's Buddhistic teaching sounded so strange to the Jews.

The theme of rebirth is apparent in many places in the New Testament.[15] Jesus spoke of his own earlier lives and his return, so adopting a clear-cut stand on the question of reincarnation. His clearest reference to a previous existence ('Before Abraham was, I am' – John 8:58) is paralleled in the oldest account of the Buddha's life, the *Nidanakatha*, where the 'Awakened One' is presented as pre-existent from the beginning.

The most important passages in the New Testament with regard to Jesus's views on rebirth have been preserved in John's Gospel (John 3:1–4, 7:9–11). Unfortunately, it has been largely mutilated by incorrect translation. Thanks to Günther Schwarz's careful work, many of those mistakes have been eliminated. In several publications the theologian set about re-establishing the original Aramaic text of the Gospels from existent Greek translations, and then used that as the basis for establishing a new German version. The fruit of those years of work is the *Jesus-Evangelium* ('The Gospel according to Jesus')[16] assembled together with his son Jörn Schwarz from all four canonical Gospels and non-biblical sources. This 'Gospel of Jesus' will time and again provide an important source of assistance in our analysis of Buddhist parallels. Quotations from the *Jesus-Evangelium* are abbreviated as 'JeEv'.

If we consider Jesus's teachings on rebirth, the real meaning becomes apparent in the corrected translation. Nicodemus, a member of the Sanhedrin, came to Jesus by night since he knew that Jesus was 'sent to us as a teacher' (JeEv 5:11). In the usual German translation, Nicodemus's conversion by night is accompanied by incomprehensible words from Jesus: 'If a man is not born from above, he cannot see the kingdom of God' (John 3:3). The Authorized Version is less enigmatic: 'Except a man be born again, he cannot see the kingdom of God.' In later

centuries the church devoted great efforts to suppressing all
New Testament references to the idea of reincarnation without
being able to eliminate them completely. In the newly assembled and correctly translated version of Jesus's words, his intentions once again become apparent. Nicodemus asks Jesus:
'What must I do to enter into the Kingdom of God?' Jesus
answered: 'Verily, verily, I say unto thee: except a man be born
again and again, he cannot be (re-)admitted into the Kingdom
of God.' Nicodemus asks: 'How can be a man be born again
and again when he is old? Can he return into his mother's
womb and be born again?' Jesus replies: 'Marvel not that I said
unto thee, Ye must be born again and again' (JeEv 5:12–16).

At issue is readmission to the Kingdom of God as the starting
and ending point of human existence. That lesson must be
viewed in connection with those passages of the Bible where
Jesus calls John the Baptist an Elijah who has come again
(Matthew 11:13–15, 17:10–13, Mark 9:11–13), and those in
which he himself is thought to be a reborn Elijah, Jeremiah or
one of the other prophets. There then remains no doubt that
Jesus was talking about physical rebirth in the Indian sense of
reincarnation. Viewed in terms of that background, a fateful
translation mistake in a well-known verse in Matthew (18:3)
must be corrected. Jesus supposedly said: 'Except ye be converted and become as little children . . .' The astonishing outcome of the corrected translation runs: 'If ye be not reborn, ye
shall not enter into the Kingdom of Heaven.'[17]

Several apocryphal declarations from the Gospel of Thomas
– to which we will often refer – clearly communicate that view.
'Jesus said: Have you then discovered the origin, so that you
inquire about the end? For at the place where the origin is,
there shall be the end' (Thomas 18). This becomes plainer still
in Thomas 19: 'Jesus said: Blest is he who was before he came
into being', and in Thomas 49: 'Jesus said: Blest are the solitary
and chosen – for you shall find the Kingdom. You have come
from it, and you shall return unto it.'

The ancient Indian, pre-Buddhist belief was that a human
being had to pass through many earthly existences in order to
attain that degree of spiritual perfection which makes possible
a 'return' to his or her own divine home. The Upanishads from
the pre-Buddhist epoch viewed that return as realization of the
understanding that the Self (*atman*) is identical with the primal
ground, with the highest divine totality (*brahman*). For the

Buddha, who rejected the idea of either a highest god or a soul, that 'return' signified finding one's way home through entering the void known as Nirvana: the end of unceasing dispersal in the separate and chance aspects of earthly existence. Soon after the Buddha died his followers diluted that radical view of things, probably also because they had difficulty in living with the idea that their revered teacher Siddhartha Gautama was gone, eternally erased from the whole of existence. A soul – inclusive of an appropriate psychology – crept back into Buddhism again as it were through the back door (in sections of the *Abhidharma*). The Buddha was transported into heaven, and Nirvana was declared to be a state of endless bliss. When Jesus was at work, those teachings within the influential school of Mahayana Buddhism were already widely disseminated. It was believed that before their earthly existence buddhas existed in a heaven and returned there after their death – until the next voluntary incarnation. Jesus's 'Kingdom of God' viewed in terms of rebirth turns out to be the Buddhists' 'Buddha Heaven'.

It is not just the contents of Jesus's conversation with Nicodemus that are eminently Buddhist; the entire biblical scene has a Buddhist parallel. Nicodemus, who received Jesus's teachings on rebirth by night, was a respected member of the administrative council and a rich young man. Buddhist texts report on a visit paid to the Buddha by night involving the rich Yasa. The Buddha taught Yasa about love, virtue, heaven and the way of redemption, making him into a convert. Perhaps the author of the Gospel according to St John wanted to incorporate Jesus's teaching about reincarnation into a teaching situation, and took the story of the Buddha and Yasa as his model. That is very probable in the light of the exceptional number of Buddhist echoes in this Gospel.

A strangely Indian rendering of the idea of reincarnation – to which Schopenhauer directed attention – is to be found in the Epistle of James (3:6). The German translation speaks of the tongue inflaming the 'circle of life' – which is another wrong translation. That should really be 'circle of births' or 'wheel of existence', which constitutes a literal translation of the Indian concept of the Wheel of Rebirths (*samsara chakra*). *Samsara* literally means 'migration', entailing life as a wandering through the world of sensory illusions. The image of the wheel of rebirths in flames inevitably brings to mind the well-known

depiction of the dancing god Shiva (*Nataraja*), who is surrounded by a wheel of flames symbolizing the dance of natural
energies (Plate 21). In the Hindu view, those forces are, like the
human body, subject to an eternal rising and fading away. The
context of this passage from the Epistle of James also betrays
its Buddhist origins. It is concerned with the right use of the
tongue, with restraining what one says since abuse of speech
is said to keep the Wheel of Rebirths in motion. The Buddha
said that right speech is one of the eight 'spokes' of the wheel
which symbolizes the Noble Eightfold Path (*Dharma Chakra*).
Anyone who does not adhere to the demands of the Eightfold
Path, inclusive of right speech, cannot become liberated since
there cannot be right thinking and action without right speech.
Such a person will once again fan the flames of the Wheel of
Rebirths. Interestingly, the passage in the Epistle of James is
preceded by words overlooked by all those who noticed the
Buddhist parallel: 'If any man offend not in word, the same is
a perfect man and able also to bridle the whole body' (James
3:2). That introduction to rebirth as punishment for malicious
speech is an exact transposition of Gautama's demands: 'Rich
in truth, diligence and well-practised discipline, and well-
spoken words – that is the highest blessing' (*Mangala-
Sutta* 5:4). The *Dhammapada* (17:11–12) says in an identical context but in reverse order to James: 'Watch for anger of the body;
bridle the body. Hurt not with the body, but use the body well.
Watch for anger of words; bridle speech. Hurt not with words,
but use words well.'

The correspondences are so clear that one must ask how
James came across the Buddhist texts or oral transmissions. A
surprising answer is provided by an instructive study demonstrating that the connection between tongue, fire and the Wheel
of Rebirths can only be understood in the light of Asoka's
edicts.[18] Obviously Asoka's Buddhist missionaries faithfully
passed on the instructions contained in the edicts, enabling the
author of the Epistle of James to reproduce them accurately
during the first century AD.

The early Christian communities still remembered Jesus's
teachings. For them belief in reincarnation was taken for
granted until it fell victim to historical error in 553, being declared to be a heretical belief at the Fifth Ecumenical Council in
Constantinople, and remaining banned from the Christian
faith up to the present day.

Hypocritical Ascetics and Cunning Prophets

The Buddhist *Dhammapada* is part of what is known as the *Khuddakanikaya* (Collection of the Small Pieces) and mainly contains Buddhist ethics. The title can be translated as 'Way of Virtue' or 'Way of the Law'. By many it is viewed as a collection of the most authentic sayings by Siddhartha Gautama. The 423 verses of the *Dhammapada* are certainly among the most impressive poetic sayings in old Indian or other literatures. The various editions are based on a very ancient compilation. The oldest were written in Pali (here abbreviated Dh), while Tibetan monasteries preserved a version written in the Prakrit dialect, known as the *Gandhari Dharmapada* (abbreviated GDh) after the Gandhara region of Buddhist high culture. Asoka's son Mahinda, who went as a missionary to Sri Lanka, brought back the Sinhalese version, the *Dhampiya*, which unfortunately no longer exists. The *Udanavarga* (Ud) is an extended collection based on the *Dhammapada*. No one knows who put together this first collection of aphorisms. Unlike the sutras, where teachings are embedded in stories, the *Dhammapada* is a collection of sayings. According to Buddhist tradition, it was created during the First Council immediately after the Buddha entered upon Nirvana. However, the oldest texts were probably first written down in the first century BC. The oral tradition they incorporate is without doubt considerably older. That is apparent from the fact that in his rock edicts Asoka makes direct use of passages from the *Dhammapada*.

We will frequently refer in this book to the *Dhammapada* and *Udanavarga* since they contain an astonishing number of elements, passages and moral views that are re-encountered in the Gospels. Striking it is, above all, that the instructions of Jesus are based on these Buddhist texts – and there is good reason for that.

It is apparent that correspondences frequently occur in certain passages. For instance, there are many parallels in Chapter 33 of the *Udanavarga*, which describes the moral attitudes and spiritual preconditions for someone who is an exemplary follower of the Buddha's path. He is called a *brahmana*, an expression that in this context is probably best translated as 'holy man'. These correlations can be viewed as an indication that at least for certain passages written models were used rather than texts merely referring to a general oral tradition.

In Matthew's version of the Sermon on the Mount (Matthew 5:21–48) there are teachings not contained in Luke. These are Jesus's six declarations beginning 'Ye have heard that it was said . . . but I say unto you'. Jesus's words about divorce can confidently be put on one side since they are just a reworking of a passage from Mark (Mark 10:11–12). Of Jesus's five declarations, the four about killing, adultery, swearing oaths and retribution are obvious borrowings from the Buddha's 'five precepts' (*pancasila*), which involve avoiding killing, taking something that has not been given, eating meat, telling lies, and poisoning oneself with alcohol and drugs (*Maha-Sudassana-Sutta* 1:16).

The Buddha time and again presented these five prescriptions as basic guidelines for his adherents. Observing them shows whether the self-control demanded by Buddhism is being achieved. Such guidelines are also given by Jesus in connection with renouncing the things of the outer world while turning inwards. That standpoint is emphasized in that Jesus links these prescriptions with control of one's words, thereby presupposing control of thoughts (and thus closing the circle with the Buddhist quotation in the Epistle of James). But this part of the Gospel does not just involve parallels with the five Buddhist prescriptions; the passage that follows offers moreover striking affinities with Buddhist texts – so we present them alongside one another here for the sake of clarity.

Man does not purify himself by washing as most people do in this world. Anyone who rejects any sin, large and small, is a holy man because he rejects sins (Ud 33:13).

Evil is done through the self; man defiles himself through the self. Evil is made good through the self; man purifies himself through the self (Dh 12:9).

Do not ye yet understand, that whatsoever entereth in at the mouth goeth into the belly, and is cast out into the draught. But those things which proceed out of the mouth came forth from the heart; and they defile the man.

For out of the heart proceed evil thoughts, murders, adulteries, fornications, thefts, false witness, blasphemies. These are the things which defile a man; but to eat with unwashen hands defileth not a man (Matthew 15:17–20).

In the passage about adultery the Gospel presents the powerful image of the eye that should be plucked out if it gives rise to sin since it is better that one limb should perish than the entire body should be cast into hell (Matthew 5:29). There is also a clear-cut Buddhist precedent for this declaration[19]: 'Whosoever has destroyed the longing for worldly goods, sinfulness, and the chains of the fleshly eye, who has torn out longing at its roots, him I call a holy man' (Ud 33:68).

We can see from these few correspondences with the sayings of Jesus that some of the moral prescriptions a Buddhist mendicant monk (*bhikshu*) had to observe recur word for word in the New Testament, embedded in another literary version. What in the Buddhist source seems like a sober instruction, a principle that should be learned by heart, is aphoristically condensed in the words of Jesus. Jesus's proclamations seem to come from discourse, while the Buddhist sayings appear to derive from written texts. We must in fact bear in mind that difference when comparing the two. If we compare a written text with speech (rather than two written texts), we must take into account the differing forms of presentation. That particularly applies to Jesus's way of speaking since it reveals a number of rhetorical characteristics. We shall return to them when we begin to look for his authentic proclamations.

Jesus's warning against false prophets, which is also to be found in Matthew's version of the Sermon on the Mount, follows on from his adoption of the five prescriptions. False prophets are only outwardly pure, pretending to perfect spiritual transformation, whereas in fact they are spiritually unclean, and thus can only be demagogues and seducers: 'Beware of false prophets, which come to you in sheep's clothing, but inwardly they are ravening wolves' (Matthew 7:15).

In the Palestine of Jesus's time there was a glut of false prophets, while in Gautama's Maghada there was an inflated number of false ascetics. Buddha warned against them in similar fashion by attacking their outer appearance symbolized by mud and rough clothing: 'Why your matted hair, fool? Why animal skins as clothing? Within yourself is a jungle, yet you embellish yourself outwardly' (Dh 26:12).

This rebuke, calling for a search for wisdom inwardly rather than putting on an outer show, seemed so important to the compiler of the Gandhari version of the *Dharmapada* that he put it at the beginning of the collection as the first verse. The age when this edition was produced may have been marked by an outbreak of religious hysteria with numerous self-appointed masters, redeemers, and prophets – not unlike the situation in Palestine during the time of Jesus – so the intention was to counter that bad development by giving great prominence to this statement.

A remarkable declaration in conjunction with Jesus's choice of disciples is to be found in the Gospel according to John. When Jesus speaks to Nathanael, the latter is startled and asks how Jesus knows him. Jesus gives the obscure answer: 'Before that Philip called thee, when thou wast under the fig-tree, I saw thee' (John 1:48). Why did Jesus see Nathanael under a fig-tree of all places? Is that an allusion to the Buddhist tree of knowledge, the Bodhi tree beneath which Gautama attained Buddhahood? The tree at Bodh Gaya beneath which the Awakened One achieved great insight belonged to the genus *Ficus religiosa* – a fig-tree. It has been suggested that this biblical passage is wrongly translated, and what Jesus really said was that he had seen Nathanael when he (Jesus) was sitting under the fig-tree. That would open up a completely new perspective, depicting Jesus as a meditating Buddha. However, an error in translation cannot be conclusively demonstrated here.

Jesus's Buddhist Miracles

Numerous relics of vedic and brahminic views on religion are to be found in Buddhism. They probably do not derive from Siddhartha Gautama but rather from the compilers of Buddhist writings for whom his teachings must have seemed too radical. It is maintained that Gautama, who originally rejected miracles and magical abilities, said of the capacities of a *bhikshu* in his discourse on the rewards of a mendicant monk's existence:

> He implements such abilities in various ways. Having become one, he becomes many; having become many, he [again] becomes one. He is able to appear, to disappear. He walks through walls, ramparts, mountains as if they were air. He can submerge in earth and re-emerge as if in water; and he walks on water without sinking as if it were earth. Sitting in the air, he moves like a winged bird.[20]

Naturally, one must assume that the attainment of such magical powers demonstrates the degree of spiritual progress, and is not intended to serve the gratification of a yearning for miracles. The Buddha – and later Patanjali, author of the Yoga

Sutras – stressed the importance of not becoming fascinated by magical abilities. Such exceptional talents indicate people who have surmounted the external world.

A later legend elucidated that symbolically in another discourse by the Buddha. The Sublime One could cross rivers effortlessly – in other words, without striving. In the non-striving state he was 'elevated' and floated as it were. In some stories the Buddha never touches the ground beneath his feet, and in the apocryphal Acts of John (93:9) we read that John observed of Jesus: 'When I walked with him, I often tried to see whether his footsteps left a trace on the ground since I had noticed he was floating – and I saw absolutely nothing.'

Two famous miracles said to have been performed by Jesus were certainly taken over from Buddhist precedents: the loaves and the fishes, and Jesus's walking on water. Perhaps that is also why they follow one another in the Gospels. The miracle of the loaves and fishes (Matthew 14:15–21, Mark 6:35–44, Luke 9:13–17) obviously derives from the introduction to *Jataka* 78. There it is reported that with the bread in his alms bowl the Buddha satisfied the hunger of his 500 disciples and all the inhabitants of a monastery, and much bread remained. Richard Garbe has drawn attention to the fact that not only is the miracle itself identical; the numbers in both narratives accord remarkably.[21] According to the New Testament accounts, Jesus satisfied 5000 people with five loaves (and two fishes), leaving twelve baskets of fragments. In the *Jataka* 500 or many more were satiated, once again leaving twelve baskets of fragments. The number 500 occurs very frequently in Buddhist texts. That circumstance and the fact of the number being less than the biblical 5000 is an unmistakable sign that this version is older and served as a model for the Bible.

In the *Dighanikaya* and the *Majjhimanikaya*, the oldest Buddhist texts, the ability to walk on water is expressly listed as one of the Buddha's many magical abilities. In the *Mahavamsa* we read how Gautama crossed the Ganges, hovering just above the surface. Walking on water as a paranormal ability was not new in the India of Buddha's time. In the Vedas we read of holy men who were said to be capable of that.

Let us once again consider the story of Buddha walking on water as handed down in the *Mahavagga*.[22] This narrative is linked with the conversion of Kassapa, the leader of a group of religious ascetics. The incident occurred during the rainy season when water was falling so violently from the skies that it was soon no longer possible to walk around dry-footed. Gautama was not interested in going for a walk but rather in meditating while walking. Special paths were established in monasteries for this important Buddhist practice. Gautama used his extraordinary abilities to keep an area free of water so that he could meditate. Kassapa was much concerned about the revered teacher. Fearful that the Awakened One could be swept away by the raging waters, he jumped into a boat to seek him. Then he saw how Gautama was walking on the water without getting wet. Kassapa was so surprised that he first disbelievingly asked: 'Are you there, great mendicant monk?' With the words 'It is I, Kassapa' the Buddha calmed the fearful man and came to the boat. Kassapa and the Buddha then started talking, and the ascetic had no choice but to accept the Enlightened One's spiritual superiority and to convert to his faith.

On one of the most impressive of Buddhist buildings, the stupa at Sanchi, there is a depiction in relief of the walking on the water. This stupa was built between the second and first centuries BC. The illustrations of the Buddha's life show how quickly these legends must have spread since the depictions assume that the stories represented were already generally known. At that time the Buddha himself was not represented because of the great reverence people showed him. His absence is a typical characteristic. The introduction of Prince Rahula before the Buddha on the Amaravati Stupa (Plate 24) depicts many people showing their reverence before an empty throne with cushions, a low bench and the impressions of two feet symbolizing the Buddha's presence. Buddha's confident walking on the water is depicted at Sanchi by way of an empty stone bench amid the flood waters. The stone bench is of course the monastic cloister path that Buddha Shakyamuni, so to speak, brought invisibly into existence.

In the New Testament texts on the walking on the water there are very strange elements which must seem completely incomprehensible to the impartial reader. Mark justifies Jesus's walking on the water as a kind of 'encore miracle'. First he performed the miracle of the feeding of the 5000 which, as we have seen, involved a Buddhist motif. But that event obviously did not impress the disciples sufficiently: 'For they considered not the miracle of the loaves' (Mark 6:52). So Jesus was forced to impress them with an even more effective miracle. He sent off his disciples by boat, and withdrew into solitude to pray. When his followers were rowing hard against the wind in the middle of the lake, Jesus walked upon the water.

The account in Mark seems alien and imposed, because Jesus is shown as performing the miracle merely in order to awaken understanding among his followers. Such behaviour in no way accords with Jesus's personality and intentions. He neither needed to impress people by way of miracles, nor was he a kind of fairground magician producing miracles one after another.

In the German Bible Jesus does not 'walk' on the water; he perambulates like the Peripatetics, the pupils of Aristotle who used to pace up and down in the covered walk of their school, the *peripatos*.[23] That expression comes closest to the events narrated in the Buddhist story, describing the meditative absorption involved in Gautama's walking across the water on an invisible path.

Jesus's disciples were upset and believed they had seen a ghost. And then followed – corresponding amazingly to the Buddhist precedent – the same words from Jesus as Buddha uttered to the astonished Kassapa: 'It is I' (Mark 6:50; John 6:20).

The theologian Norbert Klatt has impressively demonstrated that the motif of walking on water was completely alien to pre-Christian Judaism, and that the Bible passages from Job, the Psalms and Habakkuk cited by most exegetists in their interpretation of this incident cannot be related to the New Testament. Since the detailed correspondences in the accounts of the walking on water by the Buddha and Jesus are so unusually numerous we list them below, following Klatt's analysis:[24]

1. Both Jesus and the Buddha are on their own in a solitary place.
2. They are involved in religious practices (prayer/meditation).
3. They pace up and down on the water – described in the same terms in both Pali and Greek.
4. In both cases the water is rough or turbulent.
5. The narrative turns to the disciples/Kassapa.
6. On the water is a boat filled with men.
7. Those in the boat are astonished by the man walking on the water.

8. They do not know who the man walking on the water is and question him.
9. Both Jesus and the Buddha identify themselves with the words 'It is I'.
10. The men want to take the walker on the water into their boat.
11. Jesus and the Buddha enter the boat.

The correspondences are so numerous that the two stories must be viewed as almost identical.

In Matthew (14:28–33), but not in Mark and John, the apostle Peter also tries to walk on the water but starts to sink. That episode is surprisingly similar to the introduction to *Jataka* 190 where Sariputta, a disciple of Gautama, also attempts to follow his master across the water, because he cannot find the ferry-boat at the bank of the river Aciravati. He starts crossing the river in a state of profound contemplation, but when the waves get higher and he is torn out of his meditative state he begins to sink. As soon as he re-establishes his meditation, he can continue walking over the water without danger. Neither Sariputta nor Peter walked effortlessly across this treacherous element, which is only possible for someone who has attained an advanced state in the art of contemplation and trust. Peter sinks because of lack of trust, because of the 'lack of faith' with which Jesus reproaches him. This exact correspondence can only be based on a borrowing.

The Woman at the Well

The appearances of the Buddha and Jesus were socially explosive, since both called in question long-established caste systems. For a man of noble origins like Siddhartha Gautama, it must have been exceptionally unusual to lay aside inherited privileges. Nevertheless, for his 'recruitment campaign' that was highly advantageous, since his status induced many leading and esteemed people to reflect on his view of the world despite the great potential for conflict it entailed.

The Buddha may have taught his followers to keep their distance from fools and those lacking understanding, and to cultivate friendship with the discerning,[25] but for him that in no way meant disparaging certain kinds of people. It was a recommendation not to endanger spiritual progress. 'If a person finds a wise companion, steadfast and pure, he should join together with that person, surmount all corruption and be considerate and thankful. If a person does not find such a companion, steadfast and pure, he should live alone and avoid all sins, like a monarch renouncing his vast kingdom' (Ud 14:13–14).

None the less, the Buddha always treated people equally, no matter what their status, origin or caste. Jesus was Buddha's equal in that respect. He was more than once reproached for consorting with fringe groups, preferring the company of idlers, rogues, tax-collectors and whores to 'more suitable' contacts. All the same, such dealings do not seem to have been central; they were instead intended as a sign to those (the Pharisees) who thought themselves to be fine and unblemished, in their arrogance despising people of a different kind. Jesus wanted to demonstrate what the Buddha also constantly stressed: the ultimate equality of all people. Gautama pragmatically decided not to spend too much time with the narrow-minded, whereas Jesus focused on a social experiment.

On one occasion the Buddha attracted the anger of the upper classes when he accepted a courtesan's invitation to eat with her. How could the holy man dare turn down their invitation and instead sit at the same table as a prostitute? Gautama certainly also ate with persons of high standing. In his choice of table companions he was not following a programme giving precedence to the socially deprived. His attitude towards human interaction demonstrated a radical impartiality in the truest sense of the word. Jesus's attitude to the powerful religious authorities sometimes seems more rebellious and unyielding. A story about the Buddha's favourite pupil Ananda is revealing. When travelling through the countryside, Ananda met the Matangi girl Prakriti drawing water from a well. He asks her for some water. She was afraid to come into contact with him since – as she told Ananda – the Matangi caste were not allowed to approach a holy man. However, Ananda answered: 'My sister, I am not asking about your caste or your family; I am asking whether you can give me some water to drink' (*Divyavadana* 217).

The caste of the Chandala, to which the Matangi girl belonged, was the lowest in Indian society. Brahmins treated it with profound contempt. They would never have taken water from a Chandala; just the shadow of an untouchable was sufficient to ritually defile a brahmin. Even though the social systems and the historical circumstances were completely different, the Jews similarly looked down on certain peoples: the inhabitants of Samaria, the Philistines and the people of Seir. The Samaritans had attempted to preserve their own customs by establishing a holy shrine on Mount Garizim, thereby turning away from the 'dungheaps' of Jerusalem. That behaviour made leading Pharisees livid, and from that time they viewed the Samaritans as being the most repulsive of all people – as is testified in the *Book of Wisdom of Jesus Sirach* written at the start of the second century BC: 'My soul detests two peoples, and the third is not even a people: the inhabitants of Seir and the Land of the Philistines, and the foolish race that dwells in Sichem [Samaria]' (50:25).

In the New Testament there is a long narrative which initially is astonishingly similar to the story of Ananda and Prakriti. This tells of Jesus's encounter with a woman at Jacob's Well near Sychar in Samaria. Since this is in the Gospel according to John (4:5–42), it of course also contains a considerable element of spiritual symbolism. Jesus asks a Samaritan woman at the well for a drink of water. In the woman's answer we encounter the same amazement at the courage of a member of a privileged caste, or a chosen people, in turning to someone despised and rejected: 'How is it that thou, being a Jew, askest drink of me, which is a woman of Samaria?' At that point the reader would expect a brief reply such as Ananda gave – simple and beyond all prejudice, as exemplified in Jesus's aphorisms. Instead there follows a typical Johannine explanation, mystically obscure, where Jesus tells the woman that if she knew who he was, *she* would ask *him* for a drink, and he would give her 'living water'. This simple but dramatically well-shaped scene of an unequal encounter then leads abruptly to theological exposition. Everything indicates that the evangelist used an introduction from some foreign source in order to express his views on the mystical Christ. One can assume that John knew of Jesus's rejection of prejudices so it was thus convenient to know the Indian story which encapsulated this theme in an easily remembered way.

We have learned in our Christian upbringing to view such simple stories, such uncomplicated comparisons and teachings, as characteristic of Jesus. In those texts profound wisdom manifests itself in simple shape, allowing us to comprehend Jesus as a genius in the interpretation of everyday observations. Much in fact indicates that Jesus did possess such mastery. So it is disturbing to discover that some of our beloved anecdotes and aphorisms, which every child preserves in its heart from the earliest years, were not spoken by Jesus or piously invented by his disciples, but were taken over, word for word, from Buddhist traditions.

Such adoptions also include the story of the widow's mite (Mark 12:41–44; Luke 21:1–4). Its simplicity and vividness make it one of the most extensively investigated correspondences with Buddhist precedents. Hans Haas, a Professor of Religious History at Leipzig, has devoted an entire book to this theme.[26] The New Testament narrative tells of Jesus beholding how people cast money into the offertory box at the treasury in Jerusalem. A poor widow gave two lepta.[27] A priest was standing at this offertory box, charged with checking the coins and proclaiming the value of donations. Anyone close by could discover precisely how much a person had given – 'for the well-off an opportunity for display, for the poor widow a reason for shame, and for Jesus an occasion for instructing his followers'.[28] Jesus taught his disciples that a poor person's modest offering is worth more than a rich person's larger gift, who seemingly gives out of his abundance. To present such a lesson it was in no way necessary for the authors of the Gospels to mention *two* lepta. If the story is considered as an illustrated proverb, one would expect that the poor person would sacrifice one penny, and thus be praised above the rich man. In addition the tale concerns a poor widow, not any poor person.

In the Buddhist parallel (*Kalapanamandinaka* 4:22), a widow also comes to a religious assembly where she gets something to eat. She regrets her fate, being unable to give anything whilst others donate precious objects. Then she remembers that she owns *two* copper coins she found in a dung-heap. She joyously offers up these coins. An *arhat*, who can perceive people's most secret thoughts, pays no attention to donations by the affluent but sings a song in honour of the poor widow's piety.

There are many variants of this theme in Buddhist tradition. Buddhist texts viewed overall can be considered as a musical work where a single theme is presented time and again in innumerable variations. The idea that the worth of a donation is not to be measured in terms of money value but rather of the sacrifice involved for the donor also becomes clear in the story of the impoverished old woman buying oil with money she has begged so as to be able to light a lamp for the Buddha. That lamp immediately spreads a more beautiful light than all the king's many lamps.[29] In another anecdote rich men are not even capable of filling the Buddha's begging-bowl with 10,000 bushels while a poor woman fills it with a handful of flowers. In most Buddhist stories of that kind a poor person's donation, the gift of a pure heart, is rewarded. The teaching of right action (*karma*) is elucidated at the same time. The poor widow who gives the two copper coins she found receives a reward in that on her way home she meets the king returning from burying his wife, and he makes her his new consort.

The correspondences between the Buddhist tale and the Gospel narrative in terms of content, significance and syntactic characteristics are so striking that Hans Haas closed his study with the following words:

> This is not to be understood as a biographical anecdote worked up from one of Jesus's poetic teachings, as a transformed parable, but fundamentally as a legend which penetrated the realm of early Christianity from outside – and we have reason to believe from Buddhism – which was viewed in good faith as being a simple event in the Master's life and was handed down by the Christian community until Luke recorded it in writing and this was taken from his life of Jesus into the long complete second Gospel.[30]

Here we have selected only a few borrowings in predominantly narrative passages of the New Testament. In his much-praised study, Rudolf Seydel discovered no fewer than fifty-one correspondences, analysing them in depth. The theologian Van den Bergh van Eysinga thought that the following eleven correspondences were particularly convincing, and six additional ones worthy of consideration:

1. the story of Simeon
2. the twelve-year-old Jesus in the temple
3. Jesus's hesitation about being baptized (according to Matthew and the Epistle to the Hebrews)
4. the temptation
5. Mary's beatitude
6. the widow's mite

7. Jesus walking on the water
8. the Samaritan woman at the well
9. 'out of his belly shall flow rivers of living water' (John 7:38)
10. the parable of the talents (Matthew 25:14–30; Luke 19:12–27)
11. the world on fire in the Second Epistle of Peter (3:8–11).

The lesser parallels he suggests are:

12. the Annunciation (Luke 1:29–33)
13. the selection of the disciples (John 1:35–43)
14. the statement about Nathanael
15. the parable of the prodigal son (Luke 15:11–32)
16. the man born blind
17. the Transfiguration (Matthew 17:1–13; Mark 9:2–13; Luke 9:28–36)

Must one therefore – even when viewing this material very sceptically – assume that a large number of biographical elements, of parables and narratives from the life of Jesus, are fantasy? Borrowings were certainly also eagerly made from sources other than the wealth of surviving Buddhist texts. The Hellenistic legacy is demonstrated in the eclecticism of the evangelists, who drew freely on a wide range of writings and other ethnic traditions. The references to Jewish holy books, particularly the prophets, are also – viewed from the perspective of Christianity – borrowings, needed for portrayal of Jesus as the Messiah. It becomes apparent too that the representatives of the Jesus movement responsible for setting down the Gospels were primarily interested in reforming Judaism rather than establishing a new, autonomous religion. However, the fragments of various traditions were not disjointedly strung together in order to expand Jesus's life as if it were a novel. Instead this was a difficult, scholarly process deploying textual patterns from the multi-structured cultural web of these traditions.

That approach can be illustrated in the way Mark set about writing. Research has shown that the Gospel according to Mark is the result of desk work. He had spread out in front of him related stories of miracles, collections of prophetic narratives in various stages of development, an incomplete collection of Jesus's sayings, observations on the parables, the books of the Old Testament and the prophets, notes on the Christ cult, etc. Other characteristic Jewish-Hellenistic literature and Buddhist material must also have been available in his reference library. Burton L. Mack, a historian of religion, describes Mark's study as a place where a lively exchange of ideas took place and literary experiments were the order of the day.[31] Matthew and Luke, who had the result of Mark's endeavours at their disposal, operated in a similarly eclectic fashion. The same is true of the later Gospel according to John, which was also linked to an autonomous tradition with theological roots in Gnosticism and Mahayana Buddhism. But more of that later.

Seydel's thesis that the evangelists did not make direct use of legends about the Buddha but rather 'a Christianized poetic Gospel which employed the Buddhist framework and many Buddhist themes (in a musical sense) in order to be a Christian work of art similar to the Buddhist creation that stimulated the thinker into imitation'[32] is not unfounded. However, the diversity of the material taken over and the unrelated nature of the individual elements within the Gospel sequence makes the existence of such an original Christian-Buddhist Gospel seem improbable. There is no doubt that Buddhist narratives found their way into the New Testament, but up to now there has been no satisfactory explanation of how and above all why the Buddhist tradition should have been drawn on rather than others. How is the Buddhist tradition linked with Jesus's teaching, with the community of his followers and with Christianity? If this is merely a literary problem, the parallels with regard to the person of Jesus and to Christianity would be of secondary importance. In that case one would have to track down the literary structure involved – particularly in religious writing. We know from modern scholarship that our entire literary heritage is a patchwork of quotations, motifs taken over and reshaped, plagiarism, true and false copies, borrowings, mutilations and correct and incorrect translations. So how did Buddhist material get into Christian books?

Some of it certainly seems to have been taken over by the authors and editors of the Gospels and apocryphal writings from oral traditions and written texts. Buddhist sources may have been used alongside others, just because they were suitable for supplying the mythological superstructure for the religion of Christianity. But that itself provokes reflection. How did it happen that Buddhist texts were taken over to such an extent? One could assume that it occurred as part of a general

trend within Hellenistic approaches to religion and philosophy. Buddhism was especially suitable for such a process
among the Indian ideas which intellectuals employed for developing their conceptual systems. It included concepts which –
against the background of the writings of Plato and Pythagoras
rediscovered at that time – were excellently suited to the elabor-
ation of large-scale cosmological and mythological models.
However, research into the frequent use of Buddhist material
must also bear in mind the possibility that it might have been
deliberately incorporated in Christian texts in full awareness of
its origins.

So even if numerous New Testament passages are borrowings and the Gospels constitute a patchwork of highly diverse
materials, the crucial questions still remain. What do we know
about the historical Jesus? How much of the presentation of
Jesus is literary invention and how much authentic material?
On the basis of the borrowings presented here, we must
assume that more or less the entire presentation of Christ's
childhood and all the celebrated events that Christians have
learned to identify with Jesus do not correspond with the facts;
that there never was a feeding of the 5000, that Jesus never
walked on the water, that there was no meeting with a Samaritan women at a well, and that there was no teaching about the
poor widow making her donation. And how must we evaluate
the discourses of Jesus that follow Buddhist patterns? Are they
also nothing but later insertions based on Indian sources?
Answering that question is certainly the greatest challenge,
with far-reaching implications, since it is precisely in Jesus's
sayings that we encounter the most remarkable correspondences with the words of the Buddha. Just think of the passage
from John mentioned in the Preface; just remember Jesus's
views on rebirth, his moral appeals, his warning of false
prophets. Or consider the following instructions to his disciples: 'Inasmuch as ye have done it unto one of the least of
these my brethren, ye have done it unto me' (Matthew 25:40).
With the Buddha the same idea reads: 'Anyone, O monks, who
wants to stand by me should stand by the afflicted' (*Mahavagga*
8, 26:3). What if it should turn out that such declarations by
Jesus are largely authentic and Jesus himself disseminated Buddhist teachings? Then the insertion of narrative passages from
the same source must be viewed in a completely new light.

The search for real events in Jesus's life must therefore be linked with the uncovering of the authentic words of Jesus. Only then can it be decided if the appearance of Buddhist ideas in the New Testament is the outcome of writers being influenced by the spirit of the age, or whether such ideas were even introduced by Jesus himself.

The Discovery of the Lost Gospel

We do not often have the good fortune to discover in old ruins, excavations or caves ancient lost texts that enrich our fragmentary knowledge about the beginnings of Christianity. At the end of the nineteenth century, however, enormously important finds of that nature were made at Cairo and in the Near East, and the discovery in the 1940s of Gnostic texts at Nag Hammadi in Egypt and of Jewish manuscripts in the caves at Qumran on the Dead Sea are among the most sensational manuscript finds in history. Discussions about the importance of those texts continue to the present day, leading time and again to spectacular reconstructions of the environment in which Jesus lived. There are whole libraries devoted solely to work on those discoveries.

But excavation is not always necessary to get to know lost, forgotten or unknown texts. Sometimes one has the good fortune to hit upon the unknown in the peace of one's own study. Modern textual criticism is capable of dissecting texts in a variety of ways which sometimes reveal concealed sub-texts – original sources serving as a foundation for the final work, which have simply vanished for the unpractised eye as the result of multiple editorial reworkings. Nevertheless they exist, rather like a television image when the brightness control has been completely turned down – the film continues to run but nothing can be seen on the darkened screen. In the same way the original text can no longer be recognized because of all the ink eager revisers have expended on it. Experienced scholars have, however, devised methods for once again regulating the 'brightness' and restoring the concealed text.

When researchers endeavoured to ascertain which Gospel was the oldest, they made a surprising discovery. Historically, it is virtually impossible to track down the authors of the Gospels, and any findings are dependent on analysis of the text

itself. The particular theological emphasis in the Gospel according to John revealed that it must have come into being when
other influences were at work, and must therefore be the most
recent. The three Gospels by Matthew (the first evangelist
according to the canonical order in the New Testament), Mark
and Luke were related. They tell in comparable fashion of
Jesus's life, embellished to a greater or lesser extent. They are
therefore called synoptic Gospels because individual passages
of text can be viewed comparatively. Such comparisons demonstrate two revealing kinds of correspondence. The narrative
sequences in Matthew and Luke only corresponds when they
follow a story presented in Mark. That signifies that Mark must
be the oldest Gospel, and was known by the other two, who
composed their accounts of Jesus's life after Mark. But the
widely accepted view that Mark was written towards the end
of the 60s can hardly be upheld any longer. It was probably
assembled during the mid-70s, since it alludes to public events
during the Jewish War (66–73 AD). However, Matthew and
Luke, whose texts were put down around 95 AD, include a
considerable number of statements by Jesus – parables, wise
sayings, exhortations and lamentations – some of which are
common to both of them but are completely absent in Mark.
Matthew and Luke must therefore have had at their disposal
a second shared source alongside Mark, which scholars today
simply call Q as a shorthand for *Quelle* which means 'source'
in German.

When evaluating the accounts given in the Gospels, one
must bear in mind the circumstances involved. Mark wrote
over forty years after the crucifixion and the end of Jesus's
public mission; a further twenty years elapsed before the writings
of Matthew and Luke. From their perspective it is as if an author
today were to write the biography of a man who briefly caused
a sensation at the end of the 1920s and beginning of the 1930s,
basing his book on a minor work from the late 1970s and a few
other texts. And if one also imagines that there were no printed
accounts, no newspaper or television reports, it is obvious how
limited such reporting would be. In other words, the authors
of the Gospels themselves had no possibility of checking what
was true and what was invention. They had to rely on existing
texts and oral tradition. They obviously based their work largely
on source material, otherwise we would not have the synoptic
tradition and the sayings gathered in Q would never have been

uncovered. The faithfulness with which the originals were sometimes copied can be recognized from the fact that obvious contradictions are not eliminated. More precise analysis shows therefore that the two evangelists must have relied on different versions of both Mark and Q. The differences in the dual tradition of Matthew and Luke seem to derive from a mixture of oral traditions and written versions of Q.

Many historians and theologians are convinced that Q constitutes the oldest source that circulated among Jesus's followers – much older than Mark. The sayings of Jesus were probably written down for the first time by his followers immediately after the catastrophe of the crucifixion. Q is thus the lost original Gospel that preserved the sayings of the Master, and it is now gradually being extracted from the writings of the New Testament. That is an important finding since an analysis of this collection of sayings not only provides us with insight into the thinking, behaviour and sociology of the Jesus movement after its Master vanished, but also allows us to penetrate the words Jesus had given his followers along the way. This collection of sayings would certainly have been lost if Matthew and Luke had not incorporated them in their stories of Jesus's life and works – and we would never have learned about the nature of the Q movement, which existed long before Christianity came into being.

What do we learn when we restrict ourselves to filtering the Q material out of the Gospels? First, it shows us that Jesus's early followers were content with a collection of his sayings. They did not need more in order to know that they were guided in an unholy world. This was not unusual in Hellenistic times. Various collections of sayings by wise men were in circulation, and these were passed around their disciples. Even in later times when the narrative Gospels had been written down, the Jesus movement's collected sayings remained in existence and were handed down as an autonomous collection. That is indicated by the Gospel of Thomas, which we have already mentioned. This is an apocryphal text which in 1946 was discovered by Egyptian peasants in a grave at Nag Hammadi near Luxor, together with 48 other tracts from a library of Gnostic texts in Coptic (the Middle Egyptian language). Until that time we only knew of this Gospel's existence from the writings of early Christian authors.

The Gospel of Thomas is a loosely structured collection of

114 sayings by Jesus. The Q text must have been very similar in structure, and in fact many of the declarations to be found in Q are paralleled in the Gospel of Thomas. So Thomas is certainly a continuation of Q, the collection of sayings assembled by early adherents of Jesus, without any fundamental changes in the form. The many aphorisms in Thomas are for the most part less developed than parallel versions in the Gospels, which indicates an earlier level in the process of oral tradition. That is why the Gospel of Thomas has to date been an undervalued and generally little-known source for reconstructing the oldest statements attributed to Jesus. Thomas, for instance, preserves sayings that do not appear in any of the canonical Gospels, but are most probably authentic in view of their structure and contents, which relate to certain discourses from Q. So we should by no means just rely on the Gospels to find our way back to the authentic words of Jesus. Such treasures are to be found in texts that powerful forces in the Church excluded and branded as heretical.

One fact is particularly astonishing in relation to the investigation of the Buddhist sources of Christianity. The Gospel of Thomas does not merely demonstrate a close relationship with Q; it is also saturated with Buddhist ideas. Around the beginning of this century an abundance of papyrus fragments in Greek, Coptic and Arabic were uncovered near Oxyrhynchos (modern el-Behnesa) in Egypt. They included various fragments from the Gospel of Thomas, and one contained a play based on an invented episode set in India.

It was probably not chance that the Indian material was found close to the Gospel of Thomas. The texts from Nag Hammadi derive from Gnostic systems of thought, which were widespread among early Christians. These Christian Gnostics followed Jesus but rejected the administration of salvation by a hierarchy of priests and bishops. Instead they sought to attain redemption through mystical and meditative discipline – like Buddhists and yogis in India. Numerous sayings by Jesus in the Gospel of Thomas are strikingly more reminiscent of the Indian and Zen Buddhist than of Catholic Pauline theology. In her outstanding presentation of the finds at Nag Hammadi, Elaine Pagels, the American religious scholar, writes: 'Some scholars have suggested that if the names were changed, the "living Buddha" appropriately could say what the Gospel of Thomas attributes to the living Jesus.'[33] It is not surprising that

Edward Conze, the British Buddhist scholar, assumes that the Gospel of Thomas was once in use among Indian Christians, and that 'Buddhists were in contact with Thomas-Christians in South India'.[34] Even today southern Indians call themselves 'Thomas-Christians'.

Around the start of the twentieth century, research into Q was actively pursued, but then nothing more was heard. Its rediscovery since the 1970s has produced an abundance of new findings, giving us insight into both the personality of Jesus and the structure of his group of followers. So let us briefly consider the way Q is structured. Its contents are characterized by three elements: wisdom discourse, prophetic and apocalyptic declarations and, to a lesser extent, biographical material. Prophetic and wisdom traditions, against a background of an expectation of the imminent end of the world, which had been circulating in the Judaism of that time for two centuries, certainly decisively influenced Q. The question is: which strand of tradition is the original one, going back to Jesus himself? Some think that the prophetic element was decisive for Q, others the wisdom tradition. Recent research has thrown light on that problem. It shows that Q consists of three clearly distinguishable parts in terms of content, structure and objective. That signifies that Q was revised, reordered and enriched at three different periods.[35] The oldest material in the collection, known as Q^1, only comprises wisdom sayings by Jesus. The prophetic and apocalyptic texts (Q^2) were added afterwards. The story of the temptation and a number of additional linking sections (Q^3) belong to an even later date. The three layers of Q can thus be summarized as follows:

Q^1. The essential element in the initial layer consists of six wisdom discourses by Jesus. They are reminiscent of instructions to a community as they are known to us from the Egyptian, old Oriental, and Hellenistic literature. Q^1 is characterized by radical ethics, breaking with many social conventions.

Q^2. In the second phase of structuring the prophetic and apocalyptic material offers a stark contrast to Q^1. It is characterized by a symptomatic confrontation of 'this generation' and the announcement of the Last Judgement. The words about 'this generation' are directed against the Jews for their response to the preachings of Jesus. The pronouncements against Galilean towns included in this part are obviously imitations of models provided by the prophets.[36]

Q[3]. In the final revision the sayings are complemented by the addition of a biographical section with the story of the temptation.

Q was unified through these three editorial interventions, and acquired a systematic theological underpinning. Its final shape, as circulated among followers of Jesus after the Jewish War and taken over by Matthew and Luke, was a coherent, written structure of discourses and anecdotes.[37] That is demonstrated by the verbal correspondences between the evangelists and their adherence to a largely similar sequence. In addition, linguistic findings indicate that Q must have been written in Greek, and the original order of words is better preserved in Luke than in Matthew.

The 'Otherness' of Jesus

We possess so few historically indisputable accounts of Jesus that analysis of the source's sayings could become a valuable means of understanding his personality. The basic elements in his teaching are believably revealed here. However, this analysis immediately resulted in numerous new psychograms of Jesus. Some thought he was better comprehended as a rebellious apocalyptic preacher,[38] while others saw him as a wisdom teacher following the rabbinical model[39] who had even initiated 'scholastic sects'[40] as conventicles, or as a Hellenistic philosopher,[41] even as the leader of the Jewish 'Peace Party'[42], or as a peaceful revolutionary who proclaimed to the world anti-establishment wisdom in the form of parables.[43]

So who was Jesus? A philosopher, a wisdom teacher, an apocalyptic prophet, the founder of a religion, a wandering preacher, a mendicant monk? The Jesus we know from the Gospels makes his authoritative appearance as the Son of God, announces his vicarious suffering and his death on the cross for humanity, and leaves no doubt about being the promised Messiah who will initiate the end of time and the Last Judgement. Did Jesus the man really ever maintain such things? Or is most of this picture the deliberate embellishment of a Jesus Christ artificially constructed by a sect that was justifiably interested in viewing itself as the elect? Through Q – particularly Q^1 – we now have a possibility of assessing the value of this tradition, since Q grew out of a collection of their Master's words by the Jesus people themselves, who were the bearers of the tradition inaugurated by Jesus.

One thing is immediately apparent when reading the complete Q text. The followers of Jesus among whom this collection of sayings circulated were not Christians. They did not see Jesus as either the Messiah or as Christ, and did not comprehend his teachings as an attack on Judaism. They did not view his 'death'[44] as a divine event or a means of redemption, and none of them believed that Jesus had risen from the dead so as to rule over a new world. Instead they saw him as an exceptional spiritual teacher whose wisdom would help them live in troubled times.[45]

That phenotype of Jesus contrasts with the portrait presented in the narrative passages of the Gospels. If the Gospel biographies are to be believed, Jesus made his appearance to reform Judaism. As the Jewish Messiah he criticized the Scribes and Pharisees. In Jerusalem he cleansed the Temple in the name of this authority, and prophesied its destruction. He promised to his disciples that in the future Kingdom of Heaven they would have a special place which they could share in if they did penance and turned away from the wrong path. 'None of this is reflected in the sayings gospel Q. In Q there is no hint of a select group of disciples, no program to reform the religion or politics of Judaism, no dramatic encounter with the authorities in Jerusalem, no martyrdom for the cause, much less a martyrdom with saving significance for the ills of the world, and no mention of a first church in Jerusalem.'[46]

It looks as if the followers of Jesus were not aware of the cause they are supposed to have upheld. At any rate, they were far from believing that they were supposed to change the world or pave the way for a new religion. The Q material offers us a perspective that does away with the traditional view of an original community that stood up for a new faith in Jesus Christ as the Son of God and redeemer. Certainly such groupings existed, but they developed independently and much later, had nothing to do with the Q people and had no first-hand contact with Jesus's teachings and intentions.

Of course, one would be wrong to conclude that Jesus's authentic words are only preserved in Q. We also know his discourses and sayings from other parts of the synoptic Gospels, from the special features of Matthew and Luke, from the Gospel according to John, and from the apocryphal writings, particularly the Gospel of Thomas. However, through the discovery of the importance of Q^1 in relation to the editorial adaptations of Q^2 and Q^3 we gain a criterion for assessing other statements attributed to Jesus. Seeking other authentic statements by Jesus beyond Q is a rewarding enterprise currently being undertaken by the 'Jesus seminar' at Westar Institute in Sonoma, California – not just as a voyage of discovery through the labyrinth of the New Testament but also through the apocryphal texts, which also preserve sayings of Jesus.

The initial, and surprising, discovery, therefore, is that neither Jesus nor the people of Q were Christians. Q shows us that Jesus's first followers had little in common with this cult of Christ. That becomes dramatically apparent if we read the collection of Jesus's sayings which forms the oldest level of the Q material. Among the collection's most important components are parts of the Sermon on the Mount, and other Q^1 passages are closely related to those moral teachings.

In the next section we present the entire text of Q^1, following the most recent scholarly analysis by John Kloppenborg and the more accessible new version by Burton L. Mack.[47] The entire Book of Q consists of sixty-two short sections, and the twenty-one given here form the oldest layer of sayings by Jesus, amounting to all the Q^1 material as the original Gospel of Sayings cherished by the Q Jesus people.

When reading what has been handed down of Jesus's original words, it is advisable for a moment to forget all one thinks one knows about Jesus. Forget the Son of God who rose from the dead, who had come to redeem a sinful humanity through his crucifixion. Allow this material to work on you, without pre-judgements and familiar contexts. Listen to the words of the original Jesus.

The Original Jesus Speaks

[These are the teachings of Jesus]
[Seeing the crowds, he said to his disciples]

'How fortunate are the poor; they have God's kingdom.
How fortunate the hungry; they will be fed.
How fortunate are those who are crying; they will laugh.'

'I am telling you, love your enemies, bless those who curse you, pray for those who mistreat you.
If someone slaps you on the cheek, offer your other cheek as well.
If anyone grabs your coat, let him have your shirt as well.
Give to anyone who asks, and if someone takes away your belongings, do not ask to have them back.
As you want people to treat you, do the same to them.
If you love those who love you, what credit is that to you? Even tax collectors love those who love them, do they not? And if you embrace only your brothers, what more are you doing than others? Doesn't everybody do that? If you lend to those from whom you expect repayment, what credit is that to you? Even wrongdoers lend to their kind because they expect to be repaid.
Instead, love your enemies, do good, and lend without expecting anything in return. Your reward will be great, and you will be children of God.
For he makes his sun rise on the evil and on the good; he sends rain on the just and the unjust.'

'Be merciful even as your Father is merciful.
Don't judge and you won't be judged.
For the standard you use [for judging] will be the standard used against you.'

'Can the blind lead the blind? Won't they both fall into a pit? A student is not better than his teacher. It is enough for a student to be like his teacher.'

'How can you look for the splinter in your brother's eye and not notice the stick in your own eye? How can you say to your brother, "Let me remove the splinter in your eye", when you do not see the stick in your own eye? You hypocrite, first take the stick from your own eye, and then you can see to remove the splinter that is in your brother's eye.'

'A good tree does not bear rotten fruit; a rotten tree does not bear good fruit. Are figs gathered from thorns, or grapes from thistles? Every tree is known by its fruit.

The good man produces good things from his store of goods and treasures; and the evil man evil things.
For the mouth speaks from a full heart.'

'Why do you call me, "Master, master", and not do what I say?
Everyone who hears my words and does them is like a man who built a house on rock. The rain fell, a torrent broke against the house, and it did not fall, for it had a rock foundation.
But everyone who hears my words and does not do them is like a man who built a house on sand. The rain came, the torrent broke against it, and it collapsed. The ruin of that house was great.'

When someone said to him, 'I will follow you wherever you go', Jesus answered, 'Foxes have dens, and birds of the sky have nests, but the son of man has nowhere to lay his head.'
When another said, 'Let me first go and bury my father', Jesus said, 'Leave the dead to bury their dead.'
Yet another said, 'I will follow you, sir, but first let me say goodbye to my family.' Jesus said to him, 'No one who puts his hand to the plow and then looks back is fit for the kingdom of God.'

He said, 'The harvest is abundant, but the workers are few; beg therefore the master of the harvest to send out workers into his harvest.
Go. Look, I send you out as lambs among wolves.
Do not carry money, or bag, or sandals, or staff; and do not greet anyone on the road.
Whatever house you enter, say, "Peace be to this house!" And if a child of peace is there, your greeting will be received [literally, 'your peace will rest upon him']. But if not, let your peace return to you.
And stay in the same house, eating and drinking whatever they provide, for the worker deserves his wages. Do not go from house to house.
And if you enter a town and they receive you, eat what is set before you. Pay attention to the sick and say to them, "God's kingdom has come near to you."
But if you enter a town and they do not receive you, as you leave, shake the dust from your feet and say, "Nevertheless, be sure of this, the realm of God has come to you."'

'When you pray, say,
"Father, may your name be holy.
May your rule take place.
Give us each day our daily bread.

The Bodhi tree at Bodh Gaya, grown from shoots going back across the centuries to the tree beneath which Gautama achieved enlightenment.

2

The Buddha's first sermon before his five pupils at Isipatana. Kitschy modern depictions at Sarnath.

(Opposite top left) Presentation of Prince Jeta's park near Shravasti to the Buddha. Jataka scene from the Bharhut Stupa.

(Opposite top right) Asoka's lion column at Sarnath (3rd century BC). As proclaimer of the Dharma the Buddha was viewed as a roaring lion.

(Opposite below) The great Dhamekh Stupa at Isipatana (Sarnath) where the Buddha gave his first sermon.

3

4

5

6

Vulture Peak near Rajagriha where the Buddha frequently received his followers.

The Wild Boar Cave on Vulture Peak near Rajagriha where the Buddha sought shelter from rain: today it is an important place of pilgrimage for Buddhists.

7

Excavations at the Isipatana (Sarnath) monastery site.

Buddha-like statues (2nd century BC) found near Marseille.

11

12

(Above left) Mahavira, the founder of Jainism (Khajuraho).

(Above right) Buddha with the gesture of setting in motion the Wheel of Teaching (Gandhara, 2nd/3rd century).

(Opposite top) Amazing correspondence between cultures. Left: the celebrated "Proto-Shiva" - Indus Valley seal c. 2000 BC. Right: the Celtic god Cernunnos (Gundestrup cauldron, 1st century BC).

(Opposite centre left) Imprint of a characteristic Indus Valley seal (c. 2000 BC) whose characters have not been deciphered.

(Opposite centre right) Pythagoras the philosopher, the first person to bring Indian teachings to the West on a large scale.

(Opposite below left) Roman oil lamps found in Arikamedu harbour (Pondicherry Museum).

(Opposite below right) Roman sword from Arikamedu (Pondicherry Museum).

13

14

15

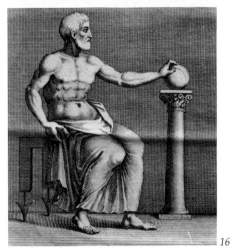

16

17

inside a burial urn (ix.i.80)

18

19

This river estuary near Arikamedu (South India) was an ideal natural harbour for Roman merchant vessels even in pre-Christian times.

The altar in the cathedral of St Thomas at Madras (South India) where relics of the apostle are worshipped.

20

Shiva Nataraja in the circle of flames. A model for ideas about reincarnation in the
Epistle of James?

Indian ascetics' self-mortification and immolation, already observed by Alexander the Great in India (from A. Roger, *Offene Tür zu dem Verborgenen Heydenthum*, 1663).

23

Cochin synagogue, today still a centre for the descendents of pre-Christian Jewish immigrants.

The empty throne symbolising the Buddha's presence (Amaravati, 2nd century).

The ruins of the once flourishing oasis of Palmyra - a staging-post for Asoka's Buddhist missionaries.

24

25

26

The base of the double-headed eagle Stupa at Taxila where Asoka's Aramaic
inscription was found.

The Dharmarajika Stupa at Taxila.

27

28 Asoka's pillar edict at Sarnath in Brahmi script (3rd century BC).

Two Indian figures (c. 200 BC) excavated at Memphis (Egypt) in 1908.

29

Alexandria in Ptolemaic times. To the right the Jewish quarter.

(Opposite top) Bodhisattva Maitreya (Ajanta cave temple, 6th/7th century).

(Opposite below) A Buddhist monk reaches across a stone wall to present King Kanishka (1st century) with a lotus blossom as a symbol of the teaching (tile at Haran).

31

32

33

34

Buddha Maitreya (Karashahar, 6th/7th century).

Jesus (Codex Aureus around 870).

Jesus (mediaeval book illustration). The mediaeval depictions of Christ demonstrate astonishing borrowings from Buddhist Maitreyas.

Bodhisattva Padmapani with lotus blossoms in the places where Jesus was wounded (Sarnath, c. 9th century).

35

36

Pardon our debts, for we ourselves pardon everyone indebted to us. And do not bring us to trial [into a trying situation]."'

'Ask and it will be given to you; seek and you will find; knock and the door will be opened for you.
For everyone who asks receives, and the one who seeks finds, and to the one who knocks the door will be opened.
What father of yours, if his son asks for a loaf of bread, will give him a stone, or if he asks for a fish, will give him a snake?
Therefore if you, although you are not good, know how to give good gifts to your children, how much more will the father above give good things to those who ask him!'

'Nothing is hidden that will not be made known, or secret that will not come to light.
What I tell you in the dark, speak in the light. And what you hear as a whisper, proclaim on the housetops.'

'Don't be afraid of those who can kill the body, but can't kill the soul.
Can't you buy five sparrows for two cents? Not one of them will fall to the ground without God knowing about it. Even the hairs of your head are all numbered. So don't be afraid. You are worth more than many sparrows.'

Someone from the crowd said to him, 'Teacher, tell my brother to divide the inheritance with me.' But he said to him, 'Sir, who made me your judge or lawyer?'

He told them a parable, saying, 'The land of a rich man produced in abundance, and he thought to himself, "What should I do, for I have nowhere to store my crops?" Then he said, "I will do this. I will pull down my barns and build larger ones, and there I will store all my grain and my goods. And I will say to my soul, Soul, you have ample goods stored up for many years. Take it easy. Eat, drink, and be merry." But God said to him, "Foolish man! This very night you will have to give back your soul, and the things you produced, whose will they be?" That is what happens to the one who stores up treasure for himself and is not rich in the sight of God.'

'I am telling you, do not worry about your life, what you will eat, or about your body, what you will wear. Isn't life more than food, and the body more than clothing?
Think of the ravens. They do not plant, harvest, or store grain in

barns, and God feeds them. Aren't you worth more than the birds? Which one of you can add a single day to your life by worrying? And why do you worry about clothing? Think of the way lilies grow. They do not work or spin. But even Solomon in all his splendor was not as magnificent. If God puts beautiful clothes on the grass that is in the field today and tomorrow is thrown into a furnace, won't he put clothes on you, faint hearts?

So don't worry, thinking "What will we eat?", or "What will we drink?", or "What will we wear?" For everybody in the whole world does that, and your father knows that you need these things. Instead, make sure of his rule over you, and all these things will be yours as well.'

'Sell your possessions and give to charity [alms]. Store up treasure for yourselves in a heavenly account, where moths and rust do not consume, and where thieves cannot break in and steal.

For where your treasure is, there your heart will also be.'

He said, 'What is the kingdom of God like? To what should I compare it? It is like a grain of mustard which a man took and sowed in his garden. It grew and became a tree, and the birds of the air made nests in its branches.'

He also said, 'The kingdom of God is like yeast which a woman took and hid in three measures of flour until it leavened the whole mass.'

'Everyone who glorifies himself will be humiliated, and the one who humbles himself will be praised.'

'A man once gave a great banquet and invited many. At the time for the banquet he sent his servant to say to those who had been invited, "Please come, for everything is now ready." But they all began to make excuses. The first said to him, "I've bought a farm, and I must go and see it. Please excuse me." And another said, "I've just bought five pair of oxen and I need to check them out. Please excuse me." And another said, "I've just married a woman so I can't come." The servant came and reported this to his master. Then the owner in anger said to his servant, "Go out quickly to the streets of the town and bring in as many people as you find." And the servant went out into the streets and brought together everybody he could find. That way the house was filled with guests.'

'Whoever does not hate his father and mother will not be able to learn from me. Whoever does not hate his son and daughter cannot belong to my school.

Whoever does not accept his cross [bear up under condemnation] and so become my follower, cannot be one of my students.
Whoever tries to protect his life will lose it; but whoever loses his life on account of me will preserve it.'

'Salt is good; but if salt loses its taste, how can it be restored? It is not good for either the land or the manure pile. People just throw it out.'
(Text from Burton L. Mack: *The Lost Gospel: The Book of Q and Christian Origins*, Element Books, Shaftesbury, 1993)

Jesus and His Buddhist Sources

The collection of sayings presented in the previous section is unified without any stylistic breaks or discontinuities of content. The original Jesus speaks of dissolving the bonds of family, of voluntary homelessness, of avoiding acknowledged ideals of purity, of simple ways of living and clothing oneself, and of begging without shame. Nowhere are there complex theological concepts or apocalyptic threats. So simple and direct are the authentic words of Jesus in Q^1 that researchers were inclined to compare them to the views of those Greek philosophers known as the Cynics – Jesus as a Cynic like Diogenes in his water-butt!

Scholars like the historian of religion Burton L. Mack have no problems with presenting Jesus as a wisdom teacher with a Cynic background, embedded in the Hellenistic spirit of the age. Viewed superficially, the contents of Q^1 support that case. Jesus's extreme positions with regard to convention, the apparently embarrassing demands ('Leave the dead to bury their dead'), and the unexpectedly critical view of society ('If anyone grabs your coat, let him have your shirt as well') are all reminiscent of the attitude of the Cynics, their lack of needs, their shamelessness, their non-adherence to conventions. Even the rhetoric he employed brings to mind the Cynics. His teaching was linguistically extremely concentrated, with brief compressed sayings, maxims, aphorisms, anecdotes, parables and what were known as *meshalim* – short, carefully formulated texts.[48] The Cynics had invented these literary forms or brought them to perfection in order to present serious rules of life in a serene and witty way as a guide to behaviour.

The church fathers were aware that this was the way some of the age's philosophers preferred to teach. To avoid Jesus being associated with these worldly teachers, Justin attributed this style to God's power, given expression in his word. The disciples must therefore have viewed Jesus as a 'teacher of truth' with an exceptional command of words, or as a 'true teacher'. In all the Gospel texts he is addressed as 'Teacher' (*didaskalos* – in the vocative *didaskale*). The German translation of Mark 12:14 runs: 'Teacher (*didaskale*), we know . . . thou teachest the way of God in truth.' According to the Gospel of Thomas, Matthew compares Jesus to 'a wise man, a philosopher' (Thomas 13).

There is no doubt that Jesus dazzled people with an unusual gift for the use of language. He spoke poetically so that the disciples could more easily learn his words by heart and retain them in their memory. For that purpose he used four poetic forms: congruence of sentence structures, rhythm, plays on words and rhyme.[49] He deployed speech to wake his listeners up. That is why he chose to present his message by way of strong contrasts and exaggerated expressions.

However, citing those similarities in order to make Jesus into a misunderstood Hellenistic Cynic philosopher in Palestine would fail to do real justice to the contents of his teaching and the circumstances involved in his impact. Jesus was active in a country where wisdom was frequently transmitted aphoristically within brief texts. He deployed that way of speaking as did the Hellenistic genre of the Cynics, and his intentions were not dissimilar to those of the Greek philosophers: presenting terse maxims directed against traditional society as a means towards the outrageous morality of a new social order. In some respects the original Jesus's teachings may be comparable with the practical wisdom of the philosophers of antiquity, but many of the themes they thought so important – education, character formation, habits, friendship, relations with women and families, ethnic themes, politics and common sense – are virtually absent from his discourses.[50]

The maxims mediated by this unusual teacher travelling around the bare landscape between Galilee and Judea certainly sounded strange, but they had nothing of the jocularity and earthiness of the Cynics. They were instead embedded in an aura of loving understanding and of a profound wish to awaken poor sleeping spirits so as to support their yearnings for liberating, redeeming realization. That is why people came together when he spoke. That is why people remembered Jesus. What he taught was revolutionary in social and psychological terms – and Buddhistic.

The historian of religion Roy C. Amore was the first person to indicate the astonishing correspondences between Q and Buddhist texts.[51] He assumed that Jesus, like the evangelists later, had access to Buddhist sources as well as traditional Jewish works, deriving some of his ideas from them. Amore's study appeared in 1978 when the three levels of adaptation in Q were not yet known. He was thus unable to offer any adequate explanation of why some of Jesus's discourses in Q sound so amazingly Buddhistic and others not at all. Today we know the answer. Later insertions into the collection of sayings served particular purposes for Jesus's followers, and were thus accepted without regard to the teachings of the original Jesus. They are only explicable in terms of the specific situation in the Palestine of that time. The declarations attributed to Jesus there are thus in no way linked with the world of Buddhist ideas. Almost without exception, the Buddhist borrowings are concentrated in Q^1 – in the words of the original Jesus.

We shall now compare those sayings with the Buddhist sources. It is interesting to see how Jesus sometimes also adhered to the poetic precedent. Some Buddhist works were written in verse. Jesus took over that form and was capable of expressing the contents even more concisely, strikingly and distinctively, so that they remained vivid in the listener's memory. Even in translations – where the poetic expressiveness of Buddhism or Jesus's words is largely lost – the original power of phrasing shines through.

This comparison will mainly be based on passages from the *Dhammapada* and the *Undanavarga*, texts presenting Buddhist moral teachings. These Buddhist models and the corresponding sections in Q^1 will be presented alongside one another to facilitate comparison. The QS abbreviations designating the Q^1 texts follow Burton L. Mack.

There are precise Buddhist precedents for the beatitudes and all the main declarations in the Sermon on the Mount, which many people believe to be the heart of Jesus's teaching.

Happily shall I live without possessions among those who possess much; among possessors live without possessions.
Happily shall I live without ties; we shall give voice to joy like the angels.
Happily shall I live without struggling anxiously among the strivers; among the strivers live without striving (GDh 167).

How fortunate are the poor; they have God's kingdom. How fortunate the hungry; they will be fed. How fortunate are those who are crying; they will laugh (QS 8).

The same ideas are to be found in the first verses of the 'Sukhavagga' section of the *Dhammapada*. Particularly striking is the moral teaching about loving one's enemy, which the Buddha emphasized in connection with non-violence.

Happily shall I live without hostility among the hostile; among the hostile live without hostility (GDh 167).

O let us live in joy, free of hatred, among the spiteful; among the spiteful let us live without hatred.
O let us live in joy, free of suffering, among those who suffer; among those who are sore troubled let us live without suffering.
O let us live in joy, free of avarice, among those filled with greed; among those who are avaricious let us live without greed.
O let us live in joy, we who are free of hindrances. Let us be like the 'Radiant Ones' who are nurtured with love (Dh 15:1–4).

Whoever counters the malicious with malice can never be pure, but he who feels no maliciousness pacifies those who hate.
Hate brings misery to humanity so the wise man knows no hatred (Ud 14:12).

I am telling you, love your enemies, bless those who curse you, pray for those who mistreat you.
If someone slaps you on the cheek, offer your other cheek as well. If anyone grabs your coat, let him have your shirt as well.
Give to anyone who asks, and if someone takes away your belongings, do not ask to have them back.
As you want people to treat you, do the same to them.

Hostility is never conquered by hostility in this world; hostility is conquered by love. That is the Eternal Law (Dh 1:5).

Surmount hatred by not hating, surmount evil with good; surmount greed through generosity, surmount lies with truth; speak what is true, do not succumb to anger, give when you are asked. Through those three steps you will come close to the gods (GDh 280–281).

Whosoever does no harm to living creatures, whosoever does not kill or participate in killing, is to be called a holy man.

Whosoever is tolerant with the intolerant, whosoever patiently tolerates punishment, and whosoever shows compassion to all creatures, is to be called a holy man (Ud 33:45–46).

If you love those who love you, what credit is that to you? Even tax collectors love those who love them, do they not? And if you embrace only your brothers, what more are you doing than others? Doesn't everybody do that? If you lend to those from whom you expect repayment, what credit is that to you? Even wrongdoers lend to their kind because they expect to be repaid.

Instead, love your enemies, do good, and lend without expecting anything in return. Your reward will be great, and you will be children of God.

For he makes his sun rise on the evil and on the good; he sends rain on the just and on the unjust (QS 9).

Various aspects of those correspondences are astonishing. Apart from the completely identical idea transmitted by Gautama and Jesus, this 'Love your enemies' quotation from the New Testament, which is perhaps Jesus's most characteristic and most-quoted, the one that shows him to be a particularly far-seeing wise man, signifies exactly the same as the Buddha's 'Surmount hatred by not hating'. The great challenge issued by the original Jesus, calling for love of one's enemies, had already been declared an Eternal Law (*Sanantana Dhamma*) by the Buddha: 'Hostility is never conquered by hostility in this world; hostility is conquered by love.'

Secondly, both Jesus and the Buddha call on people to give – on condition that they are requested to do so. Jesus says: 'Give to anyone who requests it'; and the Buddha: 'Give when you are asked.' That is striking in the context of these principles since one could also have expected that Jesus or Gautama would have encouraged giving to those in need – the poor, weak, sick. Instead both texts call for giving – irrespective of whether someone is in need – *as soon as this is requested.*

Thirdly, Jesus comes to the same conclusion as his Indian precursor. Whoever observes the commandment calling for unconditional love becomes in Jesus's words a 'child of God' and for the Buddha will 'come close to the gods'.

The parallels involved – including such details and conclusions – are so striking that it can only be assumed that Jesus studied those Buddhist basic principles very thoroughly and took them over. In the light of these correspondences it must even be asked whether Jesus had at his disposal a written copy of that passage from the *Dharmapada*, developing his teaching on such a basis.

These Buddhist moral ideas also entered into the great Indian epics. Buddha's golden rule, of which we read in such epics as the *Mahabharata* and the *Pañcatantra*, was widespread throughout Sanskrit literature: 'Listen to the essence of the Dharma, and after you have heard it, take it to heart. Do not do to others what is unpleasant to yourself.' It may be that Jesus got to know this saying as part of the stream of stories to the West, and formulated his maxim accordingly: 'As ye would that men should do to you, do ye also to them likewise.'

The correspondence of the statements, which point to the fact that Jesus had studied Buddhist texts, can also be established by the following comparison:

Judge not the mistakes of others, neither what they do or leave undone, but judge your own deeds, the just and the unjust (GDh 271–272).	Don't judge and you won't be judged. For the standard you use [in judging] will be the standard used against you (QS 10).

In the Pali version of the verse quoted (Dh 4:7) the verb *avekkheyya* is used, meaning something like 'regard from on high', 'consider', or 'reflect', whereas the Sanskrit version has *samikshe'a* – 'perceive'. In both cases the meaning entails 'precise examination' in the sense of evaluation.

When the first part of QS 10 is corrected for a possible mistranslation from the Aramaic, the result[52] is: 'Be ye therefore perfect on earth, even as Abba is perfect in heaven' (Matthew 5:48; Mark 6:36). There is also an absolute parallel to that declaration in the *Dhammapada*: 'Of you are demanded efforts. The perfect are only proclaiming.' In both cases the call to take personal responsibility for spiritual progress rather than waiting for the intervention of some external act of mercy is contrary to the Pauline teaching of redemption. The perfected, whether Abba or Buddha, are already on another level.

The Indian equivalent of a celebrated aphorism about the blind leading the blind is also astonishingly similar:

O Vasettha, those brahmins who know the three Vedas are just like a line of blind men tied together where the first sees nothing, the middle man nothing, and the last sees nothing (*Tevijja-Sutta, Dighanikaya*, 13:15).

Can the blind lead the blind? Won't they both fall into a pit? A student is not better than his teacher. It is enough for a student to be like his teacher (QS 11).

The blind are those who have not yet recognized the way of up-rightness. Buddha used that image to show that the brahmins who cling to the three Vedas have recognized nothing, so cannot be suitable teachers. The context conveyed by Jesus with aphoristic conciseness is precisely preserved: on the one hand, the blind leading the blind as a futile undertaking; and on the other, the relationship with teachers, that is the right teachers. In the Buddha's eyes, brahmins who adhere to writ-ten words are the wrong teachers for unawakened pupils – as it were, the blind leading the blind. Jesus takes up that idea by relating pupil and teacher in similar fashion.

Jesus obviously found another comparison in the *Dhammapada* for attacking the dishonest practice of judging other people in order to appear in a more favourable light oneself. The captivat-ing aspect is once again Jesus's characteristically compressed and more accessible formulation. The Buddhist texts seem like carefully formulated writings while the words of the original Jesus are renderings of those texts in living speech. When considering Jesus's sayings, one has the impression that they really are more rhetorically skilful and more vivid versions of the Buddhist originals. If he really did derive some of his declarations from written texts, it was certainly necessary to adapt the written material to the taste of the age and its public. The original Jesus demonstrated perfect mastery of the skill of concise formulation.

The faults of others are more easily seen than one's own, but seeing one's own failings is diffi-cult. The failings of others are winnowed like chaff in the wind, but one conceals one's own faults like a cheating gambler (Dh 18:18).

How can you look for the splinter in your brother's eye and not notice the stick in your own eye? How can you say to your brother, 'Let me remove the splinter in your eye', when you do not see the stick in your own eye? You hypocrite, first take the stick from

The faults of others are more easily seen than one's own. They are more easily seen because they are winnowed like chaff in the wind, but one's own failings are difficult to see. It is like a cheat concealing his own dice while showing his opponent's, drawing attention to the other's inadequacies and constantly thinking of bringing accusations against him. Such a man is far from seeing what is right, and very much worsens his unfortunate lot (Ud 27:1). your own eye, and then you can see to remove the splinter that is in your brother's eye (QS 12).

The improved retranslation of the *Jesus-Evangelism* gives even clearer expression to the detachment of the Buddhist original:

> Why dost thou remark the error in thy companion's views? Dost thou not see the self-deception in thine own views? How canst thou say to thy companion: 'Let me do away with the error in thy views'? And lo – self-deception is in thine own views. Hypocrite! First eliminate the self-deception in thine own views. And then do away with the error in thy companion's views (JeEv 11:25–27).

It can be assumed from the unified context where Jesus's authentic Q^1 sayings are taken from Buddhist texts that he derived the idea for the aphorism about the splinter in the brother's eye from the texts quoted. The teaching presented there involves an important moral obligation. It does not derive from observing other people's opinions, wrong as they may be, but solely from the Buddhist duty of awareness. The precondition for this most important of practices is constant research into oneself, becoming aware of one's own thoughts, prejudices and mistakes. That is why other Indian texts have also made the same borrowings from Buddhism. The identical idea is to be found in the great Indian epic, the *Mahabharata*: 'You see the mistakes of others even if they be as small as a mustard-seed, but you strive to overlook your own failings, be they as large as a *bilva* fruit.' (I, 96:1) Perhaps Jesus also knew that version, since in the image of the mustard-seed and the large fruit it contains the same ideas as the splinter and the stick.

Let us now turn to the demand for personal integrity where Jesus incorporated the basic elements of the Noble Eightfold Path.

No matter what a man does, whether his deeds serve virtue or vice, nothing lacks importance. All actions bear a kind of fruit (Ud 9:8).

A good tree does not bear rotten fruit; a rotten tree does not bear good fruit. Are figs gathered from thorns, or grapes from thistles? Every tree is known by its fruit.

The bad person speaks falsely, chained by his words. He who speaks ill and rejects what is truly just is not wise (Ud 8:9).

The good man produces good things from his store of goods and treasures; and the evil man evil things. For the mouth speaks from a full heart (QS 13).

The translation of the *Jesus-Evangelium* makes even clearer the way in which a person's use of words is a gauge of his or her spiritual attitude: 'Each person speaks good out of the good thoughts of his convictions. Each person speaks bad out of the bad thoughts of his convictions. The mouth speaks out of the thoughts of convictions' (JeEv 11:33–34).

Jesus's teaching is not simply a reminder of the need to act rightly. It is clearly rooted in the Indian comprehension of *karma* since it indicates that the intentions behind our words and deeds are never lost. The statements and actions deriving from inner attitudes are not individual motions but rather the outcome of constant accumulation. In other words, one cannot get rid of what has been said and done; it does not simply vanish, but continually exerts an impact. From that a personality is formed. Jesus thus points to an aspect in the development of personality that the Buddha taught his pupils through the Noble Eightfold Path as 'right speech', 'right action', and 'right conduct of life'. The image of a tree is very well chosen. If life flourishes like a tree through following the Eightfold Path, the fruits will be good. The concept of *karma* teaches in identical fashion that no deed is lost. It is gathered up in the treasure-house of the personality from which character and destiny are formed – in this and future lives. The unavoidable nature of *karma* shines out of that saying by Jesus like an echo from a verse in the *Udanavarga*: 'Just as life must end in death and all creatures are destined to die, so too must virtues and vices bear fruits as the outcome of all deeds' (Ud 1:23).

As early as the 1930s, Burnett Hillman Streeter, a well-known Oxford New Testament scholar, established that 'the moral teaching of the Buddha has a remarkable resemblance to that of the Sermon on the Mount'.[53] How right he was is apparent in the correspondences presented here (QS 8–13).

They all come from the heart of Q^1 – the Sermon on the Mount. The following comparison is also taken from there.

Just as rain penetrates a badly-covered house, so passion enters a dispersed mind. Just as rain does not penetrate a well-covered house, so too does passion not enter a well-developed mind (Dh 1:13–14).	Why do you call me, 'Master, master', and not do what I say? Everyone who hears my words and does them is like a man who built a house on rock. The rain fell, a torrent broke against the house, and it did not fall, for it had a rock foundation.
	But everyone who hears my words and does not do them is like a man who built a house on sand. The rain came, the torrent broke against it, and it collapsed. The ruin of that house was great (QS 14).

The image of rain penetrating a roof is appropriate for India, but Jesus had to adapt that example to circumstances in Palestine. The central image remained – rain as the source of catastrophe – but in the local form of torrential rivers following a downpour. The compiler of the *Udanavarga* obviously liked the *Dhammapada* comparison between the well- and badly roofed house so much that he employed it for eleven verses in Chapter 31 (Ud 31:12–22). It is used there time and again, in a multitude of transformations, to illustrate the correct spiritual attitude and the associated right actions (corresponding to the well-roofed house).

A passage from the *Mahavagga* (V, 1:26), containing instructions for mendicant monks, uses the same image as QS 14 without the house. The person who acts fully in accordance with the Buddha's teachings is compared with a rock that withstands any wind and rain.

At the beginning of the *Dhammapada* there is a verse directed against Devadatta, the 'Judas' among Buddhists, but it can also be applied to anyone who, like Devadatta, all too quickly takes pleasure in his own achievements and does not really work towards advancement – or, in Jesus's sense, hears his words but does not follow them: 'Even though he recites many holy texts, he does not act accordingly. This thoughtless man is like a cow-herd who counts other people's animals. He has no share in the blessings of the ascetic life' (Dh 1:19). The ascetic life mentioned there involves four levels of spiritual growth which the seeker must attain: first he must become one who enters the stream (*sotapanna*), then one who returns only once (*sakadagamin*), after that one who never returns (*anagamin*), and finally a holy man (*arhat*).

The concept of awareness has frequently been mentioned as a central issue along the Buddhist way. That naturally also involves attentiveness to the words of the Buddha and of *arhats*, in the same way as Jesus wished his parable to be understood. Many Buddhist texts touch on the theme that Jesus raised in the parable of the house built on good or bad foundations. The following verse exemplifies that: 'If someone has heard much but does not follow the moral law, he is not a good listener since he holds the law in contempt' (Ud 22:6).

One of the most difficult tasks for both the Buddha and Jesus was to convince serious disciples that they had to leave their families behind. The way out of entanglement in the outer world could only be gained by making a radical break with all ties, whether those were emotional or intellectual.

Those who aspire are ever striving; they do not stay in one place. Like swans leaving a lake, they move from house to house.
The only source of refuge for those who do not accumulate possessions and are careful about what they eat is unconditional freedom, knowing as they do the void of transience. Their way is difficult to follow like that of birds in the sky (Dh 7:2–3).
Whosoever has laid aside human ties, leaving behind the powers of attraction of the gods, free of all bonds, that man I call holy (Ud 33:52).

When someone said to him, 'I will follow you wherever you go,' Jesus answered, 'Foxes have dens, and birds of the sky have nests, but the son of man has nowhere to lay his head.'
When another said, 'Let me first go and bury my father,' Jesus said, 'Leave the dead to bury their dead.'
Yet another said, 'I will follow you, sir, but first let me say goodbye to my family.' Jesus said to him, 'No one who puts his hand to the plow and then looks back is fit for the kingdom of God' (QS 19).

That mysterious phrase 'son of man' must first be elucidated. This is a misunderstood interpretation of Daniel's vision where he saw the Messiah amid clouds 'like the Son of man' (Daniel 7:13). Following the tradition of Jewish apocalyptic expectations, that phrase 'Son of man' – in a vision prophesying the Messiah's glorious return, in human form, to judge the earth – was misunderstood as a messianic designation.[54] Later editors interpreted obscure sayings by Jesus in an eschato-logical context, often replacing 'I' with 'Son of man'. People were meant to believe that Jesus saw himself as the Messiah. In the original phrasing the saying by Jesus just quoted ran: 'Foxes have their holes and the birds of the heavens their nests, but I have no place where I can lay my head.'

The image that serves Jesus as an illustration of being in the world is a remarkable one. This is an unsurpassable translation of the basic Buddhist term of 'homelessness', transposed fable-like into the animal world. Such comparisons were very common in India, and, as we have shown, many such fables were taken over in the West. The god Shiva, who long before the Buddha was viewed as the prototype of the wandering ascetic, is in fact called 'the nestless' in the *Shvetashvatara-Upanishad*: 'The one who is comprehended with the heart is known as "the nestless"; he that generates coming into being and passing away is Shiva . . .'

Buddhist monks called themselves 'the homeless'. The ideal of existence on this earth as a wanderer, nowhere at home, always travelling through, was an attempt at a visual depiction and elevation into consciousness of worldly existence. Life is no more than a passing through – in the Buddhist view, a transition from one suffering existence to others within the cycle of rebirth. Nothing endures of what one owns during such wanderings, what one clings to, what one creates, cher-ishes and cares for. The precondition for breaking through this cycle is the realization of the second stage of the Eightfold Path: a complete commitment to renunciation. That fundamental pre-condition for the Buddhist had to be understood and accepted if anyone wanted to follow the Buddha's path. Jesus was equally emphatic. Only someone who sold all his possessions and followed Jesus could be perfect (Matthew 19:21). Parables and aphorisms that complement that theme are thus repeatedly encountered in the sayings of the original Jesus collected in Q[1]. They can only be explained in terms of the wealth of Buddhist precedents.

The rejection of a life of superficialities, concerned with pos-sessions, fame, honour and pleasure, could only be made attractive for people if a spiritual reward was promised in return for such renunciations. The *Udanavarga* thus cogently states: 'The disciple must renounce – for his own advantage – what the crowd sees as being profitable. If a person discovers what is of enormous advantage to himself, his greatest concern must be for his well-being' (Ud 23:9). The complete mastery exemplified by the Buddha and Jesus gave them knowledge of the rewards and gains of the inner way, and they spoke out of profound insight.

Jesus was to call the reward for such unpopular exertions 'treasures in heaven' as opposed to earthly wealth. That inner wealth can be seen as an indication of the eighth level of the Eightfold Path (right concentration): the exclusion of the outer world and focusing inwards. Nevertheless, the concept of meditation as had existed in India for centuries before Gautama could not simply be transferred to Palestine, where it was completely new. Both the Buddha and Jesus present statements about meditation in a broader context, covering the conduct of life as a whole. The Buddhist foundations of the teachings of the original Jesus appear most clearly in the uncompromising call for the renunciation of all worldly things. That is the commandment for a wandering existence as mendicant monk, unmistakably revealing Jesus to be a Buddhist.

People must store up reserves of faith since true merits cannot be taken away and no one need fear thieves. Happy are the disciples who have gained faith, and happy is the wise man when he meets such a believer (Ud 10:11).	Sell your possessions and give to charity [alms]. Store up treasure for yourselves in a heavenly account, where moths and rust do not consume, and where thieves cannot break in and steal. For where your treasure is, there your heart will also be (QS 40).
In this world the wise man holds onto faith and wisdom. Those are his greatest treasures; all other riches he pushes aside (Ud 10:9).	Seek after the treasure which does not perish, which endures in the place where no moth comes near to devour, and no worm ravages (Thomas 76).

The Buddhist 'reserves of faith' and 'faith and wisdom as the greatest treasures' were translated literally by Jesus for his contemporary listeners as 'treasures in heavenly account'. Only what points beyond the sensuously experienceable world, 'the treasures we should store up in heaven', participates in eternity and indestructibility. The Buddha emphatically demanded that this condition be both completely understood and implemented in a way of life – the ideal of the wandering monk. Jesus was equally insistent, and had to confront a wall of conventions in Jewish society where family life and progeny were considered very important. His call to abandon parents, pay no heed to relations, the dead, land or animals, must have met with intense opposition. His statements on that theme were simply a declaration of war against the age's highest views on morality, a challenge that must have led to anger and incomprehension, even among people open to his teachings. In the Gospel of Thomas Jesus offers the most succinct summary of those profoundly Buddhist instructions to his disciples, charged to disseminate his teachings by abandoning family ties and domesticity: 'Become transients' (Thomas 42).

Letting go of earthly ties, unconditional homelessness and a total focusing on the right spiritual way ('reserves of faith') recur in Jesus's splendid parable on the foolishness of possessions as derivations from Buddhist texts. Of particular interest here is the parallel with the *Majjhimanikaya*, where the sequence of events is preserved: first the dispute over an inheritance (from a dead king), and then the teaching that nothing earthly can be kept anyway so that hanging onto possessions is worthless.

The heirs are quarrelling over his property, but the King's being accords with his deeds. None of his possessions follow the dead man: no sons, wives, money, or power. Long life is not achieved through money, and old age is not frightened off by riches. Wisdom is thus better than money since it leads to perfection (*Rathapala-Sutta, Majjhimanikaya* 82).

'These children and these riches belong to me,' thought the fool, anxiously. But since no one possesses even himself, what is the point of 'my children and my riches'?

The law of humanity is that, even if people accumulate hundreds and thousands of earthly goods, they nevertheless succumb to the power of death. All stores are scattered; what was built is torn down; every-

Someone from the crowd said to him, 'Teacher, tell my brother to divide the inheritence with me.' But he said to him, 'Sir, who made me your judge or lawyer?' He told them a parable, saying, 'The land of a rich man produced in abundance, and he thought to himself, "What should I do, for I have nowhere to store my crops?" Then he said, "I will do this. I will pull down my barns and build larger ones, and there I will store all my grain and my goods. And I will say to my soul, Soul, you have ample goods stored for many years. Take it easy. Eat, drink, and be merry." But God said to him, "Foolish man! This very night you will have to give back your soul, and the things you produced, whose will they be?" That is what happens to the one who

thing that comes together must end in separation; and life must terminate in death (Ud 1:20–22).

stores up treasure for himself and is not rich in the sight of God' (QS 38).

The second correspondence with Jesus's *meshal* is provided by the rare discovery of a coherent, parable-like passage offering an astonishing parallel. It is rare because hardly any parables by Gautama have been handed down. The most frequent forms used in his poetic instructions were teaching conversations and discourses. Jesus liked using parables and *meshalim*. Parables may be relatively infrequent in the Q^1 material, where striking aphorisms predominate, but it becomes clear from the canonical and apocryphal traditions that the parable was a means of teaching that must have suited Jesus. His exceptional rhetorical talent enjoyed deployment of vivid pictorial language. *Meshalim* and parables were suitable means for transmitting teaching in a way that could be easily remembered.

Especially remarkable is the passage where Jesus gives his disciples precise instructions about what they have to do. Once they have abandoned all ties, they are called on to take his teachings into towns and villages as wandering mendicant monks.

A wandering monk should neither despise what he has received nor should he envy what others get. The envious monk does not achieve deep contemplation (Dh 25:6).

The wise man does not make friends with the unbelieving, greedy, slanderous or quarrelsome. The wise man avoids the evil (Ud 25:1).

Go. Look, I send you out as lambs among wolves.
Do not carry money, or bag, or sandals, or staff; and do not greet anyone on the road.
Whatever house you enter, say, 'Peace be to this house!' And if a child of peace is there, your greeting will be received. But if not, let your peace return to you. And stay in the same house, eating and drinking whatever they provide, for the worker deserves his wages. Do not go from house to house.
And if you enter a town and they receive you, eat what is set before you. Pay attention to the sick and say to them, 'God's kingdom has come near to you.'

> But if you enter a town and they
> do not receive you, as you leave,
> shake the dust from your feet
> and say, 'Nevertheless, be sure
> of this, the realm of God has
> come to you' (QS 20).

The strange statement that peace would be returned if the greeting is not accepted makes us stop short. Obviously the offer of peace made by Jesus's wandering monks was not just conceived as a simple greeting but also as a transmission of some special power. In fact the translation of the second part of the statement – 'If a child of peace is there, your greeting will be received' – literally means 'your peace will rest upon him'. Were the disciples called upon to give something of their truly peace-engendering power, as if it were a mediation of meditative composure? If they were rejected, they would withdraw into their inner silence, and their peace would return to them.

Jesus's encouragement of the wandering monastic life accords in all respects with the Buddha's prescriptions. The latter's followers were to set off as mendicant monks, without money or possessions. Nothing should distract them from the wish to spread the Dharma, and they should always accept the food offered them. That commandment became the Buddha's undoing when he ate a piece of bad pork given him; he did not reject the offering, even though he presumably knew it would kill him.

Also of interest are Jesus's instructions about treating people in accordance with their attitude to the teaching. If rejected, the mendicant monks were to travel onwards. Jesus did not seek the company of the stubborn at any price, and also recommended that his disciples should not stay, or strive to convince, where they were rejected. Neither Jesus nor the Buddha sought to persuade the obstinate: 'If a [Buddhist] disciple does not find a companion, either better or his equal, he should pursue a lonely way. There can be no association with fools' (Dh 5:3).

When Jesus's disciples turned their backs on places where they had not been welcome or understood, shaking the dust off their feet, they nevertheless let those who lacked understanding know that the Kingdom of Heaven (corresponding to the Dharma) had approached them. Zen Buddhism, which later brought the tradition of aphoristic teaching to a peak of mastery in riddle-like *koans*, brilliantly expresses the underlying idea: 'If you understand, things are as they are. If you do not understand, things are as they are.'

When his disciples were sent out into the world, the Buddha always stressed that they should never seem to be anything special. They should be humble, avoiding showing off with their knowledge, spiritual insight and magical powers. One of the rules for the *bhikshus* laid down that wandering monks should walk with bowed head in public. Only with that humble attitude could the goal of liberation be achieved. An echo of that attitude is present in Jesus's words: 'Everyone who glorifies himself will be humiliated, and the one who humbles himself will be praised' (QS 50).

In India wandering ascetics were nothing out of the ordinary. In Buddha's time that kind of religious search must have been widespread as a protest against the priestly religion of the brahmins. Gautama did not have to banish people's fears in bringing them onto this lonely path. He did not demand extreme asceticism or ask too much of his adherents. Nevertheless, he constantly admonished them not to fall back into the way of earthly wishes and needs since they would then lose their freedom. Ultimately, backing also had to be sought in a supportive environment for a way of life lacking all security except for that found within during deep meditation. Buddha often told his disciples how useless it was to worry about anything. He trained them in the assurance of being satisfied with everything they received or encountered. To be anxious about what tomorrow might bring, or about food and clothing, was petty, demonstrating a character that still found all too much pleasure in the things of this world. Buddhist texts contain innumerable examples of demands that we should be composed, tranquil, satisfied and free of fear: 'The upright renounce everything that is transient; the virtuous do not chatter or yearn for sensuous pleasures. Whether touched by joy or suffering, the wise show neither joyous excitement nor dejection' (Dh 6:8).

Jesus could not fall back on any comparable tradition in his country. In his time there were only isolated ascetic communities, and the tradition of hermits (anchorites) only developed in succeeding centuries. Intense persuasion was required to make clear to his followers that a life of homelessness without ties, possessions, status or recognition was worth following. He even had to console the fearful so as to save them from despair. Jesus did that in one of the most beautiful discourses in Q^1 where he spoke about the state of being free of worries. That passage absolutely breathes the spirit of Buddhistic composure as reflected in those statements where people without needs are seen as the true *bhikshus*.

Whosoever is free of worries, holding onto truth and the Dharma, will cross the sea of life, will put an end to suffering (*Mahaparinibbanasutta* 3:66).

It is difficult to follow the path of those who have accumulated nothing and live from right nourishment, those whose only refuge is unconditional freedom in recognition of the void of the transient. Their path is like that of birds in the sky.

It is difficult to follow the path of those whose appetite is satisfied and are not attached to consumption, those whose only refuge is unconditional freedom in recognition of the void of the transient. Their path is like that of birds in the sky (Dh 7:3–4).

I am telling you, do not worry about your life, what you will eat, or about your body, what you will wear. Isn't life more than food, and the body more than clothing?

Think of the ravens. They do not plant, harvest, or store grain in barns, and God feeds them. Aren't you worth more than the birds? Which of you can add a single day to your life by worrying?

And why do you worry about clothing? Think of the way lilies grow. They do not work or spin. But even Solomon in all his splendor was not as magnificent. If God puts beautiful clothes on the grass that is in the field today and tomorrow is thrown into a furnace, won't he put clothes on you, faint hearts?

So don't worry, thinking, 'What will we eat?', or 'What will we drink?', or 'What will we wear?'

For everybody in the whole world does that, and your father knows that you need these things.

Instead, make sure of his rule over you, and all these things will be yours as well (QS 39).

A translation mistake in the German version of Jesus's discourse leads to: 'Which of you by feeling worried can add even a single day to your life?' (Matthew 6:27; Luke 12:25). That should really read: 'Which of you can add just a single bone to your skeleton?' (JeEv 45:7). A similar thought is figuratively expressed in an Egyptian papyrus based on the Gospel of Thomas – and is closer to the English Authorized Version of the Bible: 'Who will add something to your stature? It is he who will give you your cloak' (POxy 655i:1–17). Later such church fathers as Origen and Clement of Alexandria presented that quotation from Jesus as: 'Ask for what is great and what is small will be added.'[55] The original Buddhist meaning was preserved there without awareness of that context: for the man who devotes himself totally to the Noble Eightfold Path, all earthly needs will be fulfilled 'of their own accord'.

Such a path would be difficult but necessary on the way towards perfection. Jesus gave expression to that conviction in his words about the cross which has to be accepted and the life which one must not strive to preserve (QS 52). The meaning of the unprecedented and supposedly difficult way Jesus demands of his followers is preserved even if the mistranslation of this passage again obscures the original Buddhist intent. According to Luke, Jesus said of anyone who wished to follow this path: 'Let him deny himself, and take up his cross daily' (Luke 9:23). The first incorrect translation involves the word 'cross'. What was actually meant was 'yoke' in its two meanings: a curved bar put across the shoulders for carrying burdens, and the collar-piece for attaching oxen to carts. Anyone who wanted to follow the way of Jesus had to submit to the yoke of his teachings. The same thought is expressed in Matthew (1:28): 'Take my yoke upon you, and learn of me.' The figurative meaning of 'duty' is also to be found in rabbinical texts as *'ôl miswôt* ('yoke of the commandments').

The second translation mistake involves the call for self-denial. In Hebrew 'he denied himself' is *jitnakker*. It is derived from the same root (*nkr*) as *jakkirem*: 'he knew her'. If the entire statement is correctly translated, it runs: 'He who wishes to follow me must know himself and bear my yoke'.[56]

The real meaning of those words in the re-established version is only to be found in a very revealing parallel from the *Dhammapada*:

When a mendicant monk, although still young, yokes himself to the Buddha's teachings, the world is illuminated like the moon freed of clouds (Dh 25:23).	He who wishes to follow me must know himself and bear my yoke.

The mistranslations urging self-denial and bearing a cross resulted in following Jesus being regarded as a terribly difficult task, full of renunciations and super-human burdens. The Church stressed the duty of self-denial so as to consolidate its position of power by depriving the mass of believers of spiritual responsibility. Such a church, founded on power, had no use for the self-assured, who took personal responsibility for their spiritual advancement, as the Buddha and the original Jesus had taught. An acceptance that such people were following Jesus's wishes would have entailed abandoning the Church's self-justification, expressed in the sacrosanct authority of its hierarchy as God's representatives on earth. However, the original Jesus had called, in Buddhist manner, for something completely different: the end of submissiveness and acceptance of self-knowledge in order to promote responsibility for one's life, actions and thinking. That was not the kind of 'bearing one's cross' that Christians were supposed to understand from the image of Jesus collapsing under the burden of the beam he was carrying. Self-knowledge would result from yoking oneself to the teachings of the Dharma. No terrible burden is involved. Once again the Gospel of Thomas preserves the authentic source of the statement: 'Jesus said: Come to me for easy is my yoke and my rule is gentle, and you shall find repose for yourselves' (Thomas 90).

The call for self-knowledge is a profoundly Buddhist characteristic. A celebrated sentence from the mouth of Zen Master Dogen-zenji runs: 'Studying Buddhism means studying ourselves. Studying ourselves means forgetting ourselves.' Self-knowledge that ultimately surmounts the ego is one of the Buddhist's objectives. Without that Buddhism is inconceivable. It receives characteristic expression in the *Udanavarga* (23:10–21). There the last two lines in each of the twelve four-line stanzas celebrate the wise man who has mastered himself because he recognized that 'the self is the ego's lord and master'.

In many of Jesus's teachings self-knowledge is said to be the basic precondition. Even though many of the original Jesus's instructions appear as practical guidelines for moral behaviour, at the same time he always pointed to the necessity of personal spiritual advancement without which there could be no morally impeccable conduct of life. Just think of Jesus's denunciation of hypocrisy in QS 12 ('How can you look for the splinter in your brother's eye . . .') or his call for integrity in QS 13 ('A good tree does not bear rotten fruit . . .').

If we look closely at Jesus's call for self-knowledge as a precondition for following the way he pointed out, the fundamental Buddhist teaching of awareness as the basis of self-knowledge becomes apparent. For the Buddhist practising awareness involves becoming conscious of all activities including such everyday automatic functions as breathing, walking, etc, adopting the meditative attitude of the pure observer. The Buddha gave precise instructions, contained in the *Satipatthana-Sutta* (*Discourse on the Awakening of Awareness*). Satipatthana ('Four Awakenings of Awareness') is the basic form of Buddhist meditation, which is mainly cultivated by Theravada schools up to the present day. Rigorous awareness meditation transforms everything that is unclear into clarity, everything that is unconscious into consciousness, and everything unknown into insight.

In this connection too the Gospel of Thomas once again turns out to be an excellent storehouse of the original Jesus's Buddhist views. The previously quoted passage about Jesus's 'gentle yoke' and 'mild rule' ends with the revealing words: '. . . and you shall find repose for yourselves' (Thomas 90). What peace could be meant if not liberation from the (illusory) constraints of outer and inner existence, a liberation that is achieved by the way of awareness meditation. According to the Gospel of Thomas Jesus also said: 'Know Him who is before your face, and what is hidden from you shall be revealed to you, for there is nothing hidden that shall not be manifest.' In a papyrus from Oxyrhynchos that saying is mediated: 'Know what is within your field of vision . . .' (POxy 654:27–31). For someone who consistently applies the Buddhist teachings of the original Jesus, 'nothing is hidden that will not be made known, or secret that will not come to light' (QS 35). At issue is the recognition of the simplest things as what they are. Anyone who has mastered a practice that sounds so simple will know everything. That is nothing but translating *Satipatthana* into action.

Jesus's words from the Gospel of Thomas make extensive use of directives about right awareness and self-knowledge, thereby demonstrating even closer links with the world of Indian thought. Self-knowledge was highly regarded in India even before the Buddha. The Upanishads are permeated by the advocacy of self-knowledge.

Just as the Buddha opposed the brahmins, Jesus opposed the Scribes who did not allow everyone access to true knowledge so as to maintain their influence, jealously clinging to religious sinecures. 'The Pharisees and the Scribes took the keys of Knowledge, and they hid them. Neither did they enter, nor did they allow those who wished to enter. But you, become prudent as serpents and innocent as doves' (Thomas 39).

Like Jesus, the Buddha attracted the anger of the dominant priesthoods through trying to mediate religious insight as an individually implemented process of realization, accessible to anyone who decides to undertake the necessary effort:

To anyone who leaves behind this world without having recognized his own real world, that is of as little use as the Veda he has not studied or some work he has avoided (*Brihad-Aranyaka-Upanishad*).

Jesus said: He who would know everything, but fails to know himself misses the knowledge of everything (Thomas 67).

The 'real world' mentioned in that passage from the Upanishads involves the spiritual, inner world, the true self (*atman*). Anyone who through meditation and religious practices succeeded in knowing his self would attain the insight that in the depths of his being he is identical with God. For the author of the Gospel according to John that presumption, so outrageous and heretical for orthodox Christians, was Jesus's profound conviction. In a scene during the feast of the dedication of the temple in Jerusalem, he presents a Jesus whose 'Indian views' almost result in his being stoned since orthodox Jews thought such views blasphemous. Jesus had dared express the idea of the identity of *atman* and *brahman* in the words: 'I and the Father are one' (John 10:30). That was in no way intended to elevate himself as the Son of God, but rather expressed the certainty that by following the rightful way everyone can experience oneness with the absolute. The evangelist also has Jesus quoting a passage in the Psalms where everyone is viewed as God's equal: 'I said, ye are gods' (John 10:34). After that Jesus had to seek safety from the first stones.

The Q^1 collection has brought to light an astonishing fact.

The most frequent, clearest and most striking correspondences with Buddhist texts – sometimes word for word – are particularly to be found in statements that derive directly from Jesus rather than being attributed to him later. The original Jesus taught Buddhist ideas, lived the life of a Buddhist wandering monk, and instructed his disciples in following the Buddhist path.

Transforming the Original Jesus into an Apocalyptic Prophet

The second layer of sayings was gathered together long after Jesus had left his followers. Among the Jesus people the sayings of their master in Q^1 were preserved as the only gospel until the period of the Jewish War (66–73 AD). Jesus was remembered as a far-sighted teacher of wisdom, independent of all conventions, moved by profound compassion for suffering human beings longing for redemption. Up to that time his followers remained a small and insignificant group, mainly spread throughout Judea and Galilee. As distress intensified in that land, war became ever more unavoidable, and their missions throughout the population found no response, they increasingly sought security in their group and in the Master's teachings.

We are very well informed about the religious and political groups and events of those decades, thanks to the testimony of Flavius Josephus. For instance, Josephus tells of certain 'charlatans and swindlers' who indulged in inflammatory speeches calling for rebellion under the pretext of 'being filled with the Holy Ghost'.[57] They were more or less successful rabble-rousers, sometimes assembled great crowds of followers, and were revered as saviours. They incited people, taking them out into the wilderness where God was expected to produce miraculous signs as an indication of liberation from the yoke of foreign rule. Obviously they wanted to repeat history with a renewed exodus into the desert. These self-designated prophets came from everywhere, from Galilee, known as a wasps' nest of insurgency, from Judea, from the land of the unpopular Samaritans, and also from Egypt, where new ideas with the potential to exert a powerful influence on an oppressed people, spread most rapidly. In Samaria, according to Josephus, there emerged a prophet who made a name for himself as a man of miracles and leader of a guerrilla band. He obviously learned his magic from his father, who had been initiated into that art in Egypt.

The Romans assumed that such 'prophets' also commanded groups of assassins. When Paul was taken prisoner, the captain believed he was the Egyptian leader of a Sicarian band (Acts 21:38). The Sicarians ('Dagger Men') were the most notorious of Zealots who had abandoned the realm of religion and taken up arms. They were the cunning underground fighters among fervent Pharisees. The Zealots ('Fanatics') were hate-filled fundamentalists, constantly ready to fight against the opponents of the Chosen People – exceeded in that respect only by the Sicarians, who resorted to arms whenever circumstances favoured that, constantly carrying weapons beneath their cloaks and simply eliminating their political opponents by stabbing them. Josephus[58] says that the Egyptian for whom the captain mistook Paul had no fewer than 30,000 followers with whom he first went into the wilderness and then to the Mount of Olives. From there he planned to capture Jerusalem in a decisive battle. He intended to do that in the same way as Joshua, the celebrated Old Testament warlord, in whose name he had come forward to further the people's destiny. At his command the walls of Jerusalem were expected to tumble, just as Jericho's had when Joshua's army blew its rams' horns, and his mob would then have been able to penetrate the city without resistance. Nothing became of that project. The Egyptian's rabble was wiped out by Felix, the Roman governor.

Another 'prophet' of that kind moved along the Jordan, promising that the river would be divided, just as it had been when under Joshua the People of Israel, following the Ark of the Covenant, had crossed over dry-footed (Joshua 3:1–17). He ended up in a Roman prison and was beheaded, just like the Jordan's most celebrated prophet, John the Baptist.[59]

The times were extremely dangerous, with both rebellion and harsh suppression by the occupying power commonplace. Strikingly many of the epoch's rabble-rousing prophets invoked Joshua ben Nun as the great mythical model of the liberator who led the Israelites against Canaan. The name Jesus is nothing other than the Greek translation of Joshua and means 'Jah is redemption'.[60] In Jewish memory Joshua re-mained the prototype of the liberator from foreign rule. Against the background of the Hellenistic belief in rebirth, people were inclined to view great personalities as different embodiments of the Chosen People's continuity of spirit. These leaders, inspired in the truest sense of the word, were thus seen by their followers as reincarnations of Joshua. It may therefore be that the name Jesus was used less as a personal name during the period than as a title or epithet for someone embodying the divinely ordained office of liberator. We must therefore express some doubt as to whether Jesus really was his name, or whether that name was given him by his followers, perhaps only around the time of the Jewish War when the land was teeming with reborn Joshuas/Jesuses. Theologians have treated that issue as a footnote so as not to endanger the uniqueness of Jesus as Christian redeemer.

The Jesus of Q^2, Q^3 and the rest of the Gospel material evidently fits into the framework of those models from the time of the Jewish War. The false prophets acted in very similar fashion to what we read of Jesus in the Gospels. He led his people into the wilderness (Matthew 15:33) and gave them a divine sign there, reminiscent of Old Testament precedents: the miraculous increase in loaves as a repetition of the won-drous provision of manna. Like other Jesuses, the Jesus of the New Testament also went to the Mount of Olives close to Jerusalem, where he told his disciples about the last days that were ahead (Matthew 24:3–36).

It must be asked in that connection how much historical credibility should be accorded to traditional accounts of Jesus. Did the Q people only call their leader Jesus so as to put him alongside the other rebellious prophets? If we assume that this interchangeable part of Jesus's biography is none the less largely authentic, then Jesus loses a considerable part of his unique-ness. He becomes merely another zealous visionary, driven by expectations of an imminent end to the world in an Israel finally freed from the foreign yoke. That picture does not, however, accord with the original Jesus of Q^1, who was filled with compassion and love, and an out-and-out pacifist. It seems probable that the Q people, the upholders of the Jesus movement, shaped the eschatological Jesus, who uttered threatening denunciations of entire cities and classes, in accordance with the age's expectations. They modelled their combative Jesus contrary to Q^1 and the Sermon on the Mount. The Jesus people wanted to build up their master retrospectively as *the* outstanding prophet, who many years previously had prophesied the ultimate victory of the righteous people of Israel, and had also initiated the last days for the chosen ones among the Chosen People.

The transition from Q^1 to Q^2 shows clearly that in threatening times the initial Jesus movement of wandering mendicant monks became an apocalyptic sect. Frustration with their lack of success gradually transformed Jesus's monks into wandering prophets, and that is recorded in corresponding changes to and enrichments of their holy book. Nevertheless, the Q community's central concern was not political domination as sought by the zealous charismatics but rather identification with socially disadvantaged groups, who in their eyes constituted God's people. When the signs of imminent war led them to believe that the rule of God was at hand, they intensified their efforts to gather together the Lord's people, thereby setting in motion a process that moved ever further away from the teachings of the original Jesus and became the doctrine of Christianity.

One demonstration of this thesis is provided by the passage already mentioned, in which Jesus, like any other prophet, led his people into the wilderness and performed the miracles of the loaves and walking on water. We have seen that both miracles were obvious borrowings from Buddhism. They do not therefore refer to actual events in Palestine, but are purely literary insertions into Jesus's biography from an Indian source, which fitted extremely well into the community's idea of 'neo-Joshuan' prophetism.

Thus began the reworking of the life of Jesus, the great Buddhist master, into a shape that accorded with the demands of the time for an intransigent religious leader. The original Jesus spoke ardently about loving one's enemy, but the new Jesus raged against the towns that resisted his teachings: 'Sodom will have a lighter punishment on the day of judgement than that town' (QS 21).

The original Jesus had persuaded his followers to be merciful and to abstain from judging, but the recreated leader thundered: 'And you, Capernaum, do you think you will be praised to high heaven? You will be told to go to hell' (QS 22).

The original Jesus, who had refused to play the judge deciding on an inheritance (QS 38), at this stage was transformed into a leader condemning 'this generation': 'When a strong man, fully armed, guards his own palace his possessions are safe. But when someone stronger than he attacks and conquers him, the stronger demolishes his defences and then plunders his goods' (QS 28).

What had happened? As we saw (QS 20), Jesus sent out his disciples to spread his teachings. In many places they were rejected and chased away, probably because people were weary, in times that were difficult enough anyway, of having to listen to announcements of salvation by yet another sect. And who was ready to love his enemies while tyrannized by Rome? The Q people had long bemoaned their preachings' lack of success – as, according to the Gospels, Jesus perhaps already regretted that his call for repentance was not heard in Galilee (Matthew 11:20–24) or Jerusalem (Matthew 23:37–39; Luke 19:41–44). Without the moral support of such an outstanding personality as Jesus, his followers were soon frustrated and sought new ways of spreading their message, ways that were adapted to fresh circumstances and the spirit of the age. We know from sociological and psychological investigations of what holds sects together, what happens to their members when objectives are not achieved. Instead of being shaken in their belief, people struggle with greater intensity than ever before, demonstrating more ardent messianic zeal on behalf of their faith.[61]

That was the situation in which the Q people found themselves, and they once again remembered their charismatic leader, whose outrageous teachings had shown them the way over thirty years previously. They staked everything on surmounting their frustration by boosting the myth of their leader, beginning by representing him as a prophet who had both promised a terrible judgement on 'this godless generation' and foreseen a dreadful war against the Romans, involving the Jewish people's final struggle against a powerful opponent. The land of Jordan had never seen such a prophet. He had to be greater than all the others: the Messiah heralded in the Old Testament was born! The people who devised this myth simultaneously provided consolation for themselves: the world of those righteous people who followed the way of 'God's Anointed' (Christ) would be spared during the resurrection on the day of judgement.

The early authors of the Christ myth certainly also had the same frustrating experiences as the Q people. They were no longer concerned with spreading Jesus's message; they wanted to give vent to their anger at not being received with open arms. A revealing insight is provided in the long speech by the apostle Stephen (Acts 6–7), the first Christian martyr. Stephen spends most of the time abusing the Jews who resisted God's intentions. Of Jesus we only learn in the last two sentences that, like all other prophets, he had been misunderstood and killed by their fathers. That is all Stephen had to say about Jesus up to the moment of his sudden vision of the son of man, which he obviously took over from Daniel.[62]

When considering the transition from Q^1 to Q^2, the question arises as to whether substantial changes could have been made in the relatively short period since Jesus's appearance, the collection of his sayings (Q^1), and the initial work on his biography including the creation of the Jesus myth. Experience shows how quickly legends about historical personalities can come into being. To take just one example, immediately after the murder of Thomas à Becket on 29 December 1170, a healing cult developed around his grave. Thomas was canonized on 21 February 1173. Among the legends that already flourished were stories about how he awoke the dead, made water shoot out of the ground by touching it with his staff, and predicted his own violent death.[63]

Times of upheaval are always good for making converts. Sects boom at moments of crisis. 'Jesus propagandists' fished the old Gospel of Sayings out of hiding, and started adding to it. They enriched it with denunciations of those social strata that opposed their missionary efforts. Their Buddhist teacher, the original Jesus from Q^1, was supplanted by a wrathful, pitiless prophet who hurled apocalyptic scenarios at 'this generation'.

Nevertheless, these writers also made use of traditional material, which had perhaps only recently come into the sect's possession. We know today that Jesus's adherents were spread throughout the country. Not all of them followed his invitation that they should take up his way as wandering monks. Some remained in their villages and towns, and educated Jesus people perhaps lived in the Greek connurbations of Decapolis. During the period of war when the sect closed ranks, it got hold of additional sayings which also derived from an early collection and must therefore be seen as authentic. These texts had been scattered in remote places, and had thus not previously been included in the Q^1 collection. Now they were incorporated together with the prophetic and apocalyptic material.

For that reason there are also further striking Buddhist parallels at this later level of Q. The wisdom sayings in this compilation are structurally and thematically identical with those of Q^1. The aphorism of the lamp and the eye from Q^2 is of interest in that context:

Whosoever has heard the law of virtue and vice is as a man who has eyes and carries a lamp, seeing everything. He will become completely wise (Ud 22:4).	No one lights a lamp and puts it under a bushel basket, but on a lampstand. And those in the house see the light.
	The lamp of the body is the eye. If your eye is good your whole body will be full of light. But if it is bad your whole body will be full of darkness. If the light in you is darkness, how great is that darkness (QS 33).
Just as a lotus blossom, scented and beautiful, can blossom on a dunghill at the side of a road, so too radiates the wisdom of the Buddha's pupils who have realized the Dharma, while normal mortals are blind (GDh 303–304).	

At this point it is appropriate to stress once again that there did not exist a single group following Jesus with a specific orientation. There were various Jesus groups which developed differently, as becomes apparent when comparing their treatment of the Sayings Source. The Q people entrenched themselves behind apocalyptic prophecies when their mission came to nothing, while the group that revered the Gospel of Thomas developed the idea of Jesus as a great esoteric teacher. The former transformed the Buddhist discourses of the original Jesus into a prophetic and apocalyptic book, and the latter made their text more metaphorical and esoteric, leaving considerably more of its Indian origins. In the Gospel of Thomas Jesus teaches that true knowledge entails self-knowledge, which in turn involves breaking away from the world. This group of Jesus's followers did not adhere to prophetism and the apocalyptic son of man. At the centre of their view of Jesus was the idea, reminiscent of the Indian concept of the *avatar*, that divine wisdom had been incarnated in Jesus so as to open the eyes of people on the way towards self-knowledge. The mythology expressed in the Gospel of Thomas is that of 'wisdom become flesh in a dark and meaningless world'.[64]

The light-dark theology evoked in the aphorism of the lamp receives expression in the Gospel of Thomas. There Jesus is a messenger from the realm of light. During the revision of this collection of sayings the metaphysics of light remained mixed with Indian ideas:

The wise man should renounce the way of darkness and follow the way of light (Dh 6:12). This world is veiled in darkness; few there can see. Only a few enter into the realm of bliss, just as only a few birds escape the net (Dh 13:8).	Because of that I say this: Whoever is emptied will be filled with light; but whoever is divided will be filled with darkness (Thomas 61).

The contents of a revealing parallel from Q^2 probably derive from an authentic saying by Jesus, which was then reshaped as a characteristically threatening passage during the time of changes:

Life is easy for someone who is shameless like a crow, slanderous and presumptuous, boastful and corrupt. Life is difficult for someone modest who always strives for purity, detached and reticent, immaculate in life and clear in understanding (Dh 18:10–11).	Strive to enter by the narrow door, for many, I tell you, will try to enter by it and will not be able. Once the owner of the house has locked the door, you will stand outside, knock at the door, and say, 'We ate and drank with you, and you taught in our streets.' But he will say to you, 'I do not know where you are from. Get away from me, all you unrighteous people' (QS 47).

Amore[65] has drawn attention to the fact that there are two successive verses in the *Dhammapada* whose content provides an exact correspondence to Matthew's references to the 'narrow gate' (Matthew 7:13–14): 'It is very easy to do what is bad and harmful for oneself. It is much more difficult to do what is beneficial and good. Whosoever perversely mocks the religion of the Arhats, the noble, and the just only prepares the way for his own destruction like the fruit of the *katthaka* reed' (Dh 12:7–8).

Amore assumes that Matthew found the sequence of two

verses in Q material, which would support the thesis that at
least part of Q consisted of a copy of the Pali *Dhammapada*. It
is only in the *Dhammapada* – not in the *Gandhari Dharmapada* or
the *Udanavarga* – that these verses follow one another in the
way that Matthew took them over. The other explanation
would be that Jesus knew the Pali version of the *Dhammapada*
and adhered to the sequence of certain didactic passages,
which his listeners faithfully wrote down.

The declaration that no one can serve two masters also be-
longs to the theme of the two ways. It is too reminiscent of
the words of the original Jesus:

One way leads to worldly gain and the other to Nirvana. Let the mendicant monk, the Buddha's pupil, seek wisdom, not worldly honours (Dh 5:16).	No man can serve two masters. Either he hates the one and loves the other, or he is loyal to one and despises the other. You cannot serve God and wealth [mammon] (QS 55).

In the Gospel of Thomas the aphorism about serving two
masters is introduced with the following sentence: 'Jesus said:
it is impossible for a man to mount two horses, for him to
stretch two bows' (Thomas 47:1). The image of the mounted
bowman sounds very Indian, and it is to be found there in
innumerable depictions of mythical warriors. In addition the
human being may be understood as contrasting with a god
who according to ancient Indian traditions was blessed
with many arms and thus probably able to span two bows
simultaneously.

The Buddhist Devil in the Judaic Wilderness

In the period after the war, when there was no longer any
external enemy, the Temple in Jerusalem had been destroyed,
and the survivors in Palestine sought new forms of self-
assertion, the Jesus movement developed to such an extent
that it could establish an autonomous tradition. The world left
by the war was a devastated environment. For centuries the
Jews had been forced to assimilate aspects of foreign culture,
and now their holy of holies was in ruins. What in one respect

seemed terrible, from another angle offered the possibility of a
fresh start. At that time the leading representatives of the Jesus
movement pushed ahead with the structuring of their sect. A
new spiritual home had to be established on a damaged foundation. Their Gospel of Sayings, to which an apocalyptic dimension had been added during all the upheavals of war, was now
intended to become the basis of a new faith – a faith that no
longer had its sights on just the salvation of the lost sheep of
the house of Israel as was originally envisaged, perhaps by
Jesus himself (Matthew 10:6), but was directed towards the
people of all religions and nations.

For that it was necessary for Jesus's activities on earth to be
recorded in writing. Producing his biography was not easy
because the Jesus people had little biographical data at their
disposal so that they could only make minor additions to their
collection of sayings. They were also too closely linked with the
tradition of Q^1 and Q^2 to be easily able to make the Jesus myth
even more enigmatic and improbable. Such tasks were taken
on by authors largely independent of the core of the Jesus
movement – by the first Christians and those later called
evangelists. The Q people did not even know of Mark, who
wrote a Jesus biography in Syria at that time. They relied on
the information that was handed down within their own ranks.
Such information was scanty, but additional material did turn
up, and it demands our attention. The most important biographical addition to the Book of Q during its last phase
(Q^3) was the story of Jesus's temptation by the devil in the
wilderness.

This story constituted a big problem for research into Q.
Some scholars even rejected the idea that it was part of Q since
it serves a completely different function from the rest of the
material. Many therefore assumed that Matthew and Luke had
independently taken the story from another source. However,
the speech passages in the narrations by Matthew and Luke
accord to such a high degree that the material must be assigned
to Q.[66]

Why was this particular biographical aspect handed down
among the Jesus people, rather than the healings and miracles
which fill the Gospels? The answer is both simple and surprising. The Q people obviously did not know any more about
Jesus's life. They seemed to have lost that knowledge already
before the war. They were very free about making additions to
the Q^1 material which are only explicable in terms of their

group's sociological situation, and for the most part could not have derived from Jesus. Yet somewhere in their ranks must have been people who knew about Jesus's Buddhist origins. Now that they were on the point of writing up and enriching Jesus's life, those people made use of Buddhist legends for the depiction of their master. The story of the temptation, added after the discourses of John the Baptist, precisely follows the Indian precedent of the temptation of the Buddha. Many researchers see this as one of the conclusive borrowings.

A very interesting aspect of Siddhartha Gautama's life story is to be found in the period immediately after enlightenment. At that moment all of his teaching was at stake. An existential crisis facing the Buddha already revealed the fundamental problem which was later to lead to a split into the two great schools of Hinayana and Mahayana. In a variant of the temptation story presented in the *Mahaparinibbanasutta*, the enlightenment is first presented as a kind of flashback. Mara, the tempter, invites the Buddha to enter upon Nirvana immediately so as to prevent his teaching being passed on. Perhaps one can assume that Shakyamuni really was uncertain about whether he should proclaim his teaching, since he saw what difficulty people had in abandoning their sensual desires and thirst for a sensuously experienceable world. The Buddha was thus not certain whether he should enter Nirvana immediately or disseminate the insights he had gained. Through his head ran the thought: 'I attained the teaching with great effort. How should I now proclaim it? Such teaching is not easy to grasp for those caught up in passions and sins. Swimming against the tide, the finely conceived, profound, difficult and precise teachings will not be seen by those subject to passion and shrouded in great darkness' (*Mahavagga* 5:3).

This is a decision between individual mastery and a dedication to general well-being, between personal salvation and an attempt at sharing insight into the ways of salvation with anyone in need of redemption. The choice in favour of propagating the teachings was later theologically founded by putting the new religion above traditional Brahminism. It was the brahminic god Brahma Sahampati who appeared before the Buddha and requested him to proclaim the teachings: 'May the Enlightened One, O Lord, proclaim the teachings; may he who is welcome speak the word. Without the teachings noble beings will go astray. They will understand the word' (*Majjhimanikaya* I, 395).

In the *Mahavagga* it is said that before Brahma Sahampati

intervened the Buddha became aware of *never previously heard* verses where he admits having received the teachings but is afraid that those caught up in passions will not *understand* and *see* them because they go against current views. Finally Gautama made up his mind to pass on this truly outrageous teaching. Jesus's promise to proclaim his message is expressed in impressively identical words. This statement is in the First Epistle to the Corinthians (I Cor. 2:9). There it is unattributed, but its origin becomes clear in the Gospel of Thomas: 'Jesus said: I will give you what no eye has seen, and what no ear has heard, and what no hand has touched, and what has not arisen in the heart of man' (Thomas 17).

The Buddha's doubts immediately after attaining enlightenment make him seem absolutely human, providing us with a means of avoiding misunderstanding that state. It could justifiably be asked how an enlightened person did not know what was to be done. However, this passage makes clear that enlightenment is not a licence for omniscience. The person concerned is still free to make wrong choices, and there is no question of infallibility in the sense of papal dominance. Perhaps that is why we in a world shaped by the Christian West often have an idea of enlightenment bordering on fantasy.

Mara represents the earthly world of appearances and of forgetting which the Buddha is striving to surmount. When Mara's persuasiveness does not achieve the objective, his three daughters, Tanha, Arati and Raga (Desire, Tenderness and Lust), make their appearance, striving to tempt the Awakened One. They constantly transform themselves into women of differing ages, but in none of these shapes do they succeed in diverting the Buddha from his path. Finally we hear in later narratives that even before Gautama's enlightenment Mara came roaring up with an army of demons so as to drive him from the place where he had sat down, resolved not to rise until he had achieved liberation. Legend says that Mara accompanied the Buddha throughout his life as a symbol of the sensuous world. We encounter him in that function several times in earlier sections of Prince Siddhartha's biography: as when he attempted to prevent the future Enlightened One from entering upon homelessness as a monk, or frequently promised to captivate him with pleasure so that he would be bound with human and divine chains.[67]

Surmounting this world by rejecting the tempter was viewed by Buddhists as an exceptionally apposite metaphor. Their literature thus contains a Sutra devoted entirely to the figure of the tempter. This *Marasamysutta* is concerned with all the variants of Mara's dealings – his constant endeavours to lead astray monks and nuns, as well as the Buddha, from the path of the Dharma. Mara only seems to be conceived as a mythological figure for the sake of more graphic description, and that certainly accorded with Indian religious thinking, used to over-extravagant worlds of gods and demons. Buddhist psychology, subtly differentiated at an early stage, identifies the tempter with the five factors (*upadanakkhandas*) which form the false personality: physicality, sensitivity, perception, emotionality and consciousness. The Buddhist monk is expected to recognize these false personalities so as not to offer Mara any targets.

Let us consider a variant of the Buddhist temptation narrative (from the *Marasamyutta*) as compared with Jesus's story in Q³:

(Buddha had withdrawn to a forest hut at Kosala in the Himalayas for solitary reflection.) Then Mara, The Evil One, knew the thought that had arisen in the Enlightened One, so he went to the Buddha: 'O Lord, may the Enlightened One reign as King, may the Perfected One reign with justice, without killing or ordering killings, without being oppressive or serving oppression, without suffering from pain or causing pain to others.' The Buddha answered: 'What doest thou have in mind, O Evil One, that thou speakest thus with me?' Mara responded: 'The Enlightened One, O Lord, has assumed the fourfold might of miracles. If the Enlightened One so wished, he could command the Himalayas, the king of mountains, to become gold, and the mountain would become gold.'

Then Jesus was led into the wilderness by the spirit for trial by the accuser.[68] He fasted for forty days and was hungry. The accuser said, 'If you are the son of God, tell this stone to become bread.' But Jesus answered, 'It is written, "No one lives by bread alone."' Then the accuser took him to Jerusalem and placed him at the highest point of the temple and said to him, 'If you are the son of God, throw yourself down, for it is written, "He will command his angels to protect you", and "They will carry you with their hands so that your foot will not strike a stone."' But Jesus answered him, 'It is written, "You shall not put the lord your God to the test."' Then the accuser took him to a very high mountain and showed him all the kingdoms of the world and their splendor, and he said to him, 'All

The Buddha turned him away: 'What would it help the wise man to own a mountain of gold or silver? Whosoever has recognized the cause of suffering, how should he succumb to desires?' Then replied Mara, the Evil One: 'The Enlightened One knows me, the Perfected One knows me,' and, grieved and discontented, he went away (*Marasamyutta* from the *Samyuttanikaya* II 10).

these I will give you if you will do obeisance and reverence me.' But Jesus answered him, 'It is written, "You shall reverence the lord your God and serve him alone." ' Then the accuser left him (QS 6).

Consider the great number of striking correspondences between the two narratives.[69] Both are preceded by glorification: Jesus was baptized and the voice came from heaven; the Buddha bathed in the river Nirañjana and gained enlightenment beneath the Bodhi tree, and the inhabitants of heaven experienced indescribable joy. Like the Buddha Jesus had reached a turning point. The Buddha was faced with a decision about whether to use the profound insights he had been granted for personal or public salvation. Jesus was making his first public appearance. He left John the Baptist, the apocalyptic prophet with a great horde of followers. Like Gautama, Jesus went to a solitary place. In those moments of peace where future actions matured, both were tempted by a skilful devil who manifested from the outside world. Both conducted a conversation with the tempter, and both were vulnerable and weak after prolonged fasting. As in Buddhist writings, the devil stands for the earthly, sensuous world. He is 'the prince of this world' (John 12:31), which the evangelist contrasts with Jesus's declaration to Pilate: 'My kingdom is not of this world' (John 18:36).

In both cases the unsuccessful tempter has to withdraw and await a more favourable moment:

The Evil One spent six difficult years, constantly following the Bohdisattva, always looking for, seeking, an opportunity to get the better of him, but he never succeeded. When he did get a chance, he had to leave frustrated and wrathful (*Lalitavistara* XVIII).

And when the devil had ended all the temptation, he departed from him for a season (Luke 4:13).

Jesus's second temptation – to throw himself down from the pinacle of the Temple – sounds strangely un-Jewish. All the references to Old Testament writings are constructed. How should such a strange action demonstrate Jesus's messianic power? That sounds much more like the abuse of magical powers, as were supposedly displayed in the arch-heretic Simon Magus's flying. That kind of temptation seems more adapted to the capacities of Indian saints who were assumed to be able to fly through the air.

Matthew's Jesus also rejects dominance of the world when this is offered by the tempter as a final trial of his steadfastness. In the *Nidanakatha* Gautama is tempted by Mara in similar fashion.[70] After the young Prince Gautama rides out of the city gate, Mara appears, promising that within seven days the Wheel of Dominance would appear before him and he would become ruler of the entire world. Gautama answers that he knows the Wheel of Dominance will appear but he would achieve Buddhahood rather than desiring power. That temptation accords completely with the narrative flow of Gautama's prophesied future. As we said earlier, Asita predicted at the Buddha's birth that Siddhartha would become either a world ruler or a 'king of religion'. The decision in favour of spiritual rule later became one of the fundamental moral precepts of Buddhism. This receives expression in the *Dhammapada*, and Jesus's identical thought in QS 52 was directly taken up by all the synoptic Gospels:

Better than reigning supreme over the earth, better than ruling heaven, better than dominating all worlds, is the reward of the *sotopatti* way (Dh 13:12).	For what is a man advantaged, if he gain the whole world, and lose himself, or be cast away (Luke 9:25).
	For what is a man profited, if he shall gain the whole world, and lose his own soul? (Matthew 16:26; Mark 8:36).

This parallel is extremely interesting. First, we can assume that it is an authentic statement by the original Jesus because of the close correspondence, in terms of content and structure, with Jesus's preceding statement (QS 52). The fact that Mark knew it is not an impediment. It must surely have been part of the original Q[1] collection of sayings, limited excerpts from which were also available to him. QS 52 is concerned with the

people following Jesus, a topic he introduces with a characteristic contrast and a radical statement about breaking off all
family relationships: 'Whoever does not hate his father and
mother will not be able to learn from me. Whoever does not
hate his son and daughter cannot belong to my school.' Then
Jesus calls on his future disciples to know themselves and to
bear his yoke. Then follows the previously quoted passage
about the fruitlessness of gaining the world while losing oneself. By this Jesus meant that in turning towards earthly things
people would lose their real lives in the sense of an existence
directed towards spiritual salvation. The verse from the
Dhammapada expresses exactly the same thoughts since 'the
reward of the *sotopatti* way' is nothing other than life on the
path towards redemption. The Pali word *sotopanna* signifies
'one who enters the stream', someone who has taken up the
Buddha's way, and is certain to attain enlightenment in a later
life.

Mara's attempt to draw Gautama onto the worldly side
accords completely with a basic problem that later – after the
Buddha's enlightenment and repeated temptations – returned
on a higher level as a decision between personal redemption
and the proclamation of the teachings with the possibility of
redeeming all suffering creatures. One seeks in vain for the
motive in the comparable biblical temptation. There is no
period of doubt (as suffered by Gautama) in the biblical tradition. After the baptism which showed him to be the Son of God
Jesus was tempted. So why the nonsensical offer of domination
of the world? Furthermore among the Jews the idea of world
rule was never proclaimed by prophets and apocalyptics as
political regency but rather as spiritual power at the end of
time. With the subordinate political role that Israel played – for
centuries tied to the apron strings of a succession of powerful
peoples – that kind of temptation seems far-fetched and incomprehensible. In India, on the other hand, the concept of
world ruler (*chakravartin*) was understood and widespread.
When Chandragupta, founder of the Maurya dynasty, mightily
expanded his kingdom, he became the epitome of the *chakravartin*. The word derives from the turning of wheels carrying
chariots victoriously over the entire world. It was also used in
Buddhism in a religious context involving 'setting in motion
the royal chariot wheel of a world empire of truth and justice'.
Later the Buddha was often depicted with his two hands in

front of the chest, one turned outwards, the other inwards, in what is called the *dhammacakka-mudra*, standing for the setting of the wheel of teaching in motion.

If one considers Jesus's Buddhist-influenced statements overall, the Buddhist moulding of motifs that developed among his disciples seems more understandable. We must even assume that some of his followers were in a sense just as 'indoctrinated' by Buddhism. The introduction of the story of the temptation by his adherents thus took place against the background of a view of their master as a buddha to whom the mythical elements in Shakyamuni's biography could be applied.

At the Jordan: the Original Jesus and the Baptist

The most serviceable record of the original Jesus is preserved in the Book of Q. We get to know the Buddhist teacher and discover the main aspects of his personality there. Nevertheless, the useable biographical data the book supplies is extremely limited. We learn nothing about Jesus's childhood. The stories we find in the Gospels and in apocryphal writings turn out, when viewed more closely, to be borrowings, mainly from India. The only biographical constant in Q involves Jesus's meeting John the Baptist, the prophet, and was added to the text during a time of war. However, there too that encounter is only indirectly mentioned.

Jesus's first public appearance is strikingly similar to the Buddha's. He appears as a disciple of John the Baptist, known as a strict ascetic and penitent. After turning his back on the palace Siddhartha Gautama sought teachers and joined Rudraka the brahmin, who was as it were his 'John'. Like Jesus the Buddha soon emancipated himself from this guru when he recognized that his teaching would not lead to liberation and true insight. He then decided to go into the wilderness in order to attain realization through strict asceticism. Jesus too went into the wilderness and fasted after being baptized by John. Five of Rudraka's followers joined Gautama, just as Jesus's first disciples were adherents of the Baptist (John 1:35–39). When Gautama gave up fasting because he saw that ascetic excesses would not lead to his objective, his followers left him, believing he had given up the search for redemption. One is inevitably reminded of the New Testament: 'John came neither eating nor drinking . . . The son of man came eating and drinking . . .' (Matthew 11:18–19). After attaining enlightenment the Buddha refound his five companions at Isipatana, converted them to his religion, and made them the first audience for his teachings.

The biographical correspondences in these episodes may not be absolutely clear-cut, but they demonstrate a remarkable intermingling. Jesus's fasting in the wilderness after baptism seems an alien element in the Gospels seeing that he had previously been presented as an 'eater' and 'drinker' in contrast to John, the typical desert ascetic. It seems as if this passage entails a mixture of genuine biographical material within various traditions: on the one hand the record as handed down by people around John, and, on the other, the evangelists' attempt to enrich Jesus's appearance on this scene with additional material (including some from Buddhist sources). We touch here on a point of exceptional importance in the history of Christianity: the environment in which Jesus lived before he freed himself, in his mid-thirties, from the shadow of the Baptist so as to proclaim his own teaching. In the development of the Gospels John justly seems an exceptionally important figure. Jesus was an unknown without any reputation. John, on the other hand, was a widely celebrated prophet. So when we encounter inserted Buddhist texts in the account of the meeting between Jesus and the Baptist rather than a completely coherent and autonomous narrative, we must assume that two traditions met here, and that both of them seem important to those who upheld memories of Jesus. They thought that Jesus should be left within the 'atmosphere' of John the Baptist while his appearance should simultaneously be mythically clad in elements from the Buddha's biography.

In the Book of Q John is introduced as the Baptist and an admonisher calling for repentance and conversion. Then comes the story of Jesus and the centurion from Capernaum whose servant he heals unseen because the soldier thinks himself unworthy of inviting such an important man into his house. John is told about this healing and sends some of his disciples to find out whether Jesus is the foretold saviour or whether another should be sought. Thereupon Jesus teaches the crowd about John, saying that he is the greatest of human beings and more than a prophet as the precursor of the Messiah heralded in sacred writings. Finally Jesus reprimands 'this generation' for despising John the ascetic and denouncing himself, who is not an ascetic, as a glutton and a drunkard. Finally there follow denunciations of the towns of Galilee.

The initial enrichment of sayings by Q^2 material is instructive in many respects. Let us for a moment consider the text as a literary invention. Its historical background is as follows. John was an exceptionally popular prophet. Crowds of people streamed to him from all over Judea, from Jerusalem, and from the entire Jordan area (Matthew 3:5). The place where he carried out baptisms, submersing all those who wished in the waters of the Jordan, was in the barren Ghor district, around three hours' walk from Qumran where a number of sectarian Jewish factions lived. The cult activities of the Qumran sects were related to those of the Baptist. Submersion was part of ritual practice at Qumran, and this purification was intended to make members aware that God will sprinkle people with the Holy Spirit just as they were purified with water, thereby making them capable of community. It is quite possible that John himself belonged to the Qumran circle, and was to a certain extent employed externally until he established an autonomous tradition. His message was eschatological and apocalyptic. He asserted that the end of time was close at hand with the dawning of God's rule and the coming of one greater, more powerful and worthier than himself. The people of Qumran similarly awaited God's kingdom with the appearance of two Messiahs from Aaron and Israel. Nevertheless, the Baptist did not promote the Qumran community. He called on people to repent and purify themselves, baptized them, and sent them on their way.

If there was a man who was viewed as a great prophet by the Jews, it was this John the Baptist. In his messianic movement people hoped for fulfilment of what had been promised. His reputation and relentlessly angry denunciations extended so far that Herod Antipas, the ruler of Galilee and Peraea, felt threatened, and had John imprisoned and later killed. If someone – particularly among those who expected a great eschatological turning point – had wanted to make known a person who was more important than the Baptist, it would have been clever to have that person legitimized by John. The Q^2 literary insert does just that. It extols the Baptist as an important prophet, makes him wonder at the miracles performed by someone greater, and adds the highly skilled rhetorical passage where Jesus himself speaks highly of John and simultaneously presents him as his own precursor. The fact that Jesus then starts to speak in denunciatory fashion, just like the Baptist, is only logical.

Viewed in this way, one could speak of a very successful fiction, aimed at making Jesus acceptable among those hoping for a Messiah. Was that the purpose of these additions during the Jewish War? Probably. This is the central moment where Jesus was transformed from a Buddhist teacher into a messianic saviour. At the same time this passage tells us that it is not a completely fictional invention but was based on a real event. The Baptist's question to his followers about whether Jesus was the promised one or not (Matthew 11:3) preserves traces of an actual occurrence. Otherwise John's doubts would not have been mentioned, and Jesus would have been immediately extolled as the messiah by the Baptist. That would certainly have been more effective for the cause. John's doubts were obviously known among his adherents so that they could not be simply ignored. That was also not possible for another reason: people hoped to gain new followers for Jesus among John's disciples.

That leads us to conclude that Jesus – by then over thirty years old – really did first make his appearance among the Baptist's followers, and with his radical Buddhist teachings about loving one's enemy, self-knowledge, and following an inner way attracted the attention of many who made the pilgrimage to the Jordan in the expectation of splendid events. There suddenly arose an unknown man who dared speak of outrageous things alongside the Baptist. Some of John's followers probably went over to Jesus at that time, constituting the initial core of disciples as the Gospel according to John says (John 1:35–39). If John's disciples, members of a baptismal sect, turned to what for them were Jesus's completely new Buddhist teachings, it was very understandable that they were on the look-out for more adherents of their new master within the ranks of the like-minded. Such people could probably only be convinced through the authority of their leader, John, so mutual manifestations of reverence between the Baptist and Jesus were invented. They obviously made such a fuss that John himself was no longer sure what he should think, and sent out his disciples to investigate the situation.

Later, after years of largely unsuccessful missionary endeavours, the Q people were probably still in touch with the baptismal sects and shared similar apocalyptic expectations. For the baptists, however, the Q^1 collection safeguarded by the Jesus movement as a precious treasure was not definitive. For them, as for the sect of the Mandaeans, John remained the sacrosanct leader figure. In the time of crisis during the Jewish War, the Q people strove to find proselytes among the not insignificant baptist communities, and attempted to intensify their persuasiveness by giving John's story a prominent place in their Gospel of Sayings. The way in which Jesus showed himself to be a follower of John and also a great admirer of this master was recorded in writing: 'I am telling you, no one born of a woman is greater than John' (QS 17). This important prophet, recognized by Jesus as the greatest, is then presented as precursor of Jesus the Messiah. Jesus's followers attempted to offer their Messiah – introduced through the authority of John himself – to the baptists, accompanied by a concealed threat should they not recognize him. After the declaration that no man was greater than John, we read, 'Yet the least in God's realm is greater than he' (QS 17). It was the followers of Jesus who could justly hope for God's kingdom. A hand was extended to the baptists: Join us in God's kingdom; follow the sign given by your master John and jump onto the train that set off when the Messiah appeared!

From that original source of legends there spontaneously came into being the traditions that remained vital in the Q community, and the New Testament accounts of Jesus's baptism are an easily comprehensible expansion of that. In the Gospels the close connection with the Baptist becomes almost obtrusive. Right at the start of his mission, the evangelists have Jesus direct the same words and admonitions towards his listeners, and use the same graphic descriptions, as John. In elucidating their inner relationship, the Gospel writers do not even shy away from attributing the completely inappropriate sermon on non-violence (Jesus's central theme) to the Baptist (Luke 3:14), the man who threatened 'the generation of vipers' that 'every tree which bringeth not forth good fruit is hewn down, and cast into the fire' (Luke 3:9). Jesus appears beside the Baptist as a similar kind of prophet with his denunciatory tongue. But was that the case? And what is to be believed about Jesus's baptism, to which there is no reference in the Q tradition?

Christian theology has particular difficulties with Jesus's

baptism. How can it be that Jesus was baptized when the baptisms conducted by John involved the forgiveness of sins (Mark 1:4)? A Jesus who needed to be purified of sin or even to enter a messianic sect by way of an initiation rite was simply impossible for Christianity. So Jesus's baptism was hurriedly interpreted as a consecration of the Messiah.

Various legends have grown up around Jesus's baptism, perhaps preserving a memory of an actual problematical situation between Jesus and John, or between their followers. It may also be that baptism was retrospectively made theologically respectable because of its outstanding importance in later Christian communities. Strikingly, neither Q nor the oldest Christian Gospel by Marcion,[71], mentions Jesus being baptized. In the Ebionitic Gospel according to Matthew,[72] however, John initially even refuses to baptize Jesus because he thinks himself unworthy of doing that for such a great man. The apocryphal Gospel of the Hebrews also tells of similar problems with baptism. Here it is Jesus's followers who urge him to be baptized, while he himself thinks that unnecessary.

If Jesus really did make an appearance among the Jordan baptists – and much indicates that he did – it may be that he decided to exert a public impact there because he hoped people would be ready to listen to what he had to teach. It was not to be expected that the Pharisees, the Scribes and the upholders of orthodoxy would take him seriously. It was the dissatisfied people, yearning for fresh spiritual impulses and driven by an inexplicable unrest, who sought out the desert prophet at the Jordan who seemed the right audience for Jesus. Whether Jesus ever met John there remains a mystery, but the Baptist learned about him and contradictory accounts of Jesus's baptism perhaps indicate that some of John's disciples urged Jesus to be baptized too.

It is at any rate interesting that the Mandaeans, the legitimate successors to the group around John, viewed Jesus as an apostate. In the Book of John, their most important religious book, John is presented as reluctantly baptizing Jesus, since for the Mandaeans the latter did wrong in establishing his own religion.[73]

The Gospel of the Hebrews, which is older than the Ebionitic Matthew, preserves a more original form where theological interventions are less apparent. There John asks Jesus to baptize him. Much about these events is historically inexplicable, especially as after the baptism (his own or Jesus's) John still had disciples who should really all have been disciples of Jesus for whom – according to the Gospels – John was only the precursor. The fact that when John was later imprisoned at Machaerus he was still not sure whether Jesus was the hoped-for Messiah demonstrates the confusion that surrounds the baptism story.

If the fragmentary Gospel of the Hebrews really is the oldest surviving account of the episode, and if the Mandaeans' Book of John is to be believed, then we gain the following picture. Before his first public appearance Jesus was on the fringes of the Jordan baptists whose intensely anti-Jewish polemics separated them from Judaism. These baptists had become a Gnostic sect where ancient Jewish washing rites had been elevated into a central baptismal ritual. John wanted to baptize Jesus as his disciple but came into conflict with that contrary thinker. This dispute must have attracted some followers to an unconventional teacher who stood up to the desert prophet. The echo of that dilemma led to divergent accounts in the writings of different sects and times. The Gospel of the Hebrews still sees Jesus as being urged by his disciples (or people close to him) to be baptized even though he himself saw no reason for it. That sounds credible, above all with respect to the Jesus we have met in Q^1, and would completely fit in with developments in the partly fictional Jesus biography to be found in the two later levels of Q. In the Gospel according to Matthew the events surrounding the baptism could no longer be hushed up because they were already circulating in various writings. It was the theological revision, making John into Jesus's precursor, which brought into the Gospel texts those contradictions that cause headaches for so many exegetists. How is it possible that after John had supposedly baptized Jesus he asked whether this was 'the man who should come', when during the actual baptism the heavens opened and a voice rang out with the remarkable words: 'Thou art my beloved Son; in thee I am well pleased'? Either that simply did not happen during the baptism, or, more probably, Jesus was not baptized.

The idea that Jesus did not believe in the necessity of such an outer sacramental action as baptism for being thought pure is apparent from another addition to Q^2. This is to be found in the denunciations of Pharisees, which in content are reminiscent of the original Jesus, and probably for that reason point to parallels in Buddhist writings. Those correspondences were merely revised so as to depict a raging Jesus – as was the trend in the adaptation of Jesus's sayings during a time of war.

You fool! Of what use are your long locks? Of what use your clothing of hides? Within yourself darkness is at home. Only outwardly you clean yourself (Ud 33:8).

Of what use is your matted hair, O fool! Of what use your clothes made of animal hides? Within yourself is a jungle, but outwardly you adorn yourself (Dh 26:12).

Shame on you Pharisees! For you clean the outside of the cup and the dish, but inside you are full of greed and incontinence. Foolish Pharisees! Clean the inside and the outside will also be clean. Shame on you Pharisees! for you love the front seats in the assemblies and greetings in the marketplaces. Shame on you! for you are like graves, outwardly beautiful, but full of pollution inside (QS 34).

Jesus uses the symbol of the cup which the Pharisees keep clean externally but allow to get dirty internally so as to emphasize the paramount importance of spiritual attitude and its expression in word and deed. We have encountered diverse variants of that theme in Q^1. The original Jesus obviously did not tire of telling people that true spiritual greatness in no way involves externalities, and does not call for any particular mortifications, rites of purification or displays of readiness for sacrifice. All its preconditions are contained in the basic principles of the Eightfold Path.

Characteristic in that context is a parallel between the account of the baptism from the Gospel of the Hebrews and a passage from the *Lalitavistara* to which Van den Bergh van Eysinga has drawn attention.[74] When his mother wants to take the young Gautama to the temple so as to present him to the gods, the boy initially hesitates but finally respects the age's religious customs. In both cases the underlying theme of hesitation followed by acceptance of the prevalent customs is identical. The connection between baptism and transfiguration in the Gospels is also interesting. The words heard from heaven on both occasions are almost identical. It seems as if the baptism was depicted in a way that derives from the transfiguration. Reflection is also provoked by the fact that the passage from the *Lalitavistara* offering a parallel to the account of Jesus's baptism ends with Gautama saying that after his transformation gods and human beings will say he was God by virtue of himself. The entire mythical ambiance of the baptism is thus paralleled in Buddha's life, underlining our assumption that Jesus was never baptized.

Jesus's answer to John's disciples who were investigating his work for their master, is also revealing. The words with which he speeds the baptists on their way mainly refer to his successes as a healer. It is an open question whether Jesus himself said these words or his followers. What is amazing is the fact that the Buddha's activities were described in exactly the same words.

The blind saw and the deaf could hear . . . The ill were healed. The hunger and thirst of the deprived were stilled. Drunkenness was taken away from the drunken. The mad regained reason. The blind could see again, and the deaf hear (*Lalitavistara* VII).	Jesus said, 'Go and tell John what you hear and see: the blind recover their sight, the lame walk, lepers are cleansed, the deaf hear, the dead are raised, and the poor are given good news' (QS 16).

His encounter with the baptists was a stage during Jesus's 'homelessness' journey. At that time he attempted with his ethical and moral teachings to speak to those opposed to the age's religious philistinism. He himself thought that baptism was unnecessary since the Buddhist view was that outer cleansings achieved nothing. It was solely inner purification that had to be striven for.

Q^1 is so uniformly Buddhistic that one cannot say Jesus picked up ideas for moral instruction here and there. He took them all from the treasure-house of Buddhist wisdom. But how did it come about that the original Jesus disseminated Buddhist teachings and wanted to propagate in Palestine the ideas which Siddhartha Gautama presented to his followers along the Ganges 500 years earlier? Where did Jesus gain his knowledge? In order to throw light on that question let us know look more precisely at the missions sent to the West by Emperor Asoka. Were the descendants of the Buddhist monks sent out by Asoka still at work in Alexandria and Syria when Jesus was alive?

Part III

THE WAY OF THE ORIGINAL JESUS

The Westward Spread of Buddhism

In the middle of the third century BC King Asoka not only sent out missionaries, but even had places of shelter and sanctuary established in distant countries. In addition he employed advisers to look after the monks' interests, protecting them against envy and persecution, and to teach respect for life and compassion for all beings. In the *Mahavamsa, Dipavamsa* and in Buddhaghosa's *Suttavibhanga* we read of the conversion of *Yavanas* (Greeks) under Asoka. In those texts the old and experienced monks (*thera*) who headed missions to early Hellenistic Greece are mentioned by name. Maharakkhito preached the *Sutta Kalakarama* to large numbers of Greeks, and it is claimed that thousands then sought refuge in the new religion. Among the missionaries selected by Moggaliputto there was even a previously converted Greek, *thera* Dhammarakkhito, who was sent to the land of the Aparantaka in the far west where he proclaimed the *Sutta Aggikhandopama*. Once again large numbers were said to have been converted, including many women.

We must assume that these accounts of missionary successes are not without historical foundation in view of the impression made by individual Buddhist ascetics in the West, such as Zarmanochegas in Athens. Nevertheless the Indian tendency towards exaggeration must be born in mind with regard to the number of converts.

Over 2000 years passed before we were able to ascertain that these accounts were not an invention, and discover the seriousness with which Asoka pursued missionization. Only in 1915 did Sir John Marshall, the famous archaeologist, discover an unusual inscription at Taxila-Sirkap in the northern Indus valley. It was found on an octagonal white marble column, written in Iranian-influenced Aramaic. It was previously known that people in these western provinces, which once belonged to Persia, made use of the official form of Achaemenidic Aramaic, and that Kharoshthi characters were employed (unlike in other parts of the country where the Brahmi alphabet was utilized), but in border areas things were much more complicated. The written characters employed different languages in various edicts, expressed sometimes Persian, sometimes Indian, and sometimes something completely different. Linguistic researchers thus had great difficulty in deciphering the Taxila-Sirkap inscription. In addition the left half was no longer decipherable, and the general state of preservation bad. This object was first thought to be a memorial to some high official. At the end of the 1940s it was suggested that it might designate a building. Only in 1958, when another Aramaic inscription[1] was found in the Kandahar province of Afghanistan, 500 miles south-west of Taxila, was the mystery of the Taxila characters gradually solved. The Kandahar inscription was a key discovery, comparable in importance to the Rosetta Stone which enabled Jean François Champollion to decipher Egyptian hieroglyphics. This inscription was in two languages, Aramaic and Greek. The text reproduces the most important contents of Asoka's celebrated rock edicts. On the basis of that discovery Helmut Humbach, a German researcher, was in 1969 able to identify the Taxila inscription as a somewhat shortened, word-for-word translation of the central passage in Asoka's Fourth Rock Edict, with its call for avoidance of killing, showing obedience to one's father, and pursuit of right conduct of life.[2] The reason why this inscription stone had been found in a wall forming part of Buddhist monks' accommodation – in the 'double-headed eagle stupa' in excavation block F at Taxila – then became apparent (Plate 26).

More discoveries of Asoka inscriptions in the 1960s in areas of Afghanistan further and further to the west made it clear how intensively Asoka had planned and pursued his arrangements for sending out missionaries. He did not just publish decrees about Buddhist missionizing; he even had edicts issued in regions beyond his immediate sphere of influence, in local languages and written characters. That infallibly reveals the extent of his foreign mission. In addition these inscriptions disclose more and more secrets which were uncovered only very recently. And who can say how many such inscriptions still await discovery on the western routes?

One of the first two Asoka inscriptions found in Afghanistan during the 1960s was completely in Greek, and thus obviously intended for the Greek-speaking peoples of the Mediterranean area. That reproduced the Twelfth and Thirteenth Rock Edicts. The other involved an Aramaic transcription of an Indian text.

This Indo-Aramaic inscription was also found at Kadahar, and is very similar to another one uncovered during the 1930s – and indecipherable at that time – at Pul-i-Darunteh in Afghanistan's Laghman valley. Only in 1966, thanks to the new discovery, was that shown to be a typical Asoka text.[3]

Finally, in 1969 Belgian ethnologists came across another completely Aramaic Asoka inscription (known as L I), also in Laghman province, which provided a great deal of information.[4] A few years later another (L II) was found nearby with contents almost identical to the first.[5] It was discovered close to the old trade route linking East and West, on a rock visible from some distance. The western route taken by caravans from Taxila, then an important centre, led over the Khyber Pass and through the Laghman valley to present-day Kabul, and from there southwards to Kandahar and on to the southern coast of the Caspian Sea. After that caravans could travel further to the west along three routes. Only now has it become clear that all these Asoka edicts appear on the land route towards Mesopotamia and on to Syria and Greece. They did not just speak of the Buddhist ethics Asoka had disseminated everywhere; they were also signposts, indicating the way to the west which the Emperor's missionaries were to take if they had been posted to the Seleucids, Ptolemies and Macedonians. Such signposts were to ease the journey of all those who similarly wanted to set out upon this important mission. Inscription L I runs: 'In that direction the place known as Tadmor.'[6] Tadmor was the old name for Palmyra. Here the way is clearly shown to the caravan town of Palmyra, the large oasis around 2400 miles west of Laghman, and the most important stage for caravans bound for Syria and Palestine (Plate 25). The next lines on inscriptions L I and L II are very difficult to interpret; there is mention of a caravan route and numbers, obviously indicating distances. Depending on how the characters are read (as Iranian or Aramaic) – and that cannot be clearly determined – L II is concerned with a bringer of religion or missionary, or with the place name of a fortress as guidance along the way.

Asoka thus chose the celebrated trading and military route by way of Palmyra for taking the Buddhist religion to the end of the Western world. We have already shown that Indian merchants already used these ways in the time of the Achaemenids. In a Hippocratic text dating from immediately

after the fall of the Achaemenids, pepper in Greece is called
peperi and viewed as being Persian. That really should be the
Indian word *pippali*. At that time many Indian products came
to Greece by way of Persia. They were brought over the Oxus
to the Caspian Sea area, from where they were taken to Pontos
Euxeinos (the Black Sea) or through Palmyra to parts of Syria,
or by way of an even more southerly route through Mesopotamia
and Arabia to the land of the Nabataeans. Ivory obviously
brought from India by such routes has been found at Pompeii.
High-quality Greco-Roman and Greco-Buddhist art was soon
produced at the flourishing oasis of Palmyra, the staging post
on this route.

The Asoka inscriptions in these areas are thus signposts
which do not indicate any ordinary trade route but rather a
spiritual itinerary. Asoka comprehended the sending out of
Buddhist missionaries as according with an inner departure
along the way of salvation indicated by the Buddha. In his
Eighth Rock Edit at Shahbazgarhi Asoka speaks about his turning towards Buddhism, remarking: 'Ten years after his in-
auguration King Devanampriya Priyadarsi went to *sambodhi*.'
What does this declaration mean? Had Asoka, converted to
Buddhism, set off on a religious pilgrimage to Bodh Gaya
(*sambodhi*), the place where the Buddha experienced enlightenment, as the Indian researcher Bhandarkar thinks? Perhaps
that interpretation is correct since Asoka speaks in this edict
ardently and in detail about a visit to adherents of the Sthaviras
Buddhist sect, which really may have happened at Bodh Gaya.
However, *sambodhi* also means insight, wisdom, intelligence,
and the awakening that is fundamental in the three higher
states of *arhat*ship. It never means the wisdom of a Buddha,
but always the insight of higher states along the way which
leads to that level of holiness. That way has been described
by Siddhartha Gautama as the Noble Eightfold Path. Perhaps
Asoka only wanted to say that in the tenth year of his reign he
decided to take up that Eightfold Path so as to attain *arhat*ship
in some future incarnation.[8]

In Buddhism spiritual alignment and outer actions accord
with one another – such as meditative walking in a cloister,
walking around a stupa clockwise or pilgrimages to places
linked with the Buddha. We can therefore assume that Asoka
intended to invite people both to follow the Eightfold Path and
to visit holy sites as pilgrims. It is thus reported in Buddhist

texts that in 249 BC Asoka, accompanied by Upagupta, a Buddhist monk, undertook an extended pilgrimage to Siddhartha Gautama's birthplace in what is today Nepal. One must view the edicts on the western route as a call to follow Buddhist teachings and as an indication that these should be transmitted to the other peoples along this route.

Asoka was in no way interested in imposition of Buddhism. He was convinced of the value of the Dharma and wanted it to be accessible to anyone who was open to this truth. He was an exceptionally tolerant ruler. After his conversion to Buddhism he may have actively supported this faith, but he did not suppress other religions. Quite the contrary: he made generous gifts to all religious communities, thereby implementing the generosity advocated by the Buddha. Buddha instructed his disciples to make sacrifices to all the gods they met with wherever they went (*Mahaparinibbanasutta* 1:31). Asoka's admonitions to travelling missionaries were in that spirit: 'Honouring one's own community of faith and criticism of another should not occur without good reason' was carved in rock in the Twelfth Edict, and so too was 'Honour a foreign community of faith as is appropriate. Acting thus, one promotes the growth of one's own faith and does good to the unfamiliar faith.'

The missionaries sent out by the Maurya king were not armed for battle for one faith and against all other religions as was generally the case with later Christian missionaries. Asoka's monks proclaimed the Dharma in distant countries without openly opposing other forms of belief. That humble approach deprived the king's Buddhists of any noteworthy success in the West. They were faced with considerable difficulties: unfamiliar morals, customs, belief systems and languages, and reservations about strangers on the part of much of the local population. A large number of hurdles had to be surmounted in order to spread the Dharma successfully. The missionaries had no choice but to proceed with great restraint. They may have lived their monastic life as they had in India but they slowly adapted to circumstances in their new environments.

In his Twelfth Edit Asoka also noted:

> Coming together is hallowing. How is that? 'Should they wish to hear the Dhamma and obey it. So be it.' That is the wish of God's Beloved [Asoka]. But what is involved? 'That believers of all faiths should be great in learning and fruitful in doing good. So be it.'

And Asoka gave his missionaries the Law of Reverence to take with them on the way they were always supposed to follow: 'More piety, many good deeds, compassion, generosity, truthfulness, purity' (Second Edict).

The content of Asoka's inscriptions is always moralistic, never dogmatic or mythological. Similarly the special feature of the 'Christian message' in the Sermon on the Mount was sought for words of salvation and parables. Here we encounter Jesus as the herald of a tremendous moral teaching. Just as the Buddhists and Asoka thought the outer forms of religion and displays of pious behaviour were not essential, and were solely concerned with living in accordance with the Eightfold Path, so too did Jesus teach a life according with the moral law – the Buddhist Dharma.

Theravadins and Therapeutae: Egyptian Buddhists

In the spring of 1908 the British School of Archaeology in Egypt started extensive excavations at Memphis. The archaeologists thus discovered a foreigners' quarter around the temple of Merenptah (Nineteenth Dynasty). This area for strangers must have existed for many centuries. The small clay heads that turned up everywhere there are the portraits of various people who had found a new home in Memphis ever since the time of Persian dominance (525–405 BC). A clear-cut distinction can be made between Sumerians, Accadians and Scythians, or Tibetans and Mongolians. Even the effigy of an Aryan woman from the Punjab and a figure sitting Indian-style with a scarf over the left shoulder were found (Plate 29). All the indications are that an Indian colony already existed in Memphis during the age of Asoka. Whether it was originally a trading outpost or whether it originated with Asoka's missionaries can no longer be determined.[9] The clay statuette of the Indian woman has been dated at around 200 BC, just a few decades after the start of Asoka's great missions.

Ten years before these excavations a gravestone from the Ptolemaic period, displaying Buddhist symbols, was discovered at Dendera in Egypt. For Flinders Petrie that discovery constituted an irrefutable indication of the influence of Buddhist missionaries in Egypt.[10]

We showed in Part I that Asoka's mission to the West profited from a cultural boom in states influenced by Hellenism; we followed the sea and land routes, and described the enormous increases in communications between Egypt and India after Alexander the Great. Under Asoka's contemporary Ptolemy II Philadelphos, Alexandria experienced its greatest blossoming. A great diversity of intellectual camps and doctrines proliferated and developed – through reciprocal stimulation and competition – their utmost potential. Dion Chrysostomos (c. 40–112 AD) confirmed that Indians lived in Alexandria immediately after the start of the new millenium in a speech where he welcomed them among his audience.[11] There is no reason to doubt that Indian communities existed in Alexandria long before Dion Chrysostomos's time, especially since they were found in Memphis, a less important town. Chrysostomos wrote that Indian traders were despised by their fellow-countrymen.[12] That statement must be seen as indicating that the Alexandrian Indians were Buddhists. In the eyes of Sunga Dynasty (c. 180–68 BC) brahmins they were heretics. In addition, brahmins themselves were forbidden to cross the sea because that entailed the risk of attracting ritual impurities and possibly losing caste membership. So it will not have been particularly difficult for the Buddhist monks in Asoka's mission to have established themselves in the existing Egyptian settlements of Indian merchants.

During the epoch leading up to the end of the old millennium the Hellenistic world underwent various political and cultural changes. Alexandria, however, remained the intellectual centre, constantly attracting people eager for knowledge, philosophers, prophets, preachers of salvation, visionaries and spiritual seekers.

The political leaders, however, were paralysed by excessive cults of power, and civil wars and rivalries developed immediately after the death of Alexander. Despite great efforts, the huge empire he left could not be maintained. The region around Taxila was lost to India again around 308 BC; in 280 there was a Celtic invasion; Cappadocia gained its independence in 260 BC; and around 230 the Parthians increasingly advanced, soon controlling large parts of Iran and extending to western

India and Syria. The subjugated peoples made life difficult for their masters, as in Egypt and later in Palestine, where around 165 BC the Maccabees resisted efforts towards extreme Hellenization. Nevertheless, these turbulent centuries before and after the start of the new millennium were shaped by a striking development. Never before had there been an epoch where foreign culture and unfamiliar ideas were so openly taken over, where East and West fused, and where philosophical systems and religions flourished to such an extent. This was plainly the age of syncretism – and the Buddhists played an important part in that.

Another clear indication of the presence of Buddhist monks in Alexandria during the Hellenistic period is to be found in the *Mahavamsa*, a Buddhist chronicle. The city of 'A'lasadda' is expressly mentioned as a colony of the Buddhist mission – and all researchers agree that 'A'lasadda' is Alexandria. We learn that a great stupa was to be erected at Ruanwelli in Sri Lanka around the mid-second century BC during the reign of Dutthagamani. For that important event Buddhist monks set off for Sri Lanka from all the areas where they had settled. From the Pallavas (Parthian) region came Mahadevo, the great wise man, with 460,000 monks, and from around A'lasadda (Alexandria) the Greek *thera* Mahadhammarakkhito with 30,000 mendicant monks. Specific mention of the Parthian and Alexandrian colony shows how important those settlements were for Buddhists. Despite the usual exaggeration, the number of monks mentioned is an expression of the importance of these two communities abroad. The Parthian community, which extended from Taxila to Bactria and far to the west, marked Buddhist missions along the Palmyra route, and the Alexandrian community indicated the settlements that were obviously close to the city along Lake Mareotis.

For Asoka's missionaries Egypt was an ideal place to go. Their way of life did not seem alien there. In the serapeum at Memphis there were male and female hermits, dedicated to study and mystical contemplation. Asceticism and celibacy were also part of the Isis cult. The ground was well prepared for a monastic community like the Buddhist one.

But what became of the Buddhist in Egypt? Were they absorbed by another culture so that their own characteristics vanished for ever, or did they maintain their tradition? From the time of Jesus we possess an exceptionally valuable account of a monk-like religious sect near Alexandria whose similarities with Buddhism attracted the attention of alert nineteenth-century religious historians. As early as 1875 Henry Longueville Mansel saw this sect, known as the Therapeutae, as uniting Alexandrian Judaism with Buddhist teachings and way of life.[13] With those Therapeutae are we really on the track of the descendants of Asoka's Egyptian mission to Ptolemy II Philadelphos?

We can count ourselves lucky that we know anything at all about the Therapeutae today. Our only source of information is a Hellenized Jew based in Alexandria. Philo (20 BC–50 AD) was a contemporary of Jesus, and in his tract *De vita contemplativa* (*On the Contemplative Life*) he left a picture of the Therapeutae community. With the establishment of Christian monks and monastic communities in the fourth century AD, church historians became interested in Philo's work and his description of the Therapeutae. Their way of life was so similar to the coenobitic rules that they were viewed as Christian monks, and in the sixth century *vita therapeutica* was even the Latin term for Christian ascetic monasticism. It was not known until the start of the eighteenth century that the Therapeutae existed long before Christianity came into being.[14] That misinterpretation saved Philo's text from destruction. Christian apologists, eager to underpin their own view of Christianity with the authority of older writings, did not hesitate to destroy unwelcome works or to stuff them with Christian additions which today have to be laboriously peeled away to reveal the original. If such improvers had realized that Philo by no means saw the Therapeutae as early Christian monks, *De vita contemplativa* would surely have been destroyed too. 'Incomparable' Christianity simply did not want to tolerate such alien precursors.

The rediscovery of the Therapeutae in the nineteenth century, and the problems the Jews and both the big Christian communities had in classifying them, led to a grotesque situation. Ultimately Jewish scholars were just as apprehensive about accepting the Therapeutae as a Jewish sect as Catholics were about calling them monks. What lay behind these difficulties? They arose from the fact that the Therapeutae constituted a disturbing historical fact for both Judaism and the Catholic church: the existence of a monk-like group linked with the Jewish settlement near Alexandria in the first century BC, a community strikingly characterized by aspects of later Christianity. Like its Buddhist equivalent, this monastic institution

involved poverty, celibacy, obedience, good deeds and compassion. There were no precursors or models for such a set-up
in either the Jewish world or in heathen religious communities.[15]

Philo made no secret of the fact that he was impressed by
the Therapeutae's way of living and their view of the world.
He presented them to his readers as being incomparably superior
to the stupid Egyptian worshippers of animals, and even to the
Greek philosophers. The latter view would have been taken as
an insult in Alexandria, the stronghold of Hellenistic intellec-
tuality, but it demonstrates the degree of importance Philo
wanted to assign to this small sect.

The Therapeutae were a religious brotherhood which had
settled on the low hills in the area south of Alexandria near
Lake Mareotis. They led a reclusive existence, completely devoted to their religious practices and studies. It seems as if they
were restricted to this region. Philo reported:

1. There were male and female Therapeutae.
2. They laid aside all worldly goods, leaving their houses,
   brothers, children, wives, parents, relatives and friends.
3. They lived away from towns in gardens, villages and remote areas, where they sought solitude – not because they
   hated humanity but so as to avoid people of a different
   kind, not mixing with them.
4. Their houses were built in an extremely modest and penuri-
   ous way, concerned with only two necessities: protection
   from the sun's heat in the summer and from cold air in the
   winter.
5. In their huts everyone had a small sacred space, known as
   Semneum or Monasterium.
6. They prayed twice a day, morning and evening, at sunrise
   and sunset.
7. They possessed old sacred writings on which they meditated a great deal. (Philo assumed that this involved works
   ascribed to Enoch and Abraham, who were viewed as
   prototypes of ascetics and hermits.) Their studies led them
   to compose songs and hymns.
8. On the seventh day they met together, ranked in accordance
   with the length of time they had spent in the community
   (rather than on the basis of their age). They ate only bread
   and drank only water. The oldest member of the order held
   a discourse. Men and women were separated by a high wall.

9. They only owned two robes, and constantly practised modesty.
10. They had no servants because for them all were equal from birth onwards. At assemblies novices served those who had belonged to the order for a long time.
11. They were vegetarians, believing that the highest degree of saintliness could only be attained by rejecting all flesh.

If it were not known that Philo was writing about the Therapeutae, one would have to believe this was a description of the life led by Buddhist monks. All the points presented are absolutely characteristic of Buddhist communities. Or did Philo really encounter in the Therapeutae the heirs of Asoka's missionaries?

The total rejection of worldly things which underlay the ideal Therapeutae existence, is of course the starting point for Buddhist beliefs. According to Philo, the Therapeutae did not prefer solitude to towns because they hated humanity; the reason was that they wanted to keep their distance from the world of those who lack insight and compassion. The Buddha instructed his followers in similar fashion: 'If a [Buddhist] disciple does not find a companion either better or his equal, he should pursue a solitary way. There can be no association with fools' (Dh 5:3).

The Therapeutae also had vegetarianism in common with Buddhists as an expression of their reverence for life. That point was particularly emphasized by Asoka, as compared with the Buddha's more moderate views. Asoka's missionaries would therefore have devoted special attention to vegetarianism, which was thus upheld in the Alexandrian settlement for many years. The religious historian Robertson Smith pointed out as early as 1894 that the development of vegetarianism among the Therapeutae and later Jewish asceticism were only explicable in terms of Buddhist influence.[16]

The fact that there were both 'monks' and 'nuns' among the Therapeutae offers another clear sign that these must have been Buddhists. The construction of their modest huts also accords precisely with the prescriptions the *bhikshus* had to follow according to the monastic rules (*patimokkha*). In early times the concentration of mendicant monks' huts around a shrine and a gathering place used to be called *vihara* (place of residence). Later *vihara* became the word used for Buddhist monasteries. Morning and evening prayers are also part of the prescribed daily routine for Buddhists,[17] and the words for Buddhist prayers are found in the *patimokkha*.

The number seven was held in high regard by both Buddhists and the Therapeutae. The seventh day, when the Therapeutae sat down together in accordance with their length of membership of the order, is an adoption of the 'Buddhist sabbath' (*uposatha*) with a day of religious observance and ceremonies for lay followers and *bhikshus* four times a month. On those days the laity wore white garments. They were called 'men clad in white' and abstained from worldly dealings and pleasures. This *uposatha* sabbath is one of the most important sacred days for Theravada Buddhism. Lay people come to monasteries to listen to a monk's (*thera*) presentation of the teachings. As with the Therapeutae, one does not become a *thera* because one has reached a certain age. Even a relatively young monk can become a *thera* if he has been a member of the order for a long time. Buddhist novices also serve longer-established members. In addition, there are very many rules and commandments regulating the separation of nuns and monks. Highly detailed prescriptions restrict the number and kind of garments a monk or nun may possess.

Philo was a cosmopolitan, Hellenized Jew. However, when God was at issue, he forgot his Hellenistic education and remembered his Jewish roots. Perhaps the Therapeutae he described with such fervour owed some of their 'Jewish' characteristics to that enthusiasm. He made quite clear that he profoundly admired this community of 'spiritual athletes', who acted from the purest motives, pursuing perfection and capable of extreme renunciation, so as to attain the highest vision of God and the truth. Can one take it amiss that he tried to portray them as being close to his own religious roots? Nevertheless, it becomes clear from his work that he himself was uncertain whether the Therapeutae were Jewish ascetics.

In his desire to denounce the gatherings of Greek philosophers (unlike those of the Therapeutae) as degenerate, noisy junketings, Philo omitted to mention what the Therapeutae lived off, as they did not own any property or go out to work. Perhaps the omission was deliberate because he thought it degrading and not part of the idealized view of the Therapeutae he wished to give. Of course the Therapeutae were mendicant monks (*bhikshus* and *bhikshunis*) like their Buddhist comrades in other parts of the world, and were thus dependent on offerings.

Philo also mentions that they were not interested in prophesies, which very much distinguishes them from Jewish sects, and is a typical Buddhist characteristic. His assumption that the writings of Enoch were among their revered texts thus seems unfounded, especially as the Enochian literature, with its vivid apocalyptic images intensively cultivated and enriched by Jewish sects during the last two centuries of the old millennium, was very much part of the prophetic and eschatological tradition – a tradition that was alien to the Therapeutae. They were only interested in the realization of a holy way of life, cultivated through individual contemplation.

The name of the sect itself proves that the Therapeutae were Buddhist monks. Philo did not know what the name really signified. The riddle has only been solved in the recent and excellent research by Zacharias P. Thundy, a specialist in the application of linguistics to religion. The word *therapeuta* is itself of Buddhist origins.[18] It is the Hellenization of the Sanskrit/Pali term *theravada*, which was the name of the Buddhist school whose members set off from Gandhara to the West. The despatch of missionaries was decided on at Asoka's council at the suggestion of Moggaliputta Tissa, who founded the Theravada order. So it was mainly Theravada monks who made their way to distant countries. In Greek there are no equivalent sounds for the labio-dental voiced fricative *v* and for the apico-dental (articulated with the tip of the tongue) fricative *ð*. Hence the Indian *v* and *ð* were changed to *p* and *t* in Greek. Thundy shows that the same displacement of sounds happened in Clement of Alexandria's Greek translation of Buddha as 'Boutta'. The *p* in Therapeuta is only the voiceless form of the bilabial voiced *b*. Thundy offers another example with the Tamil word *karuva* (cinnamon) which Ktesias translated as *karpion*. As we have seen with Theravada, the *v* is changed here to *p*.

It may not even be necessary to refer back to this displacement of sounds to explain the way the Therapeutae referred to themselves. It is conceivable that the Theravadins, who established the monastic community in Egypt, called themselves Theraputta ('Sons of the Old Ones') as a derivation from Theravada ('Teachings of the Old Ones').[19] It was probably mainly young monks who made the long, difficult and dangerous journey to Alexandria in an unknown foreign country, and their self-designation as 'Sons of the Old Ones' would have been highly appropriate.

The words 'therapist' and 'therapy', which are so familiar nowadays, were applied to the major activity of Philo's Therapeutae: healing. Only through the name given to this group did the word gain its well-known meaning in Greek. Philo thus links the name of the sect with the meaning 'healers of souls' without really comprehending the connection. That is why every now and then he also calls the Therapeutae 'supplicants' and 'beggars'. The Sanskrit word *bhikshu*, designating a Buddhist monk, means exactly the same – the literal translation would be 'beggar', someone who requests alms.

The Alexandrian Therapeutae are the Theravada Buddhists Asoka sent on a mission to Ptolemy II Philadelphos, and they really were dispatched with the express task of working as healers of people and animals. Asoka's Girnar Rock Edict states: 'In addition Piyadasi's [Asoka's] dual system of medical assistance will be introduced everywhere within the area ruled by Antiochus, the Greek king: medical assistance for human beings and medical assistance for animals, together with all kinds of medicaments suitable for humans and animals.'

The edict also proclaims that Asoka has had healing plants fetched from distant countries and planted in many places where they did not previously exist. At the start of the *Lalitavistara* the Buddha is extolled as the 'King of Medicine'. A hymn from the same passage exalts: 'O you who are experienced in healing, true doctor, swiftly transport those who suffer to the bliss of Nirvana with threefold remedies.' Healing and redemption belong together in Buddhism; they are the two fruits of a single effort. Like their master, the Buddha's followers were intended both to bring 'medicine for healing souls' through the proclamation of the Dharma and also to apply their abilities to heal bodily through progress in their meditative practices.

Philo's enthusiasm for the Therapeutae is more comprehensible in the context of his philosophical and religious tracts. There he develops chains of thought that are closely based on Indian models. He thus explains that appearances by God and the angels in the Old Testament are to be understood as a kind of *maya* or sensory illusion. He skilfully combines Indian concepts of *maya*, the deceptive world of the senses, with Platonic ideas so that as early as 1828 Isaac Jacob Schmidt was convinced: 'Various peculiar Buddhist features are to be found in

Philo.'[20] We can add that Philo learned this from the Therapeutae he so revered.

We take particular notice, of course, when Philo says that the Therapeutae would abandon their homes 'without looking back after they had left behind their brothers, children, women, parents, all their relations, all their friends and companions, and even the countries in which they were born and brought up'.[21] This passage can only be interpreted in a Buddhist context. Such a radical breaking with all human ties, especially those with the family, was inconceivable within Jewish society. Sticking together in settlements was of great importance for Judaism in the diaspora. Only one tradition involved uncompromising separation from all family ties as especially the 'way into homelessness': Buddhism. And only one man in Palestine used exactly the same words in calling on his followers to break all family contacts from one moment to the next: Jesus. The key to the mystery of how Jesus chose the words of Buddhist disciples for his teaching lies hidden in the sect of the Therapeutae. This is the crucial link.

The same passage also provides another valuable hint that Philo mentions more or less in passing. The Therapeutae-to-be did not merely leave all their relations; they also left the countries in which they were born and brought up. If that had really been a Jewish sect, such a statement would have been incomprehensible. In that case, we would assume that novices were recruited from the big Jewish communities in Egypt, which had been mainly settled in and around Alexandria since the third century BC. However, Philo lets us know that quite a few members of this sect came from *other* countries *after* they had grown up there. Obviously descendents of Asoka's Buddhist mission to Alexandria, the Therapeutae still received an influx of brothers from their home country.

The colony in Alexandria should not be viewed as a static set-up. The Buddhists at Lake Mareotis continued to maintain contacts with their fellow countrymen. This city, open to the world, was well suited to that. Sylvain Lévi, the French historian, assumes that the great trading enterprises in Alexandria were often visited by the 'adventurous priests' (as he calls the travelling Buddhist monks) who were driven beyond their national borders by curiosity and a sense of mission.[22] The Buddhists were probably attracted by fellow believers already in Alexandria, rather than by the important merchants. Ongoing exchange with their home country also led to the new ideas and texts that developed there being brought to the West.

The Bodhisattva: Idea and Dissemination

Taxila in Gandhara may well have been the place where these monks originated. It was a city whose structure, settlement and importance were comparable with Alexandria – the city where Asoka published an edict in Aramaic, the city which was the starting point for the trade routes to the West, the city which very early became the most important northern centre of Buddhism. The historic significance of Taxila-Sirkap in the sphere of East–West exchanges has been most unjustly underestimated and almost completely ignored.

Less than 30 miles from the present-day Pakistani cities of Islamabad and Rawalpindi, Taxila was then the most important city in the region, along with Pushkaravati (now Peshawar). Its name derived from Takshaka, a legendary ruler, and the city was originally called Taksha-sila, the hill of Takshaka.

Various important trade routes came together there. One originated in the Ganges plain and eastern India, and Megasthenes wrote of this Royal Road leading from Paliputra to the north-west of the empire. The other started in western Asia, reaching Taxila by way of Bactria, Kapisi, Pushkaravati near Ohind, and along the Indus. The third route came from Kashmir and Central Asia through the Srinagar valley, Baramula and Mansehera into the Haripur valley. It was mainly thanks to these three essential links that Taxila became highly important, with a growing in its population and an increase in its status.

After the introduction of a money economy by the Achaemenids (from 522 BC) Taxila was of even more interest as a trading place, linked as it was through the Achaemenid world to distant countries and even with Egypt. In many respects the city led the way in new developments. It was there that *puranas* (long pieces of silver) were first used as means of payment, thereby greatly encouraging trading. The people of Gandhara obviously took over this private form of legal tender, which was issued by the merchant guilds, from the contemporary Babylonian system of coinage.[23]

However, Taxila was by no means just a trading centre. As one of the oldest of northern India's 2000 towns, it was celebrated far and wide for its university, where the three vedas, ritual, and the 'eighteen sciences' were taught. People eager for knowledge poured into the city from all the principalities. Its fame as a centre for education is extolled in the Buddhist *Jatakas*. In those Pali texts we discover that many princes and noblemen came to be educated at Taxila from as far away as Magadha: young brahmins, Khattiya princes, and the sons of rich merchants from Rajagriha, Kasi and Kosala. Jivaka, King Bimbisara's famous court doctor who also healed the Buddha, was one of those who learned the art of medicine at Taxila under a much-esteemed teacher. Prasenajit, the ruler of Kosala, who was closely linked with events during the Buddha's lifetime, was educated there too.

After consulting contemporary accounts and archaeological discoveries, one is inclined to speak of an 'Alexandria of the East'. Sir John Marshall's excavations revealed finely carved stones, highly polished sculpture, glassware, and coins from the sixth century BC – all of a quality that was not to be exceeded in later centuries in India. New ideas of course streamed into Taxila as a centre of scholarship, and the proclaimers of fresh concepts could hope to gain a hearing. Pupils of the Buddha probably went to Taxila at an early stage so as to preach the Dharma.

We have shown how Seleucid diplomatic relations with Maurya rulers at the Maghada court gave rise to detailed reports (started by Megasthenes) about conditions in India at that time. Megasthenes was followed by Deimachos and Dionysios whose descriptions have, unfortunately, all been lost. That is particularly regrettable because these envoys certainly came to Taxila, and were in India at a time when Buddhism was on the point of achieving great significance. It can be assumed that they came into contact with Buddhists, who already lived in Magadha and also in Gandhara. That was particularly the case with Dionysios who was envoy at the court of Bindusara and later Asoka.

From Taxila there was a northern route to China as an alternative to the Silk Road. It led through the western Himalaya area between Mansehra and Thakot to the Indus, and along that way many Buddhist buildings can be found. These testify in stone to the great influence the monks exerted along the paths around Taxila. Ancient reports tell of Buddhism reaching China, and the court of Ch'in Shih-huang-ti, by way of this northern route in the third century BC. Most researchers have questioned the reliability of such accounts, but it is certainly possible that Buddhism was known in China in the centuries before the start of the new millennium.[24] One indication of this is provided by obvious borrowings from Buddhist ideas in such old philosophical tracts as the *Huai-nan-tzu*, a collection of writings by scholars around Prince Liu San, dating from the second century BC.

At any rate, the region around Taxila experienced an enormous influx of Buddhist monks in Asoka's time. After the Council's decision to send out missionaries, these Theravada monks set off in various directions to preach the Dharma. Two of Asoka's sons, Mahinda and Sanghamitta, went to Sri Lanka, and the monks Sona and Uttara to Burma.[25] Many other monks went to the upper Indus valley where they established an important culture much influenced by Buddhism, and it was from there that the mission to the West was launched. Even after the start of the new millennium, adherents of the Mahayana and Theravada schools were settled in the oasis towns of Central Asia. A form of Buddhism influenced by Hellenism developed in Gandhara and the Swat valley. From there it spread across the Oxus into the Tarim Basin.[26] That area lay on the caravan routes of the celebrated Silk Road, it is today the Chinese province of Sinkiang. In the first century AD the Bezeklik frescoes were painted there; they depicted the spread of Buddhism and showed a group of believers of different races, including a Syrian.

The Buddhist settlements in Taxila were enormously strengthened by the arrival of monks. Asoka had a large stupa erected, which bore his name. In a Buddhist text the Emperor was designated Dharmaraja ('King of the Law'), so the edifice became known as the Dharmarajika Stupa (Plate 24). This monument was probably built on top of the relics of the Buddha that Asoka had sent to all parts of the country during his lifetime. The stupa is constructed around a circular core with strengthening walls as the spokes of a wheel, thus depicting the *dharmachakra* ('wheel of the law'). The form taken by this construction was in itself intended to remind monks engaged in walking meditation there of the concept of the Dharma.

This Dharmarajika Stupa constitutes the focal point of old

Buddhist foundations. Around it are grouped many monasteries and stupas from various epochs, with the largest settlement at Kalwan, about 1¼ miles south-west of the Dharmarajika. Most of these monasteries were outside the city walls near rivers or close to spring water. They indicate the diversity of Buddhist schools established around Taxila, with scholastic exegesis of the Buddha's teachings the main occupation of learned monks. The interpretations of these different schools were gathered together in the *Abhidharmapitaka*, the most famous collection of scholastic writings.

Why is Taxila and the entire area around Gandhara of such importance for our investigation? On the one hand, because Buddhists originally set out from here to Egypt, and, on the other, because it was from here that the Therapeutae were supplied with new currents within Buddhism – developments that explain the particular manifestation of Jesus.

It was at Gandhara that the Buddhist Mahayana school was established and furthered through the writings known as the *Prajnaparamita* (*Perfection of Wisdom*). In those texts, written between around 50 BC and 150 AD, the emphasis was on mystical insight. Their authors contested the *Abhidharma* which asserted that intellectual understanding could lead to satisfactory knowledge of absolute truth. Mahayana focuses on the bodhisattva ('enlightened being'). That concept is of great importance for our thesis, since the original Jesus was not just a Buddhist preacher living as a wandering monk; more important still was the fact that he absolutely incarnated the bodhisattva.

The developments which led to this important concept got under way at a very early stage in the history of Buddhism. The foundation stones were laid during the second Buddhist Council at Vaishali, about a hundred years after the Buddha's death. At that time the teaching split into two great schools: those of the Sthavira ('Adherents of the Oldest') and those of the Mahasanghika ('Members of the Great Community' – because they constituted the majority) out of which the Mahayana school developed from the first century BC. When leading Buddhists gathered under Asoka at Pataliputra on the Ganges for the third great council in the mid-third century BC, the monks ascertained that teachings were being handed down differently within those two factions. The words of the Buddha had long been subjected to differing interpretations, and additional schools and sects had been established, adapting Buddhism to divergent theological frameworks. This third council was thus of decisive significance for the further shaping of Buddhism.

The idea of the bodhisattva became crucial in this new comprehension of religion. In terms of practical implementation, the bodhisattva surpassed the non-conceptual wisdom of the *Abhidharma*'s holy man (*arhat*) who merely sought his own redemption.[27] In the Mahayana view, on his way towards buddhahood the bodhisattva perfects six virtues: generosity, morality, patience, energy, meditation and wisdom. Generosity involves giving both material and spiritual things, and also a growth of compassion whereby the merits gained are not kept for oneself but instead made available for the redemption of other beings. After Siddhartha Gautama no one implemented those virtues so urgently as the original Jesus.

When the new millennium got under way, no absolutely clear division between Hinayana and Mahayana as yet existed. Mahayana ideas were to be found among the Theravadins, and sculptural depiction of the Buddha, which is characteristic of Mahayana, began in the Sarvastivada Hinayana school at Gandhara under Kanishka I.[28]

As a great intellectual centre and important trading place, Taxila was well suited to the communication of the new religious ideas to the West. From there the caravans of Asoka's missionaries travelled by way of Palmyra to Syria; from there the Indus valley trading routes ran to the harbour of Barbarikon where ships from the Red Sea tied up. The Buddhists took the new concepts and writings to the northern regions of Syria and Mesopotamia, and in particular to Edessa where over the years they established an inseparable link with Christianity; and they brought their new ideas by sea to their religious fellows in Egypt. The Buddhists in Alexandria remained in contact with their homeland and learned about new theological developments by way of Taxila. From that time onwards a spiritual axis linked Alexandria and Taxila, those two great cities of religious scholarship. The Therapeutae on Lake Mareotis soon strove to implement the bodhisattva ideal, living in accordance with the ethical rules (*bodhisattva-shila*) which were viewed as the precondition for that way. Historian Sylvain Lévi assumed that Buddhist propaganda managed to introduce simple, touching prescriptions of love and universal compassion into the West because the idea of the humble, self-effacing bodhisattva had spread among the Therapeutae. This teaching was directed towards the lower classes in Hellenistic society which were already inclined towards the Orient and seized by Messianic hopes. Missionary endeavours held back from the intellectual upper class, so Buddhist texts in the West did not undergo any literary regeneration.

In Palestine people no longer knew anything about the youth of Jesus because it had not been spent in that country. We have seen that almost all the New Testament stories about Jesus's childhood and youth are legendary and based on eclectically assembled texts. One of these stories is to be found in the Gospel according to Matthew and became a favourite theme for painters: the Flight to Egypt. According to the Gospel, an angel warned Mary and Joseph that Herod wanted to kill all boys under the age of two in Bethlehem after having heard from the Wise Men from the east that a star had announced the birth of a ruler over Israel. The parents thereupon took the infant Jesus to safety in Egypt and remained there for several years until Herod died.

Infanticide to remove someone predestined to succeed to the throne is a well-known motif in legends, encountered in the stories of Krishna, Moses, Zeus, Perseus, Oedipus, Romulus and Augustus, and can hardly lay claim to historical credibility. In addition, it is not clear why this little family should flee to Egypt. The distance to their home in Galilee was only about 60 miles, whereas the journey to Egypt was much further and more hazardous, taking them several hundred miles along the coast by way of Gaza. Matthew, however, knew why this inconvenient place of refuge had been chosen: in fulfilment of the Old Testament proclamation, 'I called my son out of Egypt'. Those words from Hosea (11:1) clearly refer to Moses, who led the people of Israel out of Egypt, but Matthew made use of the infanticide motif from the treasury of legends, and of the phrase 'my son' in the Jews' holy writings, to justify the fact that Jesus spent his youth in Egypt, which could not otherwise be explained.

That detail fits perfectly into all that we have presented up to this point. People knew nothing about Jesus's younger days in Palestine because he spent many of them in Egypt – with the Therapeutae. The flight to Egypt was nothing but a literary veiling of a memory about the young Jesus having been brought to the Therapeutae in Alexandria where he was educated in Buddhist teachings. An obscure tradition was pre-served and came to the surface again, embellished with that mythological adornment and artificial gloss of historical events imposed, like a crown of laurels, on anyone of importance in the history of religion or the world.

Jesus had plenty of time to make progress in Buddha's teachings among the monks at Lake Mareotis. From his later way of teaching and the impression he made on people, there can be no doubt that he was an intelligent, alert boy with a heart and mind open to the timeless insights of Shakyamuni Buddha. He would certainly have devoted considerable thought to the new ideas the *bhikshus* brought to Egypt from Taxila – to the figure of the bodhisattva out-shining every-thing. Perhaps the monks also realized what an exceptional human being the young Jesus was. They may have viewed him as a bodhisattva, educated him accordingly and then later sent him out on his homeless journey in the knowledge that an 'enlightened being' had appeared in that part of the earth to open the eyes of humanity and bring about their redemption.

We do not know how long Jesus lived with the Egyptian Buddhists. It is possible that he even travelled to India[29] – although that is not necessary as an explanation of the original Jesus's Buddhist teachings. We have seen that during his life-time the Therapeutae formed a completely intact community of Buddhist monks which preserved their sacred texts and lived in accordance with the rules and regulations of Bud-dhism. Since Jesus was a Jew the monks thought it advisable to send 'their' bodhisattva to his homeland, and Jesus was in fact later to say that he had been sent to 'the lost sheep of the house of Israel'. From time immemorial Egypt had been a place of refuge for Jews with their synagogues, schools and teachers, and Jesus also had an opportunity there to study the holy writings of Judaism. It is even to be assumed that his Buddhist teachers encouraged that. That was understandable in view of the fact that it was intended that Jesus would work among Jews, and also in view of the respect for other religions inculca-ted in their predecessors by Asoka. Whether Jesus as a twelve-year-old really did astonish priests in the Temple at Jerusalem must remain uncertain. There is, as we have shown, a Bud-dhist parallel for that, and the motif of the 'wise boy' is an archetypal pattern within heroic legends. On the other hand such an occurrence would by no means have been impossible after the thorough schooling Jesus enjoyed. In any case it would not have been advisable to return before 6 AD, when Jesus was twelve or thirteen. Archelaus, one of Herod's sons, was the cruelly tyranical Governor of Judea and Samaria until he was banished in 6 AD.

Around 30 AD, when it was time for Jesus, the bodhisattva, to return to Palestine to spread Buddhist teachings among his fellow countrymen, an appropriate way was sought. After his discipleship in Egypt he had to find out more about Jewish religious feelings and ideas, so the obvious move was to spend time with people who had some affinity with the Therapeutae. There was only one possibility – the Essenes.

The Essene Connection

Why the Essenes? First because our source, Philo, went so far as to assert that the Therapeutae and the Essenes were two groups within a single orientation. For him the Therapeutae were the theoreticians and the Essenes the practitioners. He also asserts that the Essenes in Palestine and Syria were identical with the Magi in Persia and the gymnosophists in India. 'Gymnosophists' was the name given to Indian wise men, without making any distinction between brahmins or Buddhists. The Therapeutae surely maintained spiritual relations with the Essenes, so Jesus could hope to get to know Jewish religious thinking better there than was perhaps possible in Egypt, and also to find sympathetic listeners for his own message. When Jesus made his public appearance, he did so amid the ranks of the people of Qumran and the baptists – in other words, amid Jewish sects obviously linked with the Essenes. These relationships were to characterize both the dissemination of his teachings and their mutilation. However, let us not leap ahead.

The similarity between Essene and Buddhist ideals is so obvious that by now there are an immense number of books concerned with the question of how Buddhist thought reached the Jewish Essenes. If we accept Philo's assessment, then it would have been through the Therapeutae. In the nineteenth century the theologian Adolf Hilgenfeld saw the Essenes as involving 'Jewish religious teachings fertilized by the seriousness of Parseeism and the universal characteristics of Buddhism', and as the soil 'from which the mustard-seed of the Christian world religion was to grow'.[30] Ernest de Bunsen, the Dutch researcher, assumed that Buddhist ideas were introduced to the Essenes by Jews living abroad, and that they later influenced the shaping of Christian dogmas.[31] So who were the Essenes?

Many people today believe that this question can be answered better than ever before now that the Qumran texts have been largely elucidated and many scholars accept that the inhabitants of Qumran were Essenes. In fact the texts have complicated matters, and it is only possible here to present the most important aspects of this currently unfolding, exciting period from the roots of the Western religious tradition.

Not even the origins of the term 'Essenes' have been fully clarified. Philo linked 'Essenoi' or 'Essaioi' – Pliny writes 'Esseni' – with the Greek word *hosios* ('holy'). The Greek *hosios* probably shares the same root as the Indian *isi*. Samuel Beal, the well-known expert on Buddhist literature, thinks it probable that the name of the Essenes derives from *isi* – in the plural *isi* or *isayo*.[32] The Magadhi or Prakrit word *isi* means 'saint' or 'holy man'. By adding *maha* ('great') you get *Mahesi* (the Great Saint), a title often given to the Buddha. It has sometimes been thought possible that the name originated in the *Avesta*, the holy writings of Zoroastrianism, possibly being derived from the word *ashavan* which also means 'holy' or 'pious'.[33] Another interpretation is based on the Essenes' work as healers, eliciting the name from the Aramaic *'yssyn* ('healer'), producing a suitable Semitic origin for the Greek form.[34] As was seen in discussion of the Therapeutae, holy conduct and a life as a healer belong together. The corresponding terms are themselves already related. Thus both forms of derivation can lay claim to correctness.

In their research into the community's roots and the identification of the inhabitants of Qumran as Essenes, some historians of religion have hit on the Hassidim (the Pious) as possible precursors. In the second century BC the Hassidim were a group of militant opponents of Hellenism. Others, however, believe that the Hassidim paved the way for the Pharisees; and yet others think they were the forerunners of both the Essenes and the Pharisees. All the same, the word 'Essene' cannot be shown to originate in 'Hassidim' or its Syrian equivalent.

This discussion stands and falls with classification of the people of Qumran, which causes researchers so many headaches. On the one hand, several passages in the Qumran texts indicate that spiritual healing, the healing of sins, was the community's fundamental doctrine,[35] which would bring them very close to the Essenes and the Therapeutae. On the other hand, the name 'Essenes' never occurs as a self-designation in the sect's many writings. The people of Qumran called themselves either *Bene Sadok* (Sons of Zadok) or *Ebjonim* (Community of the Poor). The latter seems to have been widespread since the anti-Pauline original Jewish Christians called themselves Ebionites. In the *Damascus Document* the people of Qumran recorded what was involved in their mission: 'The Sons of Zadok are the chosen ones of Israel, "the Called of the name", that will appear in the Last Days' (CD, Dam IV, 3:4).

Jesus appeared in the orbit of the Qumran people, and obviously there was some link between Qumranis, Essenes and Therapeutae. So we must investigate that axis in order to be able to depict the route the original Jesus took from the Therapeutae back to Palestine, and to better understand his followers' attitudes. We thus first consider the Essenes independently – leaving aside the Qumran writings and their inner connection with the Egyptian Buddhists – so as to determine the sect's origins and significance, before turning to the question of whether the people of Qumran can really be identical with the Essenes.

In his most important historical work *The Jewish War*, Flavius Josephus writes: 'Among the Jews there are three schools of philosophy – the Pharisees, the Sadducees, and finally the Essenes of whom it is generally said that they are concerned with a special form of self-hallowing.' As a sixteen-year-old Flavius Josephus decided to 'test' which of the three sects was the best, but was not really convinced by any of them. However, he had probably not summoned up the patience to last out a novitiate in even a single one of these religious groups. He may have gained some degree of personal insight into their ideas and customs but would have received most of his information from third parties. He reports that the Essenes were of Jewish origin. He emphasizes their friendly dealings with one another and their admirable sense of community. They did not think highly of marriage, but they were not completely against it. Material possessions, which they abhorred, were handed over to the sect, and neither humiliating poverty nor arrogance-engendering wealth were to be found among people who neither bought nor sold. They rejected every sensuous pleasure. Abstinence and resistance to desires were viewed as virtues. They did not use aromatic oils and always clothed themselves in white garments. They adopted a humble attitude while walking 'as if they were afraid of a teacher'. Josephus says that the Essenes were spread over several towns, while Philo maintains that they mainly lived in villages and avoided towns. The individual community groups were led by administrators, who managed their affairs. Travelling brothers could make use of the property of local communities, and were welcomed as old friends. They thus travelled without baggage and only had weapons to defend themselves against robbers. Philo stresses the Essenes' pacifist attitudes much more than Josephus, expressly mentioning that they did not produce any goods which could be employed for warlike purposes, and that they viewed violence as being godless and destructive of the laws of nature.

The Essenes did not speak about any lower worldly matters before sunrise. They followed an old custom of saying a prayer to ask God to make the sun rise. Then they washed themselves and before entering the *refectorium*, which was like a holy room for them, they put on a linen apron that seems to have had some ritualistic significance. They took a simple meal in silence, and then devoted themselves to their work until evening. Silence always prevailed in the community rooms, a silence that for people outside – as Josephus remarks – seemed like 'an awe-inspiring mysterium'. Josephus thought that the tranquillity which the Essenes radiated was a result of constantly upheld sobriety and restraint, with no more than the necessary amount of food and drink being taken.

The Essenes reached their own decisions about whether assistance should be given or compassion practised. They kept their feelings under strict control and did everything for peace. Their main occupation involved dedication to the study of their sacred writings. They also investigated medical plants and the healing properties of minerals.

A novitiate lasted a year, putting to the test the candidates' steadfastness in renunciation. After successfully completing that phase, they were allowed to come closer to the community and participate in the sacred baths. Their character was then assessed for two further years. Before the novice was admitted to the important shared meal, he had to swear to revere the godhead, practise righteousness, abstain from harming anyone either voluntarily or on command, and, above all, remain faithful to authority. In addition he vowed to love truth, uncover liars, abstain from stealing, avoid striving for sinful profit and refrain from having secrets from other members of the sect. He promised to hate the unjust and to support the struggle of the righteous. Alongside God they revered the name of the law-giver to the highest degree, and anyone who did not do so was punished with death.

Bodily things meant little to the Essenes since they are subject to transience. They felt themselves to be governed by destiny. In Josephus's description, their idea of the soul seems highly Platonic. For the Essenes the soul is said to have descended out of the finest ether to be made captive in the body, and it is only after death that it rises again on high. Then the soul of the righteous comes into a paradise beyond the ocean, while that of the evil enters a gloomy, ice-cold cave.

In these descriptions we recognize some correspondences – but also differences – with the Therapeutae. What is striking is the fact that the Essenes shared many customs and attitudes to life with the Buddhists, which accounts for the many comparisons made between the two groups.

Contempt for wealth and the establishment of communal property is a conspicuous attribute of Buddhist lay discipline. King Asoka gave all his belongings to the order and supported the sharing of goods. Caring for the body with oils is specifically proscribed in the Buddhist community. In the *Vinayapitaka* lay followers are called the 'white-clad'. Buddhist communities also have administrators (*karmadana* – 'donors of deeds') who look after a convent's general secular requirements. Taking in travellers is absolutely characteristic, since Buddhists were wandering monks who only spent long periods in monasteries during the rainy season. They were, however, also mendicant monks and as such never pursued a trade. From Chinese travellers in the early centuries of the new millennium we know that prayers were spoken in Buddhist monasteries at sunrise and sunset. The words of Buddhist prayers are to be found in the *Pattimokkha*. Samuel Beal, an ardent defender of the thesis that the Essenes carried on Buddhist ideals in Palestine, remarks: 'The Essene's rules about showing respect for older members, the taking on of novices and the actions leading to exclusion from the community are all typically Buddhistic.'[36] The shy and humble attitude of the Essenes is strikingly reminiscent of the Buddha laying down that his monks should always walk with the head lowered. The bodhisattva's self-description could be taken from an Essene rule-book: 'As a bodhisattva I keep my spirit firm and unshaken, friendly and steadfast, full of respect and reverence, full of shame and fear, calm and only concerned to serve others, in all impeccable things constantly subordinating the ego to the essence, and free of pride' (*Shikshāsamuccaya*).

The basic principles of mutual assistance, controlling outbursts of feeling, unconditional respect for all life and openness towards members of the sect are all eminently Buddhist ideas and prescriptions. The Essenes' studies of nature for medicinal purposes can perhaps also be seen as survivals of Asoka's mission which also proudly exported healing plants and medical knowledge.

For 200 years now there has been speculation about the origins of the Essenes, their roots and their influences. A great variety of views exist. Some saw the Essenes as a Jewish revivalist movement seeking to implement a universal priesthood as an expression of the true Israel (in accordance with Exodus 19:6), while others date the sect's origins back to the time of the Maccabees when some 'pure ones' imagined that the temple cult in Jerusalem had got into the wrong hands. The pure are then said to have split off and established their own community. The Qumran community is also often believed to have originated in the problems of the Maccabee period, so let us take a brief look at those historical events.

After their return from captivity in Babylon the importance of the people of Israel declined. The comparatively small population was isolated and no longer enjoyed political autonomy. With the decline of the Achaemenidic empire the protection of their liberators came to an end. Problems increased within their national borders. The people lacked a sense of purpose, and the foreign influences brought back from captivity breached the original religious tradition. The threat of losing their national identity loomed. It was probably during that period that there arose the expectation of a Messiah, an ideal ruler from the House of David. He was to bring the age of salvation as the end of history; he was to be the representative of God's rule and to restore to the people of Israel the importance they naturally claimed as the Chosen People. The joyous reception in Palestine of Alexander the Great in 332 BC must be seen against that background. Of course he was not the hoped-for Messiah, but he brought innovations which were to face Jews faithful to the law with harsh tests in the decades and centuries to come. As a cosmopolitan representative of the Greek spirit, Alexander himself was very interested in Jewish customs, morals and ideas about religion. However, the priesthood could not comprehend why he showed a similar interest in the despised religion of the Samaritans.

When Ptolemy I came to Palestine during the struggle for power in Egypt, he was also welcomed by a large part of the population. When he left again, he took a considerable number of Jews to settle in Egypt. In the spirit of Hellenistic generosity he granted them full freedom of belief since he hoped that they would decisively strengthen the part of the population devoted to him. From that time the Jews were registered in Alexandria as an established component in the population and assigned to two of the five districts. The Jewish quarter was in the northeast of the city, beyond the harbour on Lake Mereotis (Plate 30).

However Judea, which at that time comprised only the area around Jerusalem, was annexed from the start of the second century BC to the basically anti-Jewish Seleucid empire which extended as far as India. A momentous crisis developed there under Antiochos IV Epiphanes (175–164 BC). Antiochos staked everything on Hellenizing the Jews by force. He obviously hoped to achieve renewed cohesion by imposing a unified syncretistic form of religion throughout his crumbling empire. He was supported in that endeavour by the Jewish aristocrats, who enjoyed a fashionable lifestyle. The upper class was very much ready to make compromises since Hellenism promised a fresh blossoming of intellect and a comfortable existence in this backward area. Support even came from the upholders of the religious legacy of the forefathers, since the priesthood was controlled by the nobility. The high priest, Onias III, did try to resist Hellenistic innovations, but he was overthrown by his own brother Jason whose first move on taking over this office was to establish a Greek-style gymnasium in Jerusalem. Jason was contemptuous of the Temple of Jahweh and neglected sacrifices. Everywhere beyond Judea's constricted boundaries Hellenistic towns shot up overnight. Now Jerusalem was also to become a city after the Greek model. In the countryside, however, the voice of traditionalism made itself felt. A wave of national resistance swept the land. Street battles became an everyday occurrence and led to a prolonged guerrilla war.

Antiochos did not consider giving up. He hit back in a way calculated to enrage Jewish believers. On the place for burnt offerings in the holy of holies in Jerusalem's Temple he had an altar erected to Zeus Olympios; in 167 BC he issued a decree making circumcision or possession of the Torah punishable with death; and he plundered the Temple treasury and burnt down large parts of the city. Fearing for their lives, many Jews fled to the desert and the mountains. The dissolution of the cult of Jahweh and the attempt to destroy the national character by banning specifically Jewish ways of life plunged the people of Israel even deeper into a crisis of identity that had long been smouldering. In this desperate time of persecution there developed the apocalyptic writings, principally Daniel[37] and Enoch with their characteristic ideas about the 'son of man' and the sufferings of the children of Israel. The Israelites placed their faith in a reversal of the conditions that prevailed in the world. Ultimately the powerful would stand alone before God's judgement. The Book of Enoch gave expression to those expectations: 'And in that place my eyes saw the chosen ones of justice and faithfulness; and justice will reign in those days . . . and justice and right will have no end' (Enoch 39:6ff).

As the refugee problem extended over the entire country, Mattathias, an old priest at Modein, resisted the innovations. He struck down a respected citizen who wanted to make a sacrifice on the newly established heathen altar. Then he and his five sons killed the royal commissioner, destroyed the altar and fled to the mountains. There they assembled a group of the dissatisfied who called themselves the Hassidim (the Pious). By night these Jewish fundamentalists set out to kill royal officials and Hellenized Jews. Surprisingly, this small group achieved many successes of this nature. On his death-bed, Mattathias advised his followers to choose his third son, Judas, as their leader. He became known as Judas Maccabaeus, and his revolt could never be completely suppressed. When Antiochos was out of the country in 164 BC, engaged in a campaign against the Parthians, the rebels prepared for a decisive blow. Lysias, Antiochos's regent, suffered a considerable defeat. The Seleucids had no alternative but to ease the repression once again. Judas was allowed to occupy Jerusalem, religious freedom was re-established, and the Temple was purified at the winter solstice, three years after the profanation of the Temple. Today the annual Chanukka festival recalls that reinauguration.

Viewed from a neutral standpoint, the Maccabean revolt frustrated the beginnings of religious tolerance, and led to an intensification of the observation of the law under sectarians. The Essenes are said to have been one of the groups that emerged out of those struggles against the Hellenists.

From the middle of the second century the Seleucid empire increasingly disintegrated, and Rome started to show an interest in the region. Judea experienced a period of expansion into the neighbouring areas of Galilee, along the coast of Samaria, into Transjordan and even as far as Idumaea and the Hellenized Decapolis. Under the leadership of Jerusalem priests filled with new self-assurance, the Jews resorted to the same kind of ethnic suppression that the Seleucids had directed against them. Enforced Judization was pitiless and territorial integrations were violent. From 104 BC both the priesthood and royalty became hereditary. Around 70 BC the Pharisees succeeded in reversing that state of affairs because of an incompatibility of interests. After the death of Aristobulos (36 BC) the office of High Priest again fell into the hands of just a few families, but an advisory body, the Sanhedrin, was established and soon gained great political influence.

In the decades leading up to the new millennium, the Jews once again, and irrevocably, came under foreign dominance. The Romans added Judea to their empire, dispossessing the ruling dynasty of the Hasmoneans. They set the Idumaenean dynasty under Herod against its last representative, Antigonos, who allied himself with the Parthians. Then the innovations against which Mattathias and his followers had once rebelled were again introduced into the country. In the years from 39 to 4 BC Herod installed a city on the Greek model, representing the interests of Rome. This time, however, people were more circumspect. Herod behaved unobtrusively. He tolerated the office of priesthood, lived in accordance with the law, and had the Temple resplendently extended. Nevertheless, distrust spread among the population once again. It could not be denied that all these innovations were at the behest of a foreign power and subject to non-Jewish ideas. Jewish sects, whether militant or pacifist, returned to the apocalyptic writings of the Maccabean period, applying their prophesies to the present day. Never were the people of Israel more intensively permeated by messianic hopes of intervention by God as in those decades around the turn of the millennium.

Perhaps the reasons for the formation of a sectarian group that was to become the Essenes really did lie in the Maccabean era. Maybe the Essenes did come together, like the Hassidim, in opposition to Hellenization. However, events during the 200 years before the end of the millennium do not constitute a sufficient explanation for the Essenes' specific way of life and their non-Jewish convictions. Over the course of time more and more scholars have had to concede that, even if their roots do lie in the epoch of Maccabean revolt, the Essenes have no place in the development of Judaism. These scholars suggested a wide variety of influences as an explanation for that state of affairs: Alexandrian Hellenism, Iranian Parseeism, Platonic thought, Babylonian ideas and even Pythagorism. All those assumptions were intended to explain those elements which – as we have seen – were so closely linked with Buddhist monastic attitudes to life.

In that context the influence of Pythagorean ideas on the Essenes was important, especially as Pythagoras practised Indian religious thinking and monastic forms in the West. Many were more ready to attribute comparable customs among the Essenes to the geographically closer Pythagorean schools than to distant India. The comparison of the Essenes with the Pythagoreans is nothing new. The similarity was already apparent to Flavius Josephus as contemporary chronicler, who liked treating his educated Hellenistic readers to comparisons with Greek schools of philosophy. For instance, he thought the Pharisees 'approximately comparable' with the Stoics. He wrote with great conviction of the Essenes that they lived in a way that Pythagoras had implemented among the Greeks. And had not Pythagoras taught a way of life derived from an Indian source? And did not Philo also compare the Essenes with Indian gymnosophists? There is no doubt that it was a specifically Buddhist influence which led to this idiosyncratic religious community, unparalleled throughout the Jewish cultural area. It is probable that this influence came by way of the Therapeutae in Egypt whom Philo linked closely with the Essenes. All the signs are that either endeavours to expand the Alexandrian Therapeutae's mission led to successes in Judea, or Alexandrian Jews may perhaps have brought the ideas of the Therapeutae to Palestine as early as the third century BC, where they led a hidden existence in small groups. Jewish believers could be won over to the ideals of the Therapeutae without having to renounce their own forms of culture and religion. During the Hellenization crisis the Essenes become a monk-like community uniting two world-views, the Buddhist and the Jewish, faithful to the law.

The Mystery of the People of Qumran

The discovery of the scrolls in the Qumran caves led to the justifiable hope of solving the mystery of the Essenes once and for all. However, precisely the opposite happened. First, all such investigations became more difficult because the Qumran texts were only reluctantly and incompletely made available; and it now becomes apparent that the picture of the Essenes handed down by Josephus, Philo and Pliny must be revised if we still wish to maintain that the people of Qumran represent *the* Essene community. That view has the backing of those Qumran researchers whom Michael Baigent and Richard Leigh call the 'consensus' in their much-discussed book.[38] By that they mean a group of scholars who followed the Vatican's diktat in withholding certain texts from publication in order to maintain the thesis that there are no indications of a 'Christianity before Jesus' among the people of Qumran. But that view is not securely founded; matters are more complicated. But let us not jump the gun.

The origins of the Qumran sect are still obscure. The information contained in what is known as the *Damascus Document* (CD, Dam) can be interpreted in different ways. This text was not found in the caves of Qumran. It was discovered by Solomon Schechter as early as 1896 in the Caraic Geniza, a synagogue in Old Cairo. Only after the discoveries at Qumran could that document, made available in 1910, be clearly attributed to the Qumran community. The *Damascus Document* speaks of the 'Age of Anger' having begun 390 years after captivity under Nebuchadnezzar (CD, Dam 1:5). At that time a group opposed specific religious practices, cut its ties with former allies, and went into voluntary exile where it established a community of chosen members. So it may be that the Qumran group established itself as a Jewish protest movement[39] around 170 BC and set up an autonomous religious party as part of the Jewish reaction against violent Hellenization. Perhaps that was directly sparked off by the murder of Onias III, who supported the Essene aims, by Menelaus, a Hellenist, around 171 BC (2 Maccabees 4:31–38).[40]

The *Damascus Document* is so designated because the manuscript mysteriously refers to Damascus as the place of exile. Scholars dispute what Damascus refers to here. Does it refer to the city of Damascus, far to the north, beyond Galilee and the Decapolis, or was it a code, perhaps indicating where the sect originated? Taken literally, 'Damascus' could point to a time the community spent in exile close to Damascus, or to the fact that a specific group within the sect lived at Damascus. As a coded name this might also refer to Qumran – the desert settlement as place of exile. But perhaps Damascus (following Amos 5:27) points to Babylon. The solar calendar of the Qumran group seems to derive from Babylonian roots, so the sect's mysterious origins may date back to the time and place of the Babylonian captivity.

That link with Babylon should not be underestimated. For the people of Qumran the writings of Isaiah – of which Chapters 40–55 were written in exile and Chapters 56–66 afterwards – were of particular importance. The outbreak of a new time of salvation, glorifying the role played by war, was shaped by a passage in Deutero-Isaiah (Isaiah 40:3). The ritual baptismal baths implemented at Qumran in cisterns especially constructed for that purpose, and the activities of John the Baptist very close to the settlement, strengthen the presumption that the people of Qumran preserved customs they had brought from Mesopotamia. In the Land of the Two Rivers baptist communities were a long-established tradition, and in the third century AD Hippolytus, the pursuer of heretics, reported that members of sects were baptized in the flowing waters of the Euphrates. The designation of John the Baptist as a 'Nazorean' also goes back to a Babylonian term. The Assyrologist Heinrich Zimmern has shown that in ancient Babylonia *nasaru* (or *nasiru*) meant 'keeper of divine secrets'. The term seems to have been brought back to Palestine with the return from exile.

Babylon itself was of course hated by the Jews. That is why

only isolated cult practices were brought back to the homeland. But what the precursors of the Qumran people did carry back to Judea out of exile were numerous elements from their Persian liberators' Zarathustrian religion.[41] During the epoch of Babylonian captivity Zarathustra taught – probably in Bactria (modern Afghanistan) – a cosmic dualism involving Ahura Mazda (Ohrmazd), the god of light, and Angra Mainyu (Ahriman), the god of darkness. The rigorous dualism that later seemed to be the norm[42] in the Qumran texts certainly originated in Persian teachings. The important Qumran *Community Rules* (1QS) are particularly strongly marked by Iranian and Zarathustrian ideas.

Even if the Qumran material is only superficially considered, it immediately becomes apparent that these are Jewish texts. At first sight little is to be seen of foreign influences. The writings are predominantly concerned with issues within Jewish fundamentalism, the Law and the prophets. For the people of Qumran the Mosaic Law was the foundation for their thoughts and deeds. They constantly read aloud in turn, under their master's supervision, from their holy books, meditated on those passages, and interpreted texts with regard to the contemporary situation. Anyone who 'seeks the Law day and night' should never be absent, said the *Community Rules*. Despite such typically Jewish elements, the people of Qumran had an elitist view of themselves. They saw themselves as the only legitimate heirs of Moses and thus as the elect within a 'New Covenant'. They thereby made one thing clear: it was by no means sufficient to be born a Jew in order to belong to this 'New Covenant'. To implement the true Israel demanded personal effort and a full-blown initiation.

What seems on a superficial reading of their revered books to be a typical Jewish sect turns out on closer consideration to be a revivalist movement whose development is not comprehensible in terms of traditional Judaism. The reforms at Qumran were so many and so unusual that they led to a complete transformation of traditional Judaism. So if the evolution that had led to the Qumran community is not explicable within Jewish tradition, on what is it based?

André Dupont-Sommer, professor of Semitic language and culture at the Sorbonne, was one of the most influential specialists in Buddhist antiquity as well as a leading researcher into the Qumran texts. He is almost unrivalled for the insights he gained into those two worlds and for his skill in comparing Buddhists and the people of Qumran. His studies led him to conclude that the Qumran community was most certainly influenced by Buddhism.[43] He bases his case mainly on the term for community (*jachad*), which was of great importance in Qumran, and on scattered Buddhist echoes, especially in the Qumran text *The Testament of the Twelve Patriarchs*. He views the commandment of compassion, which threads through the entire work like a leitmotif,[44] culminating in an invitation to love everyone and banish hatred from their hearts (*Testament of Gad* 6–7), as a clear borrowing from Buddhism. Remarkable too are elements that derive from the ideas of Asoka's monks: compassion for all living creatures, animals as well as human beings; and the idea that God will treat everyone as he treats those nearest to him (*Testament of Sebulon* V:1–3).

Such a judgement from a respected scholar, proclaiming the Qumran people to be secret Buddhists, has particular weight and strongly supports our investigations. On the other hand, it must be borne in mind that Dupont-Sommer was one of the most determined adherents of the thesis that the people of Qumran were the same as the Essenes whose Buddhist roots are obvious.[45] So let us first investigate that view rather than precipitately combining the two groups.

Pliny's account should stop us from impulsively treating the Qumran community and the Essenes as equivalent. Pliny, whose book appeared in 77 AD, was obviously in Palestine during the war since he records the destruction of Jerusalem, En Gedi and Jericho. His description of the Essene settlement is probably as it was in the period after the war, and cannot be Qumran since its inhabitants were driven out by the Romans around 68–9 AD. From that time until at least 74 AD Qumran was occupied by Roman soldiers and not by Jews, as excavations have shown.[46]

The decisive factor is the correct translation of Pliny's Latin description of a location. He notes that the previously flourishing town of En Gedi, which at the time of writing lay in ruins, was 'below the Essenes'. Many have assumed that that meant lying to the south, thus identifying Qumran with the Essene settlement. Chirbet Qumran[47] is in fact about 20 miles north of En Gedi, but only about 12 miles east of Jerusalem. Why did Pliny mention the more distant and unknown En Gedi rather than the closer and celebrated Jerusalem? Perhaps he mentioned it for a completely different reason, since his statement could be read in a totally different way: it could be that the Essenes he was talking about lived on a hill above En Gedi. That would also solve the problem involved in the fact that Qumran had been in Roman hands for well over a decade before Pliny wrote.

Another difficulty in identifying the Qumran people with the Essenes resulted from the excavation of the cemetery there. In seven of the forty-three graves opened there were women's skeletons, and in four others children's bones. Unlike the Essenes the Qumran people were probably allowed to marry; at any rate, celibacy is not advocated anywhere in the Qumran texts. Nevertheless, we should not make too much of marriage in this context, especially as Flavius Josephus is not completely free of ambiguity with regard to Essene views on that subject. Scholars have paid little attention to an assessment by Dionysios Ben Salibi who maintained that the Essenes were married but did not touch their wives for three years. When the women became pregnant later, they were left alone for another three years. Sexual relations were thus only allowed for the procreation of children.[48]

There are other striking differences. There is no record of the Qumran community having employed the prayer to the sun used by the Therapeutae and Essenes. Nothing would have been more alien than for the Essenes to have become involved in trade. They only lived for spiritual progress. The Qumran people, on the other hand, were highly pragmatic in that respect. They were even allowed to trade with the 'sons of depravity', provided payments were made in cash (CD, Dam, XIII 14:15). The Essenes categorically rejected animal sacrifices, but the Qumran people were only opposed to the forms of sacrifice practised at that time. The Essenes were not allowed to swear oaths whereas the Qumran members could do so in specific circumstances. And unlike the Essenes Qumran clearly expected a Messiah.

The most striking difference involved attitudes towards the use of weapons in disputes. The Essenes were certainly peace-loving and for that reason were generally accepted. They only carried weapons for self-defence. The people of Qumran, on the other hand, seemed infected by the virus of zealotry, and antagonized everyone.

In the Qumran texts, heterogeneous though they may be,

the pronounced dualism which we have shown was imported from Iran cannot be overlooked: the Sons of Light stand against the Sons of Darkness (*Kittim*), truth against lies, purity against fornication. The *Community Rules* clearly state that the sect was brought up to hate the Sons of Darkness for ever. What is known as the *War Scroll* (1QM) even invokes the final battle between Light and Darkness as a holy war between believers and unbelievers. Righteous earthly warriors would then fight alongside the heavenly powers against their dark opponents who were supported by Belial and his evil crew. The final cosmic struggle would begin 'when the Sons of Light returned from emigration in the "Desert of Peoples" and pitched their tents in the wilderness before Jerusalem' (1QM I:3), and that would lead to establishment of 'the rule of a king' (1QM VI:6).

The *War Scroll* is a sober report, almost like a teaching text, constituting a remarkable contrast to the amazing events described. At any rate the book must have been held in high esteem at Qumran since four fragments of several manuscripts were found in the caves. The ideas presented in it and related texts are exceptionally close to those of the Zealots. That increasingly removes the Qumran people from the Essenes as described by Philo and Josephus.

The date of this text is of decisive importance in evaluating the Qumran people. If it were a very old text, then we have to assume that the Qumran community never consisted of peace-loving Essenes but from the start was a bellicose faction of Jewish fundamentalists. Some presume that the highly active role of the Sons of Light in the struggle indicates that the *War Scroll* must be dated to the early Maccabean period, even before the community was established at Qumran. The *Kittim* would then be Seleucid Hellenists. However, that seems unlikely. The detailed military instructions in the *War Scroll* most probably derive from a Roman war manual, which puts the date of writing in the first century AD. The *Kittim* were thus obviously the Romans.

What is to be thought of that? Did the people of Qumran undergo a transformation from gentle Essenes to Zealots deploying war-like speeches? Let us consider the age and nature of the other writings from Qumran to find an answer to that question.

Fourteen samples taken from those manuscripts were made available in summer 1990 for radiocarbon dating tests at Zurich

Technical University, employing the modern BMS method.[49] The oldest sample was first dated 405–354 BC and on another occasion 306–238 BC, and the youngest 675–765 AD.[50] That result is strange and confusing. The site was no longer inhabited after the Jewish War and the destruction of Qumran. Who would still be interested in depositing a manuscript 700 years later in a cave in this inhospitable area? It would have to be assumed that such a person knew about the other manuscripts in the caves or else his action would be meaningless. But if it was known that manuscripts were preserved in the caves, manuscripts that would certainly have been of great importance even at that time, then one must ask why they were not kept in a secure place.

Hiding scrolls in caves in the Judean wilderness was obviously a widespread practice, and not just limited to the area around Qumran. Origen reports that a manuscript was found in a cave near Jericho in the second century AD. The Nestorian Archbishop of Baghdad, Timotheus I (around 800 AD), tells of an Arab hunter who found many books in a rock-cleft, also near Jericho. The alarmed Jews identified them as biblical books and over 200 of the psalms of David. Religious writings were not only found in the wadi Qumran. Ancient texts were discovered in several wadis on the steep eastern slope of the Judean desert – at Murabba'at, Nahal Hever, Nahal Mismar, Chirbet Mird, and even the Zealot stronghold of Masada. An indication of the hiding of precious goods is provided by the *Copper Scroll* from Qumran. This is revealing in various respects. The coarse, large handwriting with irregular lines, the mention of many historical places, and the margin notes in Greek[51] are a clear sign that this text is an original and not a copy. At the end we find the information: 'In a cleft . . . to the north of Kohlat, with an opening towards the north and below graves, there is a copy of this manuscript with explanations, measurements, and details of each individual hiding place' (*Copper Scroll* XII:10–13). Details about hidden treasures, diverse books and texts hidden in many places in the Judean wilderness are recorded with pedantic accuracy. The *Copper Scroll* shows that valuable objects, including highly esteemed manuscripts, were concealed at various places in the desert which were reachable through the wadis that led from Jerusalem to the Dead Sea.

What is the significance of all this? Is it possible that not all of these writings belonged to Qumran, or were the inhabitants of Chirbet Qumran ultimately not linked with the texts at all? For any assessment of the Qumran group it is decisive whether these manuscripts belonged to a sect that lived in this area and – as archaeologist Father Roland de Vaux assumes – used the buildings as a monastery. The extent of the library is astonishing. In the eleven caves were found no fewer than 823 diverse manuscripts, with 580 in Cave 4 alone. All the texts involve religious subject-matter, and none is concerned with scientific, historical or medical themes. In Cave 7 there were only Greek writings. Among the manuscripts were canonical texts from the Hebrew Bible (so-called *Pescharim*),[52] pseudo-epigraphica (falsely attributed writings), and texts only known from Qumran, which were probably written in the community or incorporated in the library (e.g. the *Rules of the Community*, *Genesis-Apocryphon* and the *Temple Scroll*).[53]

Is it at all possible that the Qumran monks wrote this enormous amount of material? One would have to assume the existence of many hundred copyists, who in this inhospitable desert of all places had nothing else to do but transcribe holy writings. The amazing number and variety of texts indicates that they came from different centres, perhaps even from Jerusalem.

Moreover, all the Qumran manuscripts are copies with the exception of the *Copper Scroll*. Not a single one is an author's original autograph. So can we still speak of the sect's own books when we have nothing but copies? In other caves in the Judean wilderness many original texts have been found, such as letters and documents from the Bar-Kochba period (the start of the second century AD), but not a single official document was discovered at Qumran. Scholars wonder whether the lack of autographs and official documents shows that the scrolls did not belong to the Qumran community but were the remnants of various libraries from Jerusalem. The Qumran Institute at Groningen attempted to solve this mystery by way of the Groningen Hypothesis, which suggests that the manuscripts in the Qumran caves belonged to the Qumran library but were not all produced there.

What picture of the Qumran community do we gain from these contradictory facts? We know that in the Palestine of that time there were many groupings, associations and communities of interest which are not adequately designated in the well-known classifications of Sadducees, Pharisees, Essenes, etc. History has brought to light a number of other sects, and there are certainly many more about which we have no information and may never learn about. Furthermore, in the first centuries of our millennium the Qumran people could already look back on 200 years of history as an autonomous group – 200 years in their self-chosen desert solitude, where they could well have moved on from their original Essene ideas.

The fact that virtually no autographs were found indicates that the sect was dependent on other, older schools. The scrolls represent currents within old Judaism, so the texts do not necessarily all come from Qumran, and may perhaps have been put in the caves at different times. In their diversity the manuscripts characteristic of Qumran also reflect a syncretist community. The Essene elements (including the Buddhist), which certainly play a part in these writing, suggest that the Essenes were the older current from which the Qumran community derived. The Qumran books talk explicitly of a breach in the history of the sect's development, of a splitting away from a larger group. The assumptions of Florentino Garcia-Martinez, director of the Qumran Research Institute at Groningen University, who speaks of the Qumran people separating from the Essenes,[54] also tend in that direction. According to the *Commentary on Habakkuk* (1QpHab), the founding phase of the community occurred during the time when Jonathan and Simon were the high-priests. It may be that the break with the Essenes had already come under John Hyrkanus (142–104 BC) when the Qumran people followed a mysterious leader, the Teacher of Righteousness, as their 'interpreter of knowledge'. In the *Damascus Document* it is reported that those who 'recognized their sins' strayed for twenty years as if they were blind. 'Then God took note of their deeds since they sought with all their heart, and he gave them the Teacher of Righteousness to guide them along the way of his heart . . .' (CD, Dam I:10f.).

Perhaps this mysterious Teacher of Righteousness thrust his fellows towards their old roots from the period after the exile, so that Babylonian and Zoroastrian relics came to the fore again. The community's basic tone became more inflexible, tougher and increasingly permeated by an apocalyptic and prophetic spirit. When the sect settled in the Qumran area after twenty years of wandering under their Teacher of Righteousness, they did so firmly believing in the imminent arrival of the Messiah. Their beliefs and development give us reason to believe that they furthered the cause of the baptist communities close to John, whose concerns were very similar to their own.

An early separation of Qumran people and Essenes is quite possible. It cannot be definitively said whether that separation really was connected with the mysterious Teacher of Righteousness, but the many texts that refer to the community's exodus, or report on the intensification of the laws and the Teacher of Righteousness, are strikingly more recent than many people assume. For instance, the laboriously reconstructed *Miqzat Maaseh Ha-Thora* ('Some Thora Customs') presents an intensification of the law as a special feature of the Qumran *Halacha* ('Ritual Law'). This text, precipitately dated to the second century BC, is said to be Sadducean in character. It presents the earliest members of the sect as rejecting the situation after the Maccabean revolt (168–164 BC) when the Maccabeans succeeded the Zadokite priesthood. In that case the Qumran people cannot have been linked with the second-century Hassidim, the opponents of Hellenism who provided the Maccabean's priestly leadership.[55] In fact, only in one of the twenty laws can a 'demonstrable link with the ritual law of the Sadducees' be demonstrated.[56] In addition, the Hebrew idiom of the text is completely different from almost all the other known manuscripts. Hence this text can only have been written in the first century AD when the dialect employed can be shown to have existed.

The three mysterious figures who have been the object of much divergent speculation probably belong to the community's late phase: the Teacher of Righteousness, the Man of Lies, and the Wicked Priest. If the Teacher of Righteousness really had been an important founder figure, we would expect to read much more about him in the Qumran manuscripts – but little is heard of him, only in the *Damascus Document*, the *Commentary on Habakkuk*, and in a Psalms-Pescher. Those texts are among the most recent in the entire Qumran library. Palaeographic tests show that the *Commentary on Habakkuk*, the source of most of our knowledge about the mysterious teacher, dates from the first century AD.

The Man of Lies was probably a Qumran member who split away from the community. He probably spread another doctrine – false in the eyes of adherents of the Teacher of Righteousness

– and even waged war against the latter. The community of the Man of Lies, and the man himself, was often simply called *Ephraim* (Samaria). The Wicked Priest seems to have never been a member of the Qumran community. It is questionable whether he really was a historical figure or just a characteristically Hellenistic literary transposition of the Greek tyrant as a prototype of the group's opponents.

The Teacher of Righteousness must certainly have been an important leader. Some researchers assume that the *Hymn Scroll* should be attributed to his time, and that it was perhaps even written by him. One indication of that is provided by the statement: 'You have established me as a sign for the chosen ones of righteousness, and as translator of understanding wondrous mysteries' (1 QH 2:13). Such declarations, reminiscent of mystery religions together with the 'Metaphysics of Light' in the *Hymn Scrolls*, constitute obvious Hellenistic elements. If these texts really were written by the Teacher of Righteousness, he must have been a man permeated by a Hellenistic spirit alongside all the seriousness of his Jewish religiosity. The *Hymn Scroll* is as it were a book of meditation against the background of the terrors of the end of time, unparalleled in Jewish literature. What is new about the text is the Hellenistic way of spiritual conduct expressed there.[57]

After a period of wandering around aimlessly, the Teacher of Righteousness directed his Qumran flock to the right place. The few mentions of that leader and the dating of the manuscripts shift him to the first century AD. What event is entailed in the time of wandering?

During excavations at En el-Ghuweir on the western shore of the Dead Sea, 10 miles south of Qumran, archaeologists have found a building similar to the one at Chirbet Qumran, which housed another settlement of the Qumranians.[58] Like En Gedi, Ein Feshkha and the Qumran site, this was destroyed during a Parthian invasion around 40 BC. The population of En Gedi and the other oases on this western shore thus declined dramatically between 40 and 37 BC. For decades the area was almost completely abandoned. The whereabouts of the Qumran people during that period are unknown.[59] Was this the time when they were leaderless and homeless, the period of twenty years of wandering referred to in the *Damascus Document*? The return from those wanderings under the leadership of the Teacher of Righteousness could refer to the resettlement of

Qumran in the early years of the new millennium. If that was so, those who followed the Teacher of Righteousness once again took possession of Qumran, while other groups perhaps followed the Wicked Priest and the Man of Lies. The adherents of the Wicked Priest were probably opposed to Qumran being taken over by the Teacher of Righteousness's group, since they persecuted him even there on their holy day.[60]

In the land given the code name of Damascus, the people of Qumran established the 'New Covenant', an idea that only re-emerged in Christianity: 'in accordance with the laws of the members of the New Covenant in the land of Damascus' (CD Dam VI:19).

Our reconstruction thus produces the following picture of the Qumran community. The people of Qumran were a group of Jewish religious fanatics whose mythical roots were influenced by Mesopotamian and Persian ideas, and in the second century BC they were part of the Essenes. From the Essenes they mainly kept the Buddhist-derived monastic way of life and the fundamental concept of community (*jachad*). Over the course of time the Qumranians underwent an evolution. In their sectarian seclusion they distanced themselves increasingly from their original Essene characteristics. During their expulsion from Qumran when Parthians destroyed the site and the group wandered around, a more aggressive undertone developed among their ranks. An important leader, the Teacher of Righteousness, finally led them back to the caves and the community centre of Qumran, promising the beginning of the Last Days and the appearance of the Messiahs of Aaron and Israel. The 'Neo-Qumranians', who repossessed their old settlement soon after the start of the new millennium, had added a zealotistic view of the world to their dualist ideology, and were ready to employ weapons in the final battle. They had to move out of Qumran before the Jewish War. Perhaps, as in Masada, Zealots had settled there for a while, allying with a number of particularly bellicose Qumran people. Towards the end of the 60s Qumran was finally taken by the Romans. The *War Scroll*, which dates from that time and is linguistically clearly different from the *Community Rules* and the *Damascus Document*, could only have come into existence as a Zealot 'import' as part of this new spiritual direction.

The Chirbet Qumran site was really more appropriate for a fortress than a monastery. There was a fortified tower, large cisterns and a water system for long sieges. Little had remained of the Qumran people's former study areas. People were pre-occupied with something more important: the struggle against the Sons of Darkness. Josephus, fighting as a commander on the side of the Romans, confirms that the Essenes took part in combat. He probably meant the people of Qumran, who were still viewed as an Essene sect. It is not therefore surprising that archaeologists only found the remains of three desks (including two inkwells) and not a single piece of parchment. For many people this signifies that Qumran was never a monastery with an important *scriptorium* but was only a Zealot fortress. After all, just like in the caves of Qumran, a Hebrew version of the *Book of Sirach* was even discovered at Masada, the Zealot stronghold. The connection between Masada and Qumran should not be neglected. A fragment of the only recently published *Songs for the Sabbath Sacrifice*, which have been shown to originate at Qumran, even turned up at Masada.

The explanation is obvious. Before the Jewish War the former monastery with its baptismal basins and study-cells had been transformed into a fortress. The cisterns, which could hold 39,800 cubic feet, were ideally suited for storing water. In times of emergency water could also be fetched from the nearby wells at Ein-Feshkha. All important writings were stored in caves outside the site. Texts from various phases of the community thus came peaceably together. Perhaps other religious groups also learned about this outstanding hiding place and when war got under way brought some of their manuscripts to safety here.

How the Qumran Community Launched the Jesus Myth

The aim of our investigation is not to go through the Qumran material in detail, searching for its meaning. We only present it here to elucidate the relationship between the Qumran people and the Essenes, including the connection with Jesus's appearance very close to Qumran.

After his return from the Therapeutae in Egypt, Jesus perhaps spent some time with the Essenes. Later he decided to join the baptists and maybe also the people of Qumran. All those who were dissatisfied with the religious situation at that time flocked to the barren area around the Jordan. Jesus hoped they would listen to his Buddhist teachings. A statement from the Book of Q makes it clear to whom he wanted to direct his message: 'The poor are given good news' (QS 16). By that Jesus did not mean he only intended to preach to the poor; he meant the people of Qumran since they called themselves 'the Poor'. Jesus drew attention to himself with unprecedently radical views which contrasted with those of the great John. He rejected baptism and dismissed the strict asceticism taught by the Baptist. Instead he presented the Buddha's middle way, advocated love and freedom from worry, and won over both baptists and Qumranians.

It was these disciples of Jesus – former followers of John the Baptist and of the Qumran people[61] closely linked with the Johannine tradition – who wanted to convert sectarians to their new faith. Through them ideas that were familiar at Qumran found their way into the Gospels. So let us consider for a moment the 'Qumran fragments' that we encounter in the New Testament so as to see how the words of the original Jesus were transformed.

The Qumran people's relations with Iranian thought will have decisively influenced the fact that a number of characteristically Zarathustrian ideas shaped the mythology of Christianity. The doctrine of the great redeemer was particularly prominent in Zarathustra. Men were said to have been sent from God several times during the course of history, proclaiming the truth; those were the historical prophets. However, they would all be outshone by God's final envoy, the saviour, with whose arrival the Last Days began. As the saviour he was the equivalent of God himself – 'Thy equal, O Lord'.[62] Of him it is said that he would teach humanity 'the straight ways of salvation', would free the world of evil, participating in the resurrection and directing the final battle against the Evil Spirit. He would also be born of a virgin mother whom Zarathustra called 'the woman who surmounts everything'. There is no need to emphasize what importance those mythical ideas about the Final Days were to assume in Christianity.

For Qumran, the expectation of a messiah (or two messiahs)

was very characteristic. A Qumran text which foreshadowed the situation in the community of Israel at the End of Time spoke of how the Messiah would be conceived and born (1QSa 2:11). It may also be that Jesus's adherents in the Qumran group recognized this 'begotten Messiah' in their master, and Christian mythologizing later turned him into a divinely generated and resurrected Messiah. Interesting too is the fact that the text links the appearance of the Messiah with the seating order during the communal meal at the 'table of unification', which demanded that no one should 'stretch out his hand before the priest for the first portion of bread and wine since it is the priest that blesses the bread and wine, and first takes the bread. After that the Messiah of Israel stretches out his hands for the bread, and blesses the entire community of the unification, each in accordance with his dignity' (1QSa 2:17–21). It is obvious that the narrative of the last supper is a literary imitation of this eschatological meal at Qumran. It probably originated through those of Jesus's followers who still remembered the symbolic significance of the communal ritual meal from their time at Qumran. In addition, people at Qumran believed that 'the community of unification would then stand firm in truth' and, consisting of twelve perfected men, would free the country of sin (1QS 7, 1:4–7).

That is not all. In the Qumran manuscript numbered 4Q 246 there is mention of a 'Son of God', who will bring peace to earth, will be lauded in God's name as His son, and will be called 'Son of the All-Highest'.

Even the self-designations of the Qumran people were taken over by the early Jesus groups and the first Christians. They called themselves the 'Poor in Grace' or 'Poor out of Grace' (1QHod 5:22), the 'Community of the Poor' (4QPs 37,2:10), the 'Poor of Thy Redemption' (1QMil 11:9), and even the 'Poor in Spirit' (1QMil 14:7) – a designation perhaps even referred to in one of the beatitudes in Jesus's Sermon on the Mount.

Elements from mystery religions reached Qumran by way of Alexandria as something typically Hellenistic, and are to be encountered in depictions of the person of the great leader. His followers designated the Teacher of Righteousness as being the man to whom 'God has revealed all the mysteries of words as his servant, his prophet'. He is depicted as an initiate of the highest degree. That is characteristic of the Hellenistic fashion for viewing religion as an ecstatic Gnostic mystery. The idea of the darkness of the divine revelation is un-Jewish and is absent from presentations of apocalyptic ideas.[63] In the *Community Rules* initiated members are commanded 'to keep silent about the truth concerning all mysteries of knowledge' – a typical formulation in initiation in Hellenistic mystery religions. Those followers of Jesus who preserved the Gospel of Thomas as a holy text later spoke of their master as being an 'authority on the mysteries' (like the Teacher of Righteousness), who called on his pupils to do as he did: 'Jesus said: The Pharisees and the Scribes took the keys of knowledge, and they hid them. Neither did they enter, nor did they allow those who wished to enter. But you, become prudent as serpents and innocent as doves' (Thomas 39).

Time and again one is involuntarily reminded of Jesus in depictions of the Teacher of Righteousness. The Qumran people who joined Jesus naturally had a vital interest in presenting him in accordance with that model. The parallels can be summarized as follows: like the Teacher of Righteousness Jesus came forward as leader of a 'community of the New Covenant', directed his preaching and call for repentence and a change of ways to the 'last generation' as the end of the world approached, advocated fulfilment of the law (Matthew 5:17) and voluntary poverty, and denounced the high priests and Scribes. We have already come to know many of these elements as expansions of the Q^2 Sayings Source. They were thus implemented by those who followed on from disciples directly linked with Jesus. After looking through the first Qumran manuscripts, Cambridge researcher Jacob L. Teicher already assumed that the figure of Jesus had been modelled on the Teacher of Righteousness and Paul was to be seen as the Wicked Priest and Man of Lies combined.[64] That evaluation now takes on particular significance. Teicher stressed the claim to messiahship attributed to both the Teacher of Righteousness and Jesus. The Messiah longed for at Qumran was to unify priestly and royal blood – just as is maintained Jesus, who was said to descend on his mother's side from Levi and on his father's from Juda. On the Day of Judgement it would be not God but his chosen representative (Jesus/the Teacher of Righteousness) who would pass sentence on humanity. This completely un-Jewish teaching now turns out to be not a Christian speciality but rather something taken over from apostate Qumranians who concocted a Jesus myth. Jesus was by no means the mysterious Teacher of Righteousness; he was simply endowed with the Teacher's characteristics, linked with Qumran's messianic expectations, and entered history as founder of the 'New Covenant'. The ex-Qumran people and the ex-baptists, who had by then become the literary upholders of the Jesus movement in Q, used certain Qumran writings as a background for their work on the Jesus myth. That enterprise occurred only decades after Jesus had vanished, and it may well be that many of these writers had never met him. It is to be assumed that most of them were only born after the end of his public mission, and perhaps were only recruited from their previous sects by Jesus's eager Q followers during the war period. To them relating Jesus and the Teacher of Righteousness may not have seemed in any way unfounded.

As far as expectations of the End of Time are concerned, connections between Qumran and Christianity provide an interesting area for future research. The Enoch texts revered by the Qumran people, and perhaps also developed by them, were also highly esteemed in the Jesus movement. In fact the Jesus people thought so much of them that they uninhibitedly based many of the words of Jesus and the apostles on them. Here is just one example: 'In those days nations will be in turmoil and peoples will rise up on the day of their undoing' (Enoch 99:4). In his discourse on the final days, Jesus is supposed to have said: 'For nation shall rise against nation, and kingdom against kingdom' (Mark 13:8; Luke 21:10). All the motifs of Jesus's apocalyptic sermons – with prophesies of earthquakes, plague, hunger, injustice, suffering and distress – were to be found at Qumran and in the Enoch writings. Those similarities were not welcomed by Catholic theologians since they inevitably led to doubts about the originality of the supposed founder of their religion. There was thus a purge in the fourth century, in which numerous Hebrew manuscripts were destroyed and the Book of Enoch had to vanish from the canonical writings.

The first Qumran people and baptists to follow Jesus were filled with eschatological and apocalytpic thoughts. They probably listened eagerly to what Jesus had to say because the Teacher of Righteousness's proclamations to the 'last generation' about a Messiah had not been fulfilled rather than because they were profoundly convinced by his teaching. In Jesus they were confronted with such an unusual personality, above all conventions, prescriptions and legal restrictions, that they

were ready to see him as really being the man 'who was promised'. And that constituted Jesus's main problem in getting his
Buddhist message heard.

That radical ethic interested his listeners only peripherally.
They wanted to know that the redeemer sent by God had at
last come to free them from all suffering. From the start Jesus
had to struggle against his followers' messianic fanaticism.
James and John, the sons of Zebedee, even asked him to grant
them the best positions in the messianic Kingdom of Heaven
(Mark 10:35–37). Luke 4:14–30 presents the most detailed version
of the story of Jesus at the synagogue in Nazareth when he
proclaimed the coming of the Last Days but rejected people's
hopes that he might fulfil their expectations of that time. Enthusiasm turned to rage, and Jesus had to seek safety to avoid
being thrown off a cliff. It was certainly not easy to preach the
Dharma, proclaiming freedom from worry and love of one's
enemies, to people so emotionally permeated with ideas about
salvation during the Last Days, involving a messianic victory
over all opponents of the Chosen People. How could that teaching be made compatible with completely different expectations
of the future? Today we know that they could not be made
compatible, that Jesus ultimately failed, and that the Pauline
church, moving away from the ideas of the original Jesus and
elevating him instead as Christ, could never surmount the
contradiction between his teachings and the syncretist theology
of power.

The successors of the Qumran people could at least understand the original Jesus's message of compassion, and integrated
it into their view of the world which had been preserved in their
own tradition in the *Testament of the Twelve Patriarchs* from the
distant period of the Buddhist-Essene past.

In the New Testament we also encounter a whole series of
sayings by Jesus which either take up Qumran ideas or oppose
practices cultivated there. Many of them may once again derive
from the upholders of the Jesus movement, but it could also
be that Jesus himself took over various attitudes and ways of
behaviour from the community, and spoke against others. Both
are possible since the words of the original Jesus were aimed
directly at the community's members. In the *Damascus Document*
one of many ordinances regarding the Sabbath runs: 'No one
may help an animal give birth on the Sabbath. If it does so in
a ditch or a cistern, it should not be helped out on the Sabbath'

(CD Dam XI 13:14); and 'If a living person falls into the water or elsewhere, he should not be helped out with a ladder, a rope, or anything else' (CD Dam XI 16:17). Obviously Jesus had the Qumran community's raw, inhuman reading of the law in mind when he responded to the question of whether one could heal on the Sabbath: 'What man shall there be among you, that shall have one sheep, and if it fall into a pit on the Sabbath day, will he not lay hold on it, and lift it out?' (Matthew 12:11).

The original Jesus certainly also gave love of one's enemies and unconditional respect for all life as the main aspect of right action in his great Sermon on the Mount because he was all too well aware of his first followers' wrathful hatred of their foes. They were still completely caught up in the Qumran spirit of mercilessness towards the Sons of Darkness. The postscript to the sixth antithesis in Matthew's version of the Sermon on the Mount, which we have seen as part of the elucidation of Buddha's 'five precepts, is thus specifically directed against that Qumran attitude: 'Ye have heard that it hath been said, Thou shalt love they neighbour, and hate thine enemy' (Matthew 5:43). To whom could that clear statement have been directed if not to the people of Qumran – especially as extreme hatred of one's enemies was unknown among the Pharisees and Sadducees? One passage in Matthew also seems to contain a warning[65] against the theology of Qumran people as those dwelling in the wilderness: 'Wherefore if they shall say unto you, Behold he is in the desert; go not forth' (Matthew 24:26). That warning against self-proclaimed desert prophets and Qumran hopes that the Messiah would reveal himself in the wilderness came either from Jesus himself or from his followers.

Also of interest in that connection is Jesus's saying about the rock (Peter) on which he will found his church (community) (Matthew 16:18; John 1:42). That was probably added by the Jesus people since it is clearly taken from Qumran's *Hymn Scroll*. There we read: 'Thou [God] layest the "foundation" on rock' (1GH 6:25f.). In this passage the community appears as God's construction. Johann Meier[66] shows in his translation that *swd* (community) was often not distinguished from *yswd* (foundation). The later followers of Jesus who wanted to demonstrate that Jesus had founded their church borrowed the comparison from the *Hymn Scroll*.

Healing through the laying on of hands was practised at Qumran. That seems to have been a survival from the community's Essene roots. The Aramaic *Genesis-Apocryphon* states: 'He bid me come to pray for the King and to lay my hands on him that he might live ... And I laid my hands on his head and the plague left him, the evil spirit removed itself, and he lived.'[67] Immediately after his first appearance Jesus is presented as a great healer. He lays his hands on people everywhere, freeing them of illness, afflictions and evil spirits. He certainly appeared as a wandering monk who could heal, since his training with the Therapeutae included the implementation of the Buddha's call to heal people in body and soul. Nevertheless, many of the miraculous healings in the New Testament seem to be literary inventions. The practice of the laying on of hands was known to the Jesus people from Qumran, but in order to elevate their master as the most unusual of all visionaries, prophets and healers they resorted to an interesting propaganda idea that may in fact derive from his very first disciples. In order to maximize the attention Jesus quickly attracted as a healer for their mission, they spread the news about his miraculous successes everywhere, and also said that their master always insisted that those healed should tell no-one about this (e.g. Matthew 8:4, 9:30). Viewed psychologically, that was a clever move. It was thus made clear that Jesus was not any old healer but a man surrounded by mystery, about whom one should maintain silence. Of course that was the best guarantee that news about this man of miracles would spread all the more rapidly. Threats aimed at imposing silence do not sound like the original Jesus, and it is clear that this demand was not followed. The most detailed information we have about Jesus's early activities concerns precisely what should have been kept quiet – the healings.

The ill-considered way in which the disciples sometimes attributed miraculous healings to Jesus is shown in an event which supposedly happened in the Decapolis, on the eastern shore of the lake of Gennesaret. There the great healer is said to have sent the evil spirits possessing two men into a herd of swine which promptly rushed off a cliff to their death, whereupon the incensed herders understandably chased away the strange magician (Matthew 8:28–34; Mark 5:1–17; Luke 8:26–37). It is quite incredible that the original Jesus would have staged such a repulsive exhibition. The story merely demonstrates the degree of inventiveness shown by Christian authors wishing to present their master as the most important of all. In their selection of miracles they made use of tales currently in circulation about the deeds of many of antiquity's famous men of miracles, such as Epimenides, Pythagoras, Empedocles and even Plato, who was posthumously believed to be the son of Apollo. Empedocles was said to have healed the sick, awakened the dead, called up storms and predicted the future. The similarity with the miracles attributed to Jesus is sometimes amazing. Just think of the passage in which Jesus called on Peter to cast out his fishing nets once more (Luke 5:1–7). This is based on a tale about Pythagoras who told fishermen at Kroton how big their catch would be if they let down their fishing nets again.[68]

Contemporary heroes in the war against the Romans may also have served as models for this literary reconstruction at the time when most of the material was gathered together, alongside the Qumran texts and the figure of the Teacher of Righteousness. From Josephus for instance we know of the fate of Menachem, a Galilean with astonishing similarities with Jesus, in 66 AD. Like Jesus, he was a 'son of David', and as a leader of the Sicarians, he had provoked the Jewish uprising. He was born in Bethlehem, moved into Jerusalem as king, occupied the Temple, was betrayed and killed. Rudolf Augstein has drawn attention to these remarkable parallels, and speculates that Mark employed information about Menachem – a name that means 'comforter' and was later used instead of 'Messiah' – as the basis for his narrative about Jesus.[69] Interestingly, it has also been suggested that Menachem was the Qumran community's Teacher of Righteousness.[70] Since we know that the texts referring to this teacher all date from the first century AD, it is quite possible that he was a Zealot from that period.

All these parallels make it clear that the biography of Jesus was shaped by viewpoints current in militant Jewish circles and was not unique, as the Gospels would like us to believe. Against the background of an inflated number of self-designated Joshuas/Jesuses, the correspondences between the Teacher of Righteousness, Menachem and Jesus show that all three figures were products of related spiritual circles. The reason why we find so much Qumran and Johannine material in the Jesus movement's writings at levels Q^2 and Q^3 is that the Q people wanted to include Jesus in their utopias – their familiar religious ideas – as a messianic saviour. Leading ideas that had been developed in Qumran circles thus ultimately gained entrance into the Gospels. The addition of attributed but not authentic Jesus sayings to the process of forming Christian teaching and the Master's mythical biography led to the original Jesus's purely Buddhist views being increasingly pushed into the background. They did not vanish from the Gospels, but deeds and discourses, apocalyptic prophesies, mysterious proclamations of suffering to come, and claims of messiahship soon dominated to such an extent that the words of the original Jesus only constituted a small part, sunk into the background, and were only saved from being completely forgotten by the fact that their uncompromisingly moral stand shines out of the eclectic swamp of the Gospels. If we eliminate elements from the Qumran and baptismal traditions, the original Jesus reappears: the bodhisattva of universal love.

But who understood the wise man's Buddhist teachings? Probably not many people. Even his closest disciples often misunderstood him, and in the end almost all of them left him in the lurch. It is not therefore surprising that Jesus's original words were submerged, the collection of sayings was incorporated in alien contexts, and much was wrongly imputed to him. Viewed from that perspective, the story of Jesus's mission must be regarded as one of the most splendid failures in the whole of history.[71] As the transmitter of his message the original Jesus stands before us today as a loser. Not much of his message remained. His defeat was splendid because the work of Q people during the Jewish War and the propaganda of Paul (or those who hid themselves behind his name) and his epigones resulted in Jesus entering history as God and the founder of a religion that he never intended in such a form.

Indian Elements in Christianity: Monks, Churches and Redeemers

The Buddhist sources of Christianity not only become apparent through the authentic words of Jesus; they also stand out with great clarity in the development of monasticism. The monastic life always stood in opposition to the Church, and had to undergo numerous vehement confrontations with the official hierarchy over the course of history. While that official church became an administrative apparatus of spiritual and worldly power, monks attempted to live in accordance with the teachings of the original Jesus, dedicating themselves to the ideal of poverty, compassion and a mystical and meditative search. That opposition to the priesthood can be explained by the fact that the roots of Christian monasticism go back to Buddhism.

We can only make superficial mention of this theme since it is not a central aspect of our book, but it would merit extensive study. The monastic life developed during the first centuries of the new millennium in Egypt and Syria. The main precursors in Egypt were the Therapeutae who, as we have shown, were actually viewed by the old church as the first Christian monks. Their Buddhist form of monasticism must have impressed many serious seekers; even if they could only comprehend the strange teachings to a limited extent, they did see the profound seriousness with which the Buddhists turned away from the transient world of appearances, and in an inwardly directed existence devoted all their efforts to the way of redemption. That lived-out example was convincing. It influenced the Essenes and the people of Qumran. People infected by Gnostic thought also sought a comparably ascetic life in turning their backs on the world. The first imitators fell back on that extreme standpoint, which the Buddha, Jesus and the Therapeutae had already surmounted. Marcion (85–c. 260) was one of the most important champions of the ascetic ideal among Christians. His rigorous advocacy of asceticism and unconditional renunciation of sexual relations would have been of no significance for the history of monasticism and the development of the Catholic Church if he had not been so successful in attracting adherents.

Marcion was born at Sinope, where he quickly became a successful ship-owner and merchant. As a rich businessman he started to become closely interested in theological questions, advocated Gnostic ideas, and created his own holy text as a substitute for the Old Testament. As a Gnostic, he viewed the Jewish God of the Old Testament as merely the creator of the world (*Demiurge*), and since every creation was viewed as being bad that *Demiurge* was an evil god. He was opposed by the 'unknown' God, who had nothing to do with creation and belonged to the pure spirit's realm of light. That God of Love had out of his mercy sent Christ, clad in an illusory body, as redeemer of the world. Rome's theologians were not to be won over with such ideas, not even after Marcion had donated an enormous sum of money to the community of the Church of

Rome. Around 144 he was excommunicated and his teachings were branded as heretical. But he was not discouraged; he founded an anti-Catholic counter-church, which Justin in the mid-second century had to concede was spread across the whole earth. Even though Marcion was the arch-heretic for Catholics, they had to face up to his church, which in the second and third centuries had more power and influence than this.

In Asia Minor where many believers flocked to Marcion, his ascetic religion exerted a great influence on the Christian monastic communities that were coming into being. In the third century Syrian ascetics left the familiar world of social ties and traditional ways of life to live in the desert as anchorites (hermits). These lonely ascetics in fact looked back on a long-established tradition in that area. John the Baptist was such a desert ascetic, and so too was a certain Banus, of whom Flavius Josephus reports that he only ate fruits, clothed himself in leaves and constantly bathed in cold water so as to remain pure.

The first person to lead a company of like-minded people into the middle Egyptian desert was Antony in the second half of the third century. He thereby established the first colony of hermits, which gave birth to the idea of monastic existence in the Christian world-view. Numerous hermit colonies were then set up in Egypt – in Leontopolis in the Nile delta under Hierakas, in the Nitrian desert under Amun, in the Scetian desert under Makarios the Egyptian (c. 300–80), and in Upper Egypt under Palaimon.

Actual monasticism was established by Pachomios (c. 292–346), who came from the upper Thebaid in Egypt. Pachomios joined Palaimon's colony of ascetics and around 320 founded a monastery at Tabennisi near Dendera, whose rules were long binding on coenobitic communities. After that he endowed eight further monasteries and two nunneries. From Egypt, the country where Asoka's Buddhists first established monastic rules and ways of life, Christian monasticism spread to the other Mediterranean countries. Believers travelled from all over the place to the country of the Nile to gain ideas for their own cloistered communities. Pachomios's rules were to provide an important model for the monasteries set up by Basil, Cassian and Benedict of Nursia.

The rules of Basil (330–79), with their emphasis on asceticism, denial of self-will and unconditional obedience, shaped

Greek monasticism, while Cassian (*c.* 360–430) transmitted the ideals of Egyptian monasticism to Gaul and Benedict of Nursia (480–547) formulated Cassian's ideas in that stricter form that became authoritative for the entire later Western tradition. The obligation to reside in a monastery (*stabilitas loci*) was laid down there for the first time.

The practice of *meditatio* already played an important part for Pachomios's monks.[72] They spent their free time learning divinely inspired writings instead of devoting themselves to all-too-human trivialities. Here we clearly encounter the line of descent from the Jewish Christian tradition, influenced by the Therapeutae and the Essenes, to Egyptian and Syrian monasticism.[73] The practices of *vigiliae* (vigils), *meditatio* and *lectio continua* (continuous reading aloud) followed by these early monks had great similarities with the regulations written down in Qumran's *Community Rules* (1QS 6:6–8).

The original precursors of Christian monasticism, the Therapeutae in Egypt, were still totally dedicated to the Buddhist ideal of monkhood. They may not have had to alternate between times of wandering and periods of residence in a monastery, as was necessary in India where the rainy season made wandering difficult and dangerous, but they were certainly mobile. So there was no necessity for Jesus to live in a monastery-like community, and he could follow a wandering life in accordance with Buddhist traditions. The communal settlements in the simple huts of the Therapeutae, the Essenes, and later the people of Qumran (who lived in caves)[74] were the result of a need to withdraw from the society of unbelievers.

However, Buddhist elements are unmistakable even in the fifth-century monastic rules drawn up by Benedict of Nursia. Buddhist monastic practice is called *trishiksha* ('threefold schooling'). It consists of training in morality (*shila*), schooling of the spirit through meditation (*samadhi*), and the training of wisdom through the study of written texts (*prajña*). Benedictine practice comprises the three corresponding elements: *opus manum*, *opus dei*, and *lectio divina*.

Shila entails more than just a moral way of life; it involves the whole of everyday behaviour towards fellow humans, animals and inanimate objects. The reverence the Benedictine displays towards the world is expressed in the *opus manum*, and is most apparent in careful field-work and the cultivation of fruits. *Samadhi* signifies concentration, relating to attitudes in meditation and worship. The Benedictine parallel is the *opus dei* (God's work) – the daily programme of the liturgy and the mass. Just as the Buddhist rises early so as to satisfy the continuous alertness of the Buddha state, so too does the Benedictine in order to direct constant attention towards Christ's possible return at any time. *Prajña* means study of the *sutras* and *shastras*, which should lead to wisdom once that knowledge has been inwardly absorbed. The *lectio divina* similarly involves tranquil and attentive listening to the recitation of holy texts. In both cases these three disciplines are mutually complementary.

Eastern influences did not just enter into monasticism; they reached the totality of religious life in the West. That is why the Pauline church, which developed alongside monasticism, had to compete during the first centuries of its existence with many other religions, philosophies and mystical movements until the struggle was finally decided in favour of the Catholic Church by the Roman Emperor in the fourth century AD. The suppression of non-Pauline cults only succeeded, however, through Christians taking over a large number of rituals, festivities, temples, sacraments and mythologies. In the course of its early history Christianity thus integrated selective influences from apocalypticism, the mysteries, Gnosticism, Eastern ideas about religion and even concepts from philosophers ranging from Plato to Proclus.[75] Among the most striking borrowings from Buddhism we encounter the Roman Catholic ceremonial with tonsures, rosaries, incense, bells, the worship of relics, monasteries, distinctions between novices and ordained monks and nuns, confessions and celibacy. The incomprehensible term 'rosary' even derives from an incorrect translation of the Indian word *japamala* ('prayer beads'). *Japā* with a long *a* at the end means 'rose' while *japa* with a short *a* signifies 'prayer'. Even the number of beads in a rosary is the same as in the Buddhist equivalent.[76]

The art historian James Fergusson has demonstrated that various details in early Christian churches – such as the nave and side-aisles, the pillars, the semi-domed apse and the cross-shaped ground-plan – were all taken over from Buddhism. As an example he takes the rock temple of Karli (78 BC), whose arrangement and dimensions are very similar to the chancel of Norwich Cathedral and of the Abbaye aux Hommes at Caen. Where Christian churches have the altar, Buddhists have the *dagopa*, a canopy or little cupola sheltering the relics of an *arhat* in the same way as the relics of a saint are preserved in an altar.[77]

In its early years the Christian church's mightiest competitor was a movement that came to Egypt from the East two hundred years before Jesus, reached Rome around the turn of the millenium[78] and soon became the Roman Empire's most important religion – the cult of Mithras, a god from the pantheon of the Indians and Persians. Vedic India worshipped Mithras as a patron of human relationships (friendships, marriages, contracts), the preserver of heaven and earth and a combatant of lies and error. In Persia, where he was the messenger of Ahura Mazda, the god of light, he appeared in the sky at dawn and then crossed the firmament in a chariot drawn by four white horses. As mediator between the worlds of light and darkness, as humanity's ally in the struggle against evil, and as the soul's guide in its ascent to eternal life, Mithras was soon identified as the redeemer prophesied by Zarathustra until as the sun god, who at the end of time would appear as a human being, he finally became the supreme godhead and started his triumphal progress across the Greco-Roman world – at the same time as the Buddhist savour Maitreya in the East.

The parallels involved in are very interesting if we consider the etymology of the name Maitreya. The word means 'friendly, loving' and is derived by way of *maitri* ('friendship, empathy') from *mitra* ('friend, ally'), the Sanskrit form of Mithras. Used as a personal name, Maitreya even means 'Son of Mitra'.[79] Like Maitreya, Mithras is said to be waiting in heaven for the End of Time, when he will descend to earth. According to legend, the redeemer will be born of a virgin, a goddess, thrusting through an animal skin to the light of day. His birth will be watched by shepherds, who will worship the newly born. His earthly mission of vanquishing the world of evil culminates in his victorious struggle with the bull in the presence of two gods, Cautes and Cautopates, with whom Mithras forms a divine trinity. From the body of the dying bull grow corn (bread) and grapes (wine)[80] until Mithras finally mounts to heaven in the sun-chariot and is enthroned by the god of light as ruler of the world so as to return to earth, awaken the dead and pass judgement.

The legend does not specify whether this birth is a past or future event. For those who believed in Mithras, however, he was the 'coming one' whose arrival was celebrated every year on the night of 24–25 December, when the community had its most important festivity. Another big annual festival was held at the start of spring. The weekly divine service was held on Sunday, the day of the god. The most important cult activity was a meal of wine and bread – offered as consecrated wafers bearing the sign of a cross. The Mithras cult had six other sacraments which correspond completely with those of the Catholic Church – including a slap during confirmation. The spiritual leader of the hierarchically organized Mithras religion was entitled *Pater Patrum*, 'Father of Fathers' – like the Roman Pope whose Church of St Peter was built over a Mithraic cult site.

When at the beginning of the fourth century Emperor Constantine declared Catholic Christianity to be the state religion, he had no alternative but to take over the liturgy of the popular Mithraic church (whose stronghold was in southern Germany). Christmas was declared to be the feast of Jesus's birth, and from that time church services were on Sunday with rituals taken over from the Mithras cult. 'The mass is nothing other than the celebration of these [Mithraic] mysteries . . . The *Dominus vobiscum* is literally the utterance of acceptance: *chron-k-am, p-ak*.[81]

Ex Oriente Lux: The Way of Knowledge

The enforced confrontation with and integration of Eastern ideas into Christian self-comprehension was a result of the continuing advance of Iranian and Indian culture into the Hellenistic area. The early Jesus movements integrated this material so as to weave a suitable theological garment for the figure of Jesus.

The fertile soil from which these ideas sprouted is known as Gnosis. Gnosis grants us an insight into the workshop of some of the evangelists and into the ways in which the Buddhist material, which turns up in the New Testament independently of the discourses of the original Jesus, could gain access to the writings of Christianity.

Gnosis is difficult to define because it is a very complex and enormously interesting religious phenomenon. It came into being in the encounter with the syncretistic movements which during the Hellenistic period spread throughout the Middle East from Egypt by way of Syria to Asia Minor. From the East Gnostic systems were mainly shaped by Iranian dualism; from Babylon astrological symbolism was taken over; from India flowed a multitude of models including the idea of rebirth and of a god and redeemer coming down to earth; from Egypt, Syria, Greece and Rome came elements of magic and aspects of the mystery religions; and from Jewish concepts the mythological forms of the creation story were put together. This diverse collection of fragmentary ideas was mixed together to make a dish that began to ferment when exposed to the philosophical schools of neo-Platonism and neo-Pythagoreanism.

Gnosis means 'knowledge', and is in fact the exact Greek translation of the Sanskrit word *bodhi* from which 'Buddhism' derives. Just as the Buddhist based his religion on knowledge of his own state and from that experience attained knowledge of what was higher, so too the Gnostic strives to come closer to the Kingdom of God in similar fashion. Gnosis, like Buddhism, viewed itself as the opposite of a religion based on belief: knowledge (*gnosis*) against belief (*pistis*). The foundation of Gnostic thought involves insight into a far-reaching dualism: this world is a place of darkness, forgetting and evil. A Naassene psalm runs: 'Through ignorance the world is a place of terror and of mourning.' This world was formed by a 'wicked god' who corresponds to the creator god of the Old Testament. The act of creation itself involved breaking away from the 'good god', that 'Unknown God' who commands the spirit's realm of light and is in no way involved in desecration through creation. However, it is maintained that a spark of this good god is implanted in human beings as a seed. The common man loses himself amid the multiplicity of earthly desires – the Buddhist would say in thirst for life – and thus does not achieve insight. The Gnostic, however, recognizes his true spiritual home by turning towards the invisible light within himself. He or she turns away from all worldly things and directs all strivings towards the spiritual realm. It goes without saying that Buddhism, with its turning away from the world and its spiritual practices, constituted an incomparable model for Gnosis. Basilides's Gnostic system, for instance, is full of Buddhist influences.[82] Characteristically, one of the charges brought against Gnostics by such people as Hippolytus, the eager hunter of heretics, was that they were infiltrated by Indian ideas.

The significance of Gnostic thought can be measured by the fact that the oldest of the church fathers developed the structure of the 'true' Roman Catholic Church in the course of their struggle with Gnosticism and its condemnation as heresy. In that process Catholic theology ultimately also had to take on Gnostic ideas. This theology was mainly advanced in Alexandria, the centre of Gnostic teachings. It was there that such church fathers as Clement of Alexandria (*c.* 150–214) and Origen (*c.* 185–254) lived and worked. Clement was not just familiar with the spiritual world of India; he also knew the Buddha's teachings. What he had to say about the transmigration of souls, for instance, speaks for itself: 'We, however, exist before the laying of the world's foundations since we existed earlier because of our being in God, we the rational creatures of the Divine Logos through which we are ancient . . ..'[83] 'In so far as one birth follows another, it wants to lead us, gradually but continually, towards immortality.'[84]

Origen, Clement's pupil and successor, and the founder of systematic Christian theology, had a teacher called Ammonius Sakkas or Ammonius the Saker. It remains uncertain whether 'Saker' derives from the Scythians of Iran, who conquered northern India in the middle of the first century AD and regenerated Buddhism under their emperor Kanishka, or from 'Shakya', thus pointing towards a Buddhist monk.[85] At any rate Origen, one of the most important early Christian theologians, could have gained his knowledge of India directly from a Buddhist teacher.

Interestingly, in his studies of Gnosticism and Buddhism Origen went back to the ideas of Philo, who we come to know as a great reverer of Buddhist ideals. He therefore developed a Christian exposition of divine manifestation through the examination of the materialization of the Buddha as presented in Mahayana teachings. We here encounter instructive attempts at finding a theological theory for a Jesus who was supposed to be both human and God – a theory whose foundations were laid in the spiritual homeland of the original Jesus. The *Mahasanghika* had already taught that the historic Buddha was the incarnation of a supernatural, transcendent Buddha. From that the Mahayana philosophers developed the Buddhology of the *trikaya*, the teaching of the Buddha's three bodies. According to that teaching, out of the cosmic principle of the impersonal, featureless original Buddha (*adi* Buddha) emerges a personal

Buddha living in heavenly spheres (*dhyani* Buddha), who is then incarnated on earth as a human Buddha (*manushi* Buddha) in order to redeem living creatures with his teachings about the sufferings of existence. It is with the help of these three bodies that the Buddha is constantly present in three different states:

1. *dharmakaya*, the 'body of the Great Order', the absolute Buddha identical with transcendent truth, the primal ground of all being
2. *sambhogakaya*, the 'body of bliss', the body of a buddha in the heavenly Buddha paradise
3. *nirmanakaya*, the 'body of transformation', the earthly form taken by a Buddha

The *nirmanakaya* is the mortal earthly body with which a Buddha appears in the human world. It is conceived as an illusory body, which the Buddhist texts call a 'body of transformation'. This idea particularly attracted the Gnostic school of Docetism. According to that, Jesus only took on an illusory body on earth. They thought the crucifixion unimportant, since it merely involved that false body or someone other than the true Jesus. The teachings of Marcion, the old Church's great opponent, were also permeated by Docetic ideas. Such convictions are to be found, idiosyncratically, in many passages of Paul (Romans 8:3; Philippians 2:7; 2 Corinthians 5:16). That is grist to the mill for those who boldly speculate that Paul's epistles are largely Marcionite forgeries. The Buddhist moral prescriptions found in the Epistles are explicable on that basis. The Gnostic spirit of the age was like a sponge, soaking up all suitable religious convictions from the great river of oral tradition flowing from East to West. In Paul we read: 'Recompense for no man evil for evil' (Romans 12:17), and in the *Mahabharata* (3, 198:43): 'Do not respond to evil with evil.' And the Indian proclamation: 'Whatsoever someone sows, that will he harvest' (*Mahabharata* 12, 287:44) in the Epistle to the Galatians (6:7) becomes: 'Whatsoever a man soweth, that shall he also harvest.'

With the *sambhogakaya*, the 'body of bliss', a Buddha exists in a buddha paradise beyond earthly existence. It is the 'radiant body' of the 'Pure Land'. This idea turns up again in Gnostic circles where there is talk of a 'light-body' which is slipped over the soul, like a garment, on its return home to the realm of light. The most beautiful poetic expression of that idea

is found in the 'Song of the Pearl' in the Christian Acts of
Thomas. Even after the earthly illusory body has died, a Buddha can also bless a pious person with the *sambhogakaya* in a
supernatural world. In the Gospel of Thomas, which incorporated such influences in further developing Jesus's Q sayings,
we read: 'Jesus said: If someone asks you: "Where are you
from?" answer: "We came from the light, from where the light
originated by itself"' (Thomas 50).

Philo took over the idea that the *sambhogakaya* is only perceptible by bodhisattvas, and applied it to believing Jews before the
advent of the Kingdom: they were led by a divine manifestation only visible to those who were saved. Henri de Lubac, the
important Catholic theologian who drew attention to the links
between early Christian theology and Buddhism (for which the
Vatican imposed a ban on his writing), shows that Origen also
incorporated the Buddhist notion of the three bodies in his
system.[86] Origen made distinctions with regard to Jesus's
forms of manifestation between the 'divine form' (corresponding to the *dharmakaya*), the 'form of the servant' (*nirmanakaya*),
and that form which became visible to those present during the
transfiguration on the mountain (Matthew 16:1f; Mark 9:1),
which accords with the *sambhogakaya*. One of Origen's texts
(with considerable Buddhist borrowings) even ends with the
same words as those used in the *Lotus of Good Law* when the
Buddha concludes his discourse on skill in method (*Upaya*).[87]

Plotinus (205–70), the philosopher who furthered Gnostic
ideas and founded Neo-Platonism, was a contemporary of
Origen, and in his system of thought he deployed so many
Indian ideas that it almost seems like a variation of the Samkhya philosophy. Perhaps he visited India accompanying the
army of Gordian III, the Roman Emperor.

While apocryphal Christian literature was equally permeated
by Gnostic and Buddhist thinking, the Gospels could not completely escape such influences either. The first conflated Gospel
in Syrian or Greek, known as the Diatesseron (Greek: 'through
four'), was assembled by Tatian around 170. According to
Irenaeus, Tatian was the leader of the Encratics, who were
sectarian Christians who did not marry and preached the renunciation of meat. Paul attacked them for having fallen away
from belief (1 Timothy 4:1–4). Perhaps they represented a religious attitude closer to the beliefs of the original Jesus, and it
was rather Paul himself who had fallen away, since Hippolytus

maintains that the Encratics derived their doctrine from the Indian gymnosophists![88] Hippolytus knew what he was talking about, as he was one of the first church fathers to leave us a detailed account of brahmins and their beliefs.[89] The church authorities found a harmonization of the Gospels on such a basis unacceptable. Early in the fifth century all copies of the Diatesseron were destroyed, including the commentary by Ephraem. Only after alternative versions were no longer available did leading churchmen bring out their own version of the four New Testament Gospels, declaring them to be canonical – after the elimination of extensive passages thought to be undesirable.[90]

A large part of the Gospels was probably written in or around Alexandria where Gnosticism, infiltrated by Buddhism and Zoroastrianism, was strongly represented. Additional Buddhist material flowed through those channels, finding acceptance independently of the mission of the original Jesus.

One Gospel stands out for its borrowings from Buddhism – the Gospel according to John. We mentioned at the start of this book that J. Edgar Bruns, the American researcher, termed John's subject matter and theology 'Christian Buddhism'. Bruns's work shows that the author of that Gospel made use of a great deal of Buddhist material. The figure of the 'disciple whom Jesus loved' is one of its striking aspects. Nowhere in the other Gospels is there someone serving a similar function. For John the favourite disciple was a central figure, guaranteeing the authenticity of the Johannine interpretation of Jesus's teachings. The beloved disciple was the true witness, chosen by the Master to receive his special love (John 13:23). He alone kept faith until the bitter end (John 19:26). He saw (John 19:35) and wrote down what happened (John 21:24). In antiquity the author of this Gospel, identified as the disciple Jesus loved, enjoyed a high reputation as a comprehensive source and arbiter among evangelical literature. It was even asserted that John had translated Matthew from Hebrew to Greek. John was simply viewed as a guarantor of Jesus's words and thoughts.

The idea of the disciple was widespread in ancient times. Moses had Joshua, Elijah Elisha, Jeremiah Baruch, Socrates Plato, Peter Mark, Paul Luke, and later (and largely legendary) John had Prochorus. But none of these was the guarantor for their master's religious message. In the best cases they were faithful secretaries. There exists only one real parallel to the beloved disciple in religious writings, and that is Ananda, Gautama's favourite pupil, who was also the only guarantor that the Buddha's teaching was accurately handed on.[91]

When Ananda faithfully reproduced all of his master's discourses during the first council, he fulfilled the request Gautama made when still alive: 'O Ananda, remember my words, the words of the Buddha, and repeat them publicly at many meetings' (*Amitayur-Dhyana-Sutra* 1:7). Before all his disciples the Buddha said of Ananda: 'For a long time, Ananda, you have been very close to me through acts of love, friendship and goodness, which never change and exceed all measure' (*Maha-parinibbanasutta* II:145). It was also Ananda who remained at his master's side when Devadatta made his last fruitless attack on the Buddha's life after all the other followers had fled – just as John stood alone under the cross.

In the Gospel according to John we also re-encounter the concept of the Maitreya, the last earthly Buddha embodying all-embracing love. The Johannine Christ prophesies the coming of the Paraclete as a comforter, just as Gautama once said of the Maitreya: 'He will be the last one to attain the great spiritual light, and will be called the Buddha of brotherly love (Maitreya)'.[92] On the theological level, according to Bruns, Ananda corresponds exactly to the Paraclete, the Holy Spirit as comforter, who 'shall teach you all things, and bring all things to your remembrance, whatsoever I have said unto you' (John 14:26).

The idea of Maitreya being the Buddha of the world to come probably first arose at Taxila where the Buddha's prophecy that Maitreya would be incarnated has a long tradition. From there it reached the centres of Christianity by the usual routes. The extent to which Maitreya, the bodhisattva, shaped Christian thought is shown in artistic depictions. Maitreya is characteristically portrayed sitting with his feet resting on the ground (Plate 31). That pose, completely atypical within Buddhist iconography, demonstrates his readiness to rise, at the appropriate moment, from his seat in the Tushita heaven and come into the world. As a result of the far-reaching meeting of religions in the areas between Gandhara and Syria, that form of depiction was taken over for the triumphant Christ Pantocrator as found in the Byzantine art of late antiquity and the early Middle Ages. The correspondences range from the frontal depiction by way of the seated position with splayed knees to almost identical hand positions (*mudras*), which in the Christian context are enriched with a book – the Gospel (Plates 33 to 35).

The Buddha Jesus: Inter-Religious Encounters

When Catholicism was made into the state religion of the Roman Empire, the days of those religious groups which did not want to submit to the diktat of Emperor and Pope were numbered. In some remote areas in Europe a number of Gnostic groups managed to survive until the Middle Ages, but they too were finally brutally destroyed by the Roman Church. Other communities fled from Syria and Persia, where they were persecuted by the Zarathustrian church, to the East – to the shores of southern India and to the Tarim Basin, then a centre of Buddhism and today Sinkiang in China. Texts from the fourth century, found at the oasis of Turfan, show that the new arrivals obviously did not feel any great incompatibility with Buddhist teachings. In those places the Christian-Gnostic and Buddhist communities both lived in harmony and even used the same sacred buildings. A Buddhist Jesus-Messiah Sutra was created here; Buddha was depicted here as the Good Shepherd Jesus,[93] and it was from here that the Buddha finally became a saint of the Catholic Church through the legend of Barlaam and Joasaph.

John Damascenus (675–749 AD), a church scholar, reported for the first time on the strange story of an Indian king who was a confirmed opponent of Christians. Astrologers predicted that a son would be born to him who would accept the new teachings of Christianity. Fearful that this prophesy would be fulfilled, the father had this son brought up so that he was completely cut off from the outside world. The king granted the boy wealth and all the pleasures a profane life had to offer. One day a Christian hermit gained access to the court and taught the Prince the Christian message. The youngster had himself baptized, renounced all his worldly possessions, and followed his master into the wilderness. It is obvious that this story is a Christian reinterpretation of the childhood and youth of Buddha Shakyamuni as presented in the *Lalitavistara*.

Out of this intermingling of Christianity and Buddhism there developed in the area between Syria and India the idiosyncratic concept of the 'Buddha Jesus', which no longer seems odd to us. One is tempted to say that the circle has been closed. Jesus was once again brought back to that spiritual place where he originally set out to assist the suffering on their way towards redemption; not, however, by Christians – at least as comprehended by the Church which in the years since the third century had been taking shape – but by heretics who followed one of history's most interesting founders of religions: Mani.

Mani (216–276) grew up in the Jewish-Christian baptist community of the Elchasaites in Mesopotamia and saw himself as the Paraclete. The religion he brought into existence, which we today call Manichaeanism, attempted to unify, and to surpass, Christianity and Buddhism. As an 'apostle' of Jesus, Mani set off on extended missionary journeys. On one of those trips he reached the Indus valley and Baluchistan, where he converted the local ruler to his faith. In India he came across the concept of reincarnation and incorporated it into his edifice of ideas. His followers soon became a mighty company. Later the *Great Hymn to Mani* called him the 'Buddha Mani',[94] and in the *Book of the Coming of the Buddha* the return of Mani as Jesus is prophesied.

Among the blossoms produced through Buddhism and Christianity from the Gnostic-Manichaean system were Mani, addressed as 'Buddha Jesus', and the Realm of the Redeemed, conceived as a sphere of light where the 'King of Nirvana' reigned. This king was seen as the father of light, composed of the four Dharma bodies of purity, light, energy and wisdom. The Iranian concept of the 'fourfold god' was thus interpreted in Buddhist terms and integrated in a Christian context.

An important investigation into another Gospel whose implications have not been recognized was put forward by R.E. Osborne, a historian of religion. His profound analysis demonstrates that the Gospel according to Matthew was written at Edessa under the influence of Zoroastrian and Buddhist elements.[95] Edessa was an important market on the land route from Gandhara to Syria, and had close contacts with nearby Palmyra. Not only had Asoka's missionaries already been in Edessa; there were also important Jewish and Christian colonies there. Edessa constituted a typically heterogeneous Hellenistic society whose intellectuals flirted with the fashionable

Gnostic and Eastern religious systems. The many Buddhist echoes (apart from Q material) that Matthew worked into his Gospel probably came about because of that influence. One could even speculate that Matthew told of the wise men from the East and the flight to Egypt because he knew the underlying tradition from people in Edessa to whom the original Jesus's Buddhist origins were known. This tradition may also have been influenced by a comparable story from the Buddha's life, since we read in the *Lalitavistara* of how five foreign wise men (*rishis*) made a pilgrimage to the infant Buddha, worshipped him and extolled him as king and god.

Christian legend soon transformed the wise men into three kings, calling one of them Caspar, a name derived by way of the Armenian Gathaspar from Gundofarr (Greek Gondophares). Gondophares was the Indo-Parthian King of Gandhara who was visited by the apostle Thomas (see p. 75). Hence legend tells of a Buddhist king from India making a pilgrimage to the newly born Jesus.

Do we hear in Matthew's account and in the associated legends a faint echo of the arrival of Asoka's missionaries in the Near East, or can we comprehend them as an allegory for the advent of Buddha's teaching in Palestine? Is Matthew taking into account Edessan memories of the original Jesus when he suggests that a new Buddha had been born in the House of David? An old Turkish text indicates that the presents brought by the three wise men – gold, frankincense and myrrh – are symbols for the three jewels of Buddhism: Buddha, Dharma, sangha.[96]

The recurrence of trinities – three kings, three jewels – is one of those remarkable parallels between Christian and Buddhist thought: the threefold training (*trishiksha*), the three baskets (*tripitaka*) in which the written canon is assembled, and of course the most holy element in ancient Buddhism, the three jewels (*triratna*). Taking refuge in this holy trinity is at the centre of the Theravada cult up to the present day. Christian theology has the trinity of Father, Son and Holy Spirit, whereby the Son, the second person, is equated with the *Logos*, and the third person, the Holy Spirit, is at work in the community of the faithful. In Buddhism the community of the faithful is the *sangha*, while the Sanskrit word Dharma corresponds to the Greek *logos* – a central concept in Greek philosophy ever since Heraclitus. The introduction to the Gospel according to John –

'In the beginning was the Word [*Logos*] . . .' – could therefore be presented in a translation that sounds like a quotation from Buddhist writings: 'At the foundation [of all things] is the Dharma'. The Buddha's teaching of the three bodies (*trikaya*) also demonstrates many analogies with Christian theology regarding the trinity.[97] We are reminded here of Origen's important doctrine of threefold astuteness – literal, moral and mystical astuteness.

Out of the doctrine of the three bodies Mahayana developed a belief in a large number of Buddhas – 'unending in number like grains of sand in the Ganges' – which incarnate on earth time and again in human form. A transcendental *dhyani* Buddha is assigned to each world epoch (*kalpa*), and from that manifestation derive a heavenly *dhyani* bodhisattva and an earthly teaching Buddha. The heavenly Buddha in the present aeon is Amitabha ('the Immeasurable Splendour'). His human form is the historic Buddha Siddhartha Gautama, who is seen as the earthly son of Amitabha. His bodhisattva, his spiritual son, is Avalokiteshvara ('the Lord who looks down with compassion').

The worship of Amitabha illustrates how much original Buddhism has changed. The Buddha taught that redemption had to be achieved through one's own efforts. The new doctrine proclaims that redemption becomes quicker and easier through the assistance of a Buddha from beyond this world.

The first written record of the Amitabha legend is contained in the *Sukhavativyuha Sutra* from the first century AD. The text tells of how Amitabha reached Sukhavati, the 'Pure Land', a paradise situated in the West of the universe. In a previous aeon Amitabha (as the monk Dharmakara) is said to have taken a vow to become a Buddha himself once his good works made him capable of bringing into being a buddhaland without suffering. That 'happy land' (Sukhavati) should be a place where all those reborn would mature to Nirvana and achieve enlightenment. After innumerable incarnations as a boddhisattva, Dharmakara finally attained liberation. Since that time he, as Amitabha, has been the ruler of Sukhavati in his Buddha paradise where everyone is reborn who asks that of him before dying. In Sukhavati there are no desires, no suffering, no pain and no property. All its inhabitants live in lotus blossoms and devote themselves exclusively to reaching Nirvana. The Pure Land is, however, not yet Nirvana. Here each person on the threshold of the great redemption experiences his or her last incarnation. In Sukhavati he or she finally reaches Nirvana through Amitabha's instructions.

Bodhisattva Avalokiteshvara, the incarnation of compassion, assists Amitabha in that task. According to legend he has eleven heads and a thousand arms and eyes with whose help he, in his unlimited mercy, can save all those who turn to him. The thousand arms symbolize *upaya* – skill in exposition of the teachings. *Upaya* is the activity of the absolute in this world, most completely expressed in mercy. The compassionate bodhisattva can take on various forms in order to bring suffering humanity to salvation. He thus slips into the shape of other religions' gods and appears as, say, the Hindu god Shiva so that non-Buddhists also get to know the liberating truth of the Dharma. The German Buddhist scholar, Hans Wolfgang Schumann, simply calls him 'the primal image of help towards redemption whose most outstanding quality is compassion. By helping people to destroy greed, hatred and illusion in themselves, he makes liberation from the cycle of rebirths easier for them.'[98]

With the increasing idolization of the Mahayana Buddhas, Sukhavati soon became a substitute for Nirvana, since it is much more comprehensible for believers than an abstract dissolution into the nothingness of Nirvana. The perfect utopia of the Pure Land gave people an idea of what was meant by a life without desires and suffering. The Pure Land cult, which demanded nothing of its adherents except firm belief in the Sukhavati paradise and the all-embracing mercy of Amitabha, became a mass religion in the third century and extended from India to eastern Asia. Here from the seventh century Amitabha[99] and Avalokiteshvara became popular gods – a development equivalent to the gradual idolization of the human being Jesus within Christianity. In China and Japan Avalokiteshvara is worshipped in a female form as the compassionate goddess Kuan-yin or Kwannon. In Japan followers of Amitabha finally did away with monasticism since the illuminated Buddha's unlimited compassion was after all available to everyone. In Tibet the lama viewed as the earthly incarnation of the bodhisattva became under the title Dalai Lama his country's secular and spiritual leader. In the seventeenth century the Dalai Lama of the time gave his master the honorary title of Panchen Lama, and declared him to be a reincarnation of Amitabha himself.

When the Jesuits came to Japan in the sixteenth century to convert heathens to Christianity, they were horrified to discover that other Christians had obviously been there already and won over the majority of the population. They thought that the Amitabha cult with its doctrine of 'only belief counts' was a variant of Protestantism they so hated. Perhaps the Jesuits were not completely wrong. The analogies between the Christian trinity and the Buddhist doctrine of *triratna* and *trikaya* point to the two philosophies having a shared origin. Just as the heavenly Amitabha appeared on earth as Gautama to save suffering humanity, so too did God have his son Jesus born as the Redeemer. Amitabha's heavenly son who works among humanity as does the Holy Ghost in Christianity, is Avalokiteshvara. In fact the *Sukhavativyuha-Sutra* extols the compassionate bodhisattva as Amitabha's 'Mighty Buddha Son'. People have also wondered whether the small lotus blossoms on the hands and feet – where traditional iconography depicts Avalokiteshvara as Padmapani ('Lotus Hand') – might represent the crucifixion scars of Jesus, who was elevated to the status of bodhisattva after his death in India (Plate 36). The magical phrase the faithful employ for calling on Avalokiteshvara is the celebrated '*Om mani padme hum*'. According to Schumann, *om* and *hum* characterize 'the beginning and the end, symbolizing totality, just like alpha and omega, the first and last letters of the Greek alphabet, in Christianity'.[100]

Epilogue

The Church, which can no longer simply shut itself off from the arguments concerning Buddhist elements in Christianity, has recently been attempting to appear understanding, extending one hand and simultaneously warding off with the other. In a book on Buddha and Christ recently published by the Vatican university, it is said: 'The truths preached by the Buddha are Providence's preparation for the pronouncement. They involve enlightenment within human beings, and require the revelation of Christ for their fulfilment.'[101] The author hastens to add that Jesus Christ commanded his followers to baptize all peoples in the name of the Father, the Son and the Holy Ghost, which turns his journey to the realm of Buddhism into a concealed missionary project.

Buddhists, however, do not seem to feel in any way incomplete without the 'revelation of Christ'. That is not surprising since the 'revelation of Christ' is nothing but the 'revelation of Paul'. However, the revelation of Jesus is already Buddhist.

Buddhist sources in Christianity can no longer be denied, even though they have been crushed under the weight of theologically prescribed reworkings. What is more important though is the fact that this Buddhist material was originally disseminated by Jesus himself. That discovery adds a completely new dimension to the discussion of Buddhism in the New Testament: the true teachings of Jesus, his Buddhist teachings.

Christianity – and even the Christian message – is completely different from what Jesus taught. The deeper scholars penetrated into the Q sayings, the clearer became the differences between what the original Jesus tried to communicate and what his adherents' propaganda made out of it. When the layers of supplemented and invented events, sayings, parables and aphorisms in Jesus's life and teachings fell away, one thing became obvious: the unembellished teachings of the man Jesus was the Buddhist Dharma.

Jesus proclaimed the Dharma when he returned to Palestine from the Therapeutae and fell among the Jordan sectarians. He refused to be baptized, and opposed both orthodoxy and sectarian extremes. Like the Buddha he rejected strict asceticism and taught the middle way, the way of unlimited reverence and awareness, of composure in the face of real dangers and fantastic apocalyptic scenarios. As answer to hatred and violence he advocated love and serenity, and he countered the fear of existence by speaking of freedom from anxiety and trust in spiritual leadership. He encouraged his followers to be modest at all times, never to show off and elevate themselves, and he instructed them to give away all their property, to break ties with family and friends, and to proclaim the truth of the Dharma as homeless wandering mendicant monks.

His first followers were enthusiastic. Jesus was so uncharacteristic, so different from the prophets who everywhere wanted to gain converts for their cause. These disciples followed Jesus in fierce trust. But they did not understand. They were too caught up in their messianic hopes. They excessively wanted their master to be the Messiah, they excessively wanted to participate in his redemption. The brief time that Jesus remained was not sufficient to establish the Dharma in his listeners' awareness. Jesus had to vanish after the ill-fated crucifixion, when friends saved his life. Palestine had become a place where his existence was at risk. His followers unsuccessfully sought to disseminate the basic principles of his teachings in towns and villages. They were chased away and ridiculed. Hardly anyone gave them serious attention. They soon realised what a terrible vacuum had been left. For the Jesus movement it was fortunate that confrontation with the Romans led to open conflict. In that 'end of the world' atmosphere, with people's utopian yearning for a kingdom of the just, Jesus could be incorporated in an apocalyptic current. He was taken over by sectarian fanaticism, which turned the Buddhist master into the Messiah and Redeemer.

The many myths about Jesus came into being alongside the development of a multiplicity of Jesus communities, which based themselves on different texts and traditions, representing diverse social classes and language groups, and flourishing in contrasting social environments. The evolution of those social groups was similar to the development of other societies. Research into the development of Q brought to light the diversity of myths upheld in Jesus groupings until they cohered to form what we have learned to call Christianity. The congregations of Christ devised only some of the mythologies surrounding Jesus. They mainly took shape on the basis of the epistles attributed to Paul which centre around the *kerygma*, the proclaimed word of God: Jesus's death on the cross as a sacrifice for others and his resurrection to cosmic authority. That mythological presentation became the foundation of the Christian church, and the Christian generally views and judges Jesus against that background. This Jesus myth arose in northern Syria, and it succeeded in almost completely eliminating memories of the original Jesus, replacing them by the cult of Christ.

It is Jesus's real concerns, which were threatened with eternal oblivion, that can celebrate genuine 'resurrection' at present. Now we can recognize that in Jesus the same heart beats, touched by the same love for humanity and determined by the same feeling of compassion for all beings, as in the life and teachings of Gautama Buddha, the Awakened One.

Notes

Part I INDIA AND THE WEST

1 Grimm (1917).
2 Nestle (1947), p. 89.
3 Overbeck (1919).
4 Quoted from *Der Spiegel* No. 14, 1966.
5 Scholars do not agree about the Buddha's exact dates. See Schumann (1988), pp. 22ff.
6 Mahavagga, I, 3, 4.
7 Samyuttanikaya, LVI, 11.
8 d'Eypernon (1946), p. 95.
9 Mylius (1988), p. 184.
10 Müller (1870). See also Walhouse (1879).
11 Holwell, *Original principles of the ancient Brahmans*. London, 1779.
12 Schmidt (1828).
13 See Schomerus (1932), p. 104.
14 Seydel (1882), ibid (1897).
15 Van Eysinga (1909), Garbe (1914), Schomerus (1932).
16 Edmunds (1902).
17 Jaspers (1949), p. 33.
18 Jaspers (1949), p. 22.
19 Radhakrishnan (1952), p. 134.
20 Gadd (1932), p. 191.
21 Scheil (1925), pp. 55f.
22 Wheeler (1968); Dales (1968).
23 See Delougaz (1952); Pigott (1948).
24 See Lemberg-Karlovsky (1972).
25 Lemberg-Karlovsky (1970).
26 See Oppenheim (1954).
27 Golzio (1983), p. 11.
28 In fact a pre-form of the classic Sanskrit that developed later.
29 Vendryes (1948).
30 Rahn (1933).
31 Heine-Geldern (1938); De Hevesy (1938).
32 See Schomerus (1932), p. 65.
33 *Illustrated Weekly of India*, Bombay 7.11.1992 and 27.2.1993; *Sunday*, Calcutta 12.9.1993; *Amrit Bazar Patrika*, Calcutta 7.1.1994.
34 Dulaurier, (1907) p. 132.

35 See 2 Chr 9,10; 1 Kings 9:26–28 and 10:11; on Gold from Ophir see Isaiah 13:12.

36 1 Kings 10:22.

37 See on David: 2 Sam 8:13; 1 Kings 11:15ff.; on Solomon: 1 Kings 11:14–22.

38 Kennedy (1898), pp. 254f. See also Caldwell (1913), pp. 88f.

39 Lassen, Vol. II (1849), p. 589.

40 Bibby (1969).

41 Kennedy (1898), p. 249.

42 Bühler (1896).

43 Eschatology is the doctrine of the Last Things and the End of Time.

44 Winston (1966), p. 190.

45 See Strabo, xvi, c.3, par. 3, Lassen, Vol. II (1849), pp. 601–2.

46 See Boyce (1982), p. 199.

47 See Lassen, Vol. II (1849), pp. 581–4 and pp. 593–6.

48 See Beal (1882), p. 143.

49 Garbe (1894) pp. 85–105.

50 Schroeder (1884).

51 Schroeder (1884), p. 22.

52 Clements, *Strom.* 1, 304, B.

53 Schroeder (1884), p. 37.

54 Pythagoras's Theorem says that in a right-angled triangle the square of the hypotenuse equals the sum of the square of the other two sides.

55 Cantor (1880), pp. 540ff.

56 Schroeder (1994), p. 92.

57 See Reese (1914).

58 It is uncertain whether Alexander thus heard about the Ganges or merely about the Satledsh, which was only a few days' march away.

59 Bhandarkar (1955), pp. 27f.

60 See Raychaudhuri (1953), pp. 299f.

61 See Lassen, Vol. II (1849), p. 713.

62 Quoted from Snelling (1991), p. 106.

63 See Bhandarkar (1955), p. 43 f.

64 Droysen, Vol. III (1836), p. 353.

65 Filliozat (1949).

66 McCrindle (1879).

67 Strabo, *Geograph.* II, v, 12.

68 The aloe that Nicodemus and Joseph of Arimathea used for healing Jesus also came from Socotra.

69 A spice often mentioned in *Periplus* of which there must have been many varieties.

70 Jouveau-Dubreil (1941), pp. 26–9.

71 Pattabiramin (1946), p. 5f.
72 *India Abroad*, 12 May 1989, p. 22.
73 Kersten (1994).

Part II   JESUS – THE BUDDHIST

1 Amore (1985), first published in 1978.
2 Thundy (1993).
3 Lillie (1887), p. 181.
4 Thundy (1993), p. 270.
5 Thundy (1993), pp. 79–128.
6 See Seydel (1882), p. 106.
7 In the Proto-Gospel of James Jesus is born in a cave.
8 Thundy (1993), pp. 108f.
9 See Mus (1935), pp. 475ff.
10 See Campbell (1953).
11 See Klatt (1982), p. 106.
12 Garbe (1914), pp. 49f.
13 See Thundy (1993), p. 116.
14 See Gruber (1982); Gruber (1985).
15 Otto Flink (*Schopenhauers Seelenwanderungslehre und ihre Quellen*) mentions the following passages: Mt. 14:1–2; 1 Cor 15:35–55; Mt. 17:9–13; Lk 9:7.8.19; Mk. 9:9–13; Mt. 19:28–30; John 3:3 and 8. He believes the idea of karma is expressed in John 9:2–3; Mt. 19:30; Mt. 5:4.26; Mk. 10:29–31; Lk. 18:29–30.
16 Schwarz and Schwarz (1993).
17 Schwarz (1990), p. 46.
18 Philonenko (1972).
19 See Amore (1985), p. 66.
20 *Dighanikaya*, II, 87; *Majjhimanikaya* 6.
21 Garbe (1914), p. 60.
22 See Klatt (1982).
23 Klatt (1982), p. 149.
24 Klatt (1982), p. 192.
25 See the whole of section 25 of the *Udanavarga* 25:1–25.
26 Haas (1922).
27 A lepton was the smallest Greek coin.
28 Schwarz and Schwarz (1993), p. 380.
29 Beal (1882), pp. 172f.
30 Haas (1922), p. 78.
31 Mack (1987), pp. 322f.
32 Seydel (1897), p. 36.
33 Pagels (1981), p. 17.
34 Conze (1953).

35 Kloppenborg (1987); Kloppenborg (1988).

36 Kloppenborg (1987), p. 37.

37 Kloppenborg (1987), p. 87. See also Funk and Hoover (1992).

38 Hengel (1981), pp. 57–60.

39 Riesner (1988), Riesner (1991).

40 Judge (1960/61).

41 Mack (1993).

42 Borg (1984), pp. 234–7.

43 Crossan (1973); Breech (n.d.).

44 We put Jesus's 'death' in inverted commas here since we have shown elsewhere that Jesus did not die on the cross. See Kersten and Gruber (1994); Kersten (1994).

45 See Mack (1993), p. 4.

46 Mack (1993), p. 5.

47 Kloppenborg (1988); Mack (1993), pp. 73–80.

48 Gerhardsson (1991).

49 Schwarz (1991); Riesner (1988), pp. 392–404.

50 Carlston (1980).

51 Amore (1985).

52 Schwarz (1991).

53 Streeter (1932), p. 41.

54 Schwarz (1986).

55 Origen, *De oratione* 2:2; 14:1. Clement, *Strom.* 1:24.

56 Schwarz (1990), p. 65.

57 Flavius Josephus, *Jewish War, II*, 13:4.

58 Flavius Josephus, *Jewish War, II*, 13:5.

59 Flavius Josephus, *Jewish Antiquity*, 20:5, 1.

60 See Robertson (1965), p. 80.

61 Festinger, Schachter, Riecken (1956).

62 See Piper (1989), p. 191.

63 This example comes from Aune (1991), p. 224, who cites Fontenrose (1966), pp. 15–19.

64 Mack (1993), p. 183.

65 Amore (1985), p. 163.

66 See Kloppenborg (1987), p. 246f.

67 *Nidanakatha* VII, 114; *Mahavagga*, I, 11–13.

68 Greek *diabolos* is the persecutor/accuser.

69 See Klatt (1982), p. 141.

70 See Rhys Davids (1880), pp. 83f.

71 Tertullian, *Adv. Marc.* IV, 7–8.

72 Epiphanes, *Haer.* 30, 13. The Ebionites were a Jewish Christian sect.

73 See Lidzbarski (1915), pp. 103–9.

74 Van Eysinga (1904), p. 29.

Part III THE WAY OF THE ORIGINAL JESUS

1 Schlumberger et al. (1958).
2 Humbach (1969).
3 Beneviste et al. (1966).
4 Dupont-Sommer (1970).
5 Davary and Humbach (1974).
6 Dupont-Sommer (1980), p. 709.
7 Bhandarkar (1913).
8 Rhys Davids (1898).
9 Flinders Petrie (1908).
10 Flinders Petrie (1898), p. 54. See also Salomon (1991), p. 736.
11 Oratio XXXII, 40. See *Dio Chrysostom* III. H. Lamar Crosby, trans. Loeb Classical Library, London, 1940, pp. 209–11.
12 Oratio XXXV, 23.
13 Mansel (1875), pp. 31f.
14 See the book by Montfaucon (1709).
15 Dupont-Sommer (1980), p. 710.
16 Smith (1894), pp. 302f.
17 Beal (1882), p. 165.
18 Thundy (1993), p. 245.
19 Thomas Gotterbarm drew our attention to that idea.
20 Schmidt (1828), p. 17.
21 Philo, *De vit. con.* 2.
22 Lévi (1893), p. 47.
23 Kennedy (1898), p. 277.
24 See Zürcher (1959).
25 Müller-Hess (1913).
26 Klimkeit (1985).
27 See Dayal (1931), pp. 18f.
28 Mukherjee (1988), p. 89.
29 See Kersten (1993).
30 *Zeitschrift für wissenschaftliche Theologie*, X, 1867, p. 110.
31 Bunsen (1880).
32 Beal (1882), p. 163.
33 Modi (1933), p. 211.
34 Vermes (1960), p. 441.
35 Vermes (1960), p. 443.
36 Beal (1882), p. 165.
37 Koch (1980), pp. 8f.
38 Baigent and Leigh (1991).
39 Talmon (1993).
40 Beckwith (1980).
41 See Winston (1966).

42 Dexinger (1993), p. 46.
43 Dupont-Sommer (1980).
44 Dupont-Sommer (1980), p. 714.
45 Dupont-Sommer (1960).
46 See Roth (1965).
47 *Chirbet* means 'ruin'.
48 See Brock (1977).
49 See Kersten and Gruber (1994), pp. 55f.
50 Bonani et al. (1991).
51 Golb (1993).
52 A *pescher* (plur. *pescharim*) is a text that comments on Old Testament writings, relating them to the present day. The idea is that
   the Bible is a treasury of prophetic truth, which when rightly interpreted provides answers and guidelines for any contemporary
   situation.
53 See Dexinger (1993).
54 Garcia-Martinez and Van der Woude (1990).
55 Schiffman (1990), pp. 64–73.
56 Golb (1993), p. 97.
57 See Bardtke (1956/57).
58 Bar-Adon (1977).
59 Charlesworth (1980).
60 See 1QpHab XI:5–8. For the Wicked Priest that was a normal
   weekday because the people of Qumran used a different calendar
   from other Jews.
61 See Hjerl-Hansen (1959).
62 See Jackson (1898).
63 See Schneider (1967).
64 Teicher (1951).
65 Hjerl-Hansen (1959), p. 495.
66 Maier and Schubert (1992), p. 211.
67 1QGenAp 20,21f,29; see also Flusser (1957).
68 Porphyrios, *De vita Pythagorae*, § 25, Jamblichos, *De vita Pythagor-
   ica*, VIII § 36.
69 Augstein (1972), p. 362.
70 See Roth (1965).
71 As in Carl Amery (1990, pp. 108ff), inventor in his oppressive
   novel *Das Geheimnis der Krypta* of the science of Spaghistics, a
   systematics of losers and defeats.
72 Riesner (1991), pp. 205f.
73 See Daumas (1967).
74 Fluctuations in temperature were more bearable in the caves. The
   Chirbet Qumran site was only the community centre.
75 Meyer (1991), p. 438.
76 Garbe (1914), pp. 123f.

77 Quoted from Lillie (1887), p. 206.
78 According to Plutarch in 67 BC by way of Kilikien, Paul's home.
79 Monier-Williams (1889).
80 In the legend's Iranian-Indian homeland this was the sacred plant *Soma* (Old Persian *Haoma*). See Schütze (1972), p. 139.
81 Volney (1860), pp. 185f.
82 Kennedy (1902); see also Lubac (1937), p. 337.
83 Clement *Admonition* I, 6.
84 Clement *Strom.* I V 160, 3.
85 See Seeberg (1941).
86 Lubac (1937), p. 341. See also Benz (1951); Przyluski (1937).
87 Origen, *Contra Celsum*. See Lubac (1937), pp. 348f.
88 Hippolytus, *Refut.* VIII.
89 Hippolytus, *Refut.* I, 21.
90 Kee (1970), p. 250.
91 Bruns (1973/74), pp. 236f.
92 See Kern (1963).
93 See Klimkeit (1983).
94 See Band and Gabain (1930).
95 Osborne (1973/74).
96 See Röhrborn (1971). See also Klimkeit (1980).
97 See also Falk (1937).
98 Schumann (1990), p. 187.
99 *Amituo-fo* (China) and *Amida* (Japan).
100 Schumann (1980), p. 190.
101 Nguyen (1987), p. 129.

Bibliography

Amery, C.: *Das Geheimnis der Krypta*. Munich, Leipzig, 1990.

Amore, R. C.: *Two Masters, One Message*. Kuala Lumpur, 1985.

Aufhauser, J. B.: *Buddha und Jesus in ihren Paralleltexten*. Bonn, 1926.

Augstein, R.: *Jesus Menschensohn*. Munich, 1972.

Aune, D. E.: 'Oral Tradition and the Aphorisms of Jesus'. In: Wansbrough, H. (Ed.): *Jesus and the Oral Gospel Tradition*. Sheffield, 1991, pp. 211–65.

Baigent, M. and Leigh, R.: *The Dead Sea Scrolls Deception*. Munich, 1991.

Band, W. and A. von Gabain: Turkische Turfantexte III. *Sitzungsberichte der Preuss. Akad. der Wiss.* Berlin 1930, pp. 183–211.

Bar-Adon, P.: 'Another Settlement of the Judean Desert Sect at Ein el-Ghuweir on the Shores of the Dead Sea'. *Bulletin of the American Schools of Oriental Research*, 277, 1977, pp. 1–25.

Bardtke, H.: 'Das Ich des Meisters in den Hodajoth von Qumran'. *Wissenschaftliche Zeitschrift der Universität* Leipzig, 6, 1956/57, pp. 93–104.

Baur, F. C.: 'Apollonius von Tyana und Christus'. *Tübinger Zeitschrift für Theologie*, 1832.

Beal, S.: *Abstract of Four Lectures in Buddhist Literature in China*. London, 1882.

Beckwith, R. T.: 'The Significance of the Calendar for Interpreting Essene Chronology and Eschatology'. *Revue de Qumran*, 38, 1980, pp. 167–202.

Beneviste, E., A. Dupont-Sommer, C. Caillat: 'Une inscription indo-araméenne d'Asoka provenant de Kandahar (Afghanistan). *Journal Asiatique*, 1966, pp. 437–470.

Benz, E.: 'Indische Einflüsse auf die frühchristliche Theologie'. *Akademie der Wissenschaften und der Literatur*, Mainz: Geistes- und Sozialwiss. Klasse, Jg. 1951, Nr. 3. Wiesbaden, 1951.

Bergh van Eysinga, G. A. van den: *Indische Einflüsse auf evangelische Erzählunngen*. Göttingen, 1904.

Berve, H.: *Gestaltende Kräfte der Antike*. Munich, 1949.

Bhandarkar, D. R.: *Ashoka*. Calcutta, University of Calcutta, 1955.

—: 'Sambodhi in Ashoka's Rock Edict VIII'. *Indian Antiquary*, XLII, 1913, pp. 159–60.

Bibby, G.: *Looking for Dilmun*. New York, 1969.

Bonani, G., M. Broshi, I. Carmi, S. Ivy, J. Strugnell, W. Wölfli: 'Radiocarbon Dating of the Dead Sea Scrolls'. *Atiqot*, 20, 1991, pp. 27–32.

Borg, M. J.: *Conflict, Holiness and Politics in the Teachings of Jesus.* New York, 1984.

Boyce, M.: *A History of Zoroastrianism.* Vol. II. Leiden, Cologne, 1982.

Brech, J.: *The Silence of Jesus.* Toronto, n.d.

Brock S. P.: 'Some Syriac Accounts of the Jewish Sects'. In: Fischer, R. H. (Ed.), *A Tribute to Arthur Vööbus: Studies in Early Christian Literature and its Environments, Primarily in the Syrian East.* Chicago, 1977, pp. 265–76.

Broshi, M.: Qumran – die archäologische Erforschung. In: J. B. Bauer, J. Fink and H. D. Galter (Ed.): *Qumran. Ein Symposion.* Graz, 1993, pp. 63–72.

Brown, W. N.: *The Indian and Christian Miracles of Walking on the Water.* Chicago, London, 1928.

Bruns, J. E.: Ananda: 'The Fourth Evangelist's model for "the disciple whom Jesus loved"?' *Studies in Religion,* 1973/74, pp. 263–43.

—: *The Christian Buddhism of St John.* New York, 1971.

Bühler, G.: *Indische Paläographie. Grundriß der Indo-Arischen Philologie und Altertumskunde.* Strasbourg, 1896.

Bunsen E. de: *The Angel-Messiah of Buddhists, Essenes, and Christians.* London, 1880.

Caldwell, R.: *A Comparative Grammar of the Dravidian or South-Indian Family of Languages.* London, 1913.

Campbell, J.: *The Hero with a Thousand Faces.* New York, 1949.

Cantor, M.: *Vorlesungen über Geschichte der Mathematik.* Vol. I, Leipzig, 1880.

Carlston, C.: 'Proverbs, Maxims and the Historical Jesus.' *Journal of Biblical Literature* 99, 1980, pp. 87–105.

Charlesworth, J. H.: 'The Origin and Subsequent History of the Authors of the Dead Sea Scrolls: Four Transitional Phases Among the Qumran Essenes'. *Revue de Qumran,* 10, 1980, pp. 213–23.

Charlesworth, M. P.: *Roman Trade with India: A Resurvey.* Studies in Roman Economic and Social History in Honor of Allan Chester Johnson. Princeton, 1951.

Chattopadhyaya, N.: *Indische Essays.* Zürich, 1883.

Conze, E.: *Der Buddhismus. Wesen und Entwicklung.* Stuttgart, 1953.

Crossan, J. D.: *In Parables.* New York, 1973.

d'Eypernon, T.: *Les paradoxes du bouddhisme.* Paris, 1946.

Dales, G.: 'Of Dice and Men'. *Journal of the American Oriental Society,* 88, 1968, pp. 14–22.

Dani, A. H.: *The Historic City of Taxila.* Paris, 1986.

Daumas, F.: La solitude des Thérapeutes et les antécédents égyptiens du monachisme chrétien'. In: *Philon d'Alexandrie.* Paris, 1967, pp. 347–59.

Davary, I. G. D. and Humbach, H.: 'Eine weitere aramäoiranische Inschrift der Periode des Asoka aus Afghanistan'. *Akademie der*

Wissenschaften und Literatur, Mainz. Abhandlungen der geistes- und sozialwissenschaftlichen Klasse, 1974, pp. 3–16.

Dayal, H.: *The Bodhisattva Ideal in Buddhist Sanskrit Literature*. London, 1931.

De Hevesy, G.: 'The Easter Island and the Indus Valley Scripts'. *Anthropos*, 1938.

Delougaz, P.: *Pottery from the Diyala Region*. University of Chicago Oriental Institute Publication, Vol. LXIII, Chicago, 1952.

Dexinger, F.: '45 Jahre Qumran – ein kritischer Forschungsbericht'. In: J. B. Bauer, J. Fink and H. D. Galter (Eds.), *Qumran. Ein Symposion*. Graz, 1993, pp. 29–62.

Driver, G. R.: *The Judean Scrolls*. Oxford, 1965.

Droysen, J. G.: *Geschichte des Hellenismus*, 1836. (Republished Basel 1952–4).

Dulaurier, E.: 'Etudes sur la relation des voyages faits par les Arabes et les Persans dans l'Inde et à la Chine'. *Journal Asiatique*, IVme série, 1907, p. 132.

Dupont-Sommer, A.: *Die essenischen Schriften vom Toten Meer*. Tübingen 1960.

—: Essénisme et Bouddhisme', *Académie des Inscriptions et Belles-Lettres*. Comptes rendus des séances de l'année 1980, Nov-Dec., pp. 698–715.

—: 'Une nouvelle inscription araméenne d'Asoka trouvée dans la vallée du Laghman (Afghanistan). *Comptes rendus des séances de l'Académie des Inscriptions et Belles Lettres*. 1970. pp. 158–73.

Edmunds, A. J.: *Buddhist and Christian Gospels now first compared*. Philadelphia, 1902.

Faber, G.: *Buddhistische und neutestamentliche Erzählungen. Das Problem ihrer gegenseitigen Beeinflussung*. Leipzig, 1913.

Falk, M.: 'Origine dell'equazione ellenistica logos-anthropos'. *Studi e materiali di storia delle religioni*, XIII, 1937, pp. 166–214.

Festinger, L., Schachter, S., Riecken, H. W.: *When Prophecy Fails*. Minneapolis, 1956.

Fillozat, J.: *La doctrine brahmanique à Rome au IIIe siècle*. Paris, 1956.

—: 'Les échanges de l'Inde et de l'empire romain aux premiers siècles de l'ère chrétienne'. *Revue Historique*, 201, 1949, pp. 1–29.

Flavius Josephus: *Der jüdische Krieg*. Munich, 1987 (4th ed.) Trans. Hermann Endrös.

Flinders Petrie, W. M.: *Dendereh*. London, 1898.

—: 'The Peoples of the Persian Empire'. *Man*, 71, 1908.

Flusser, D.: 'Healing Through the Laying on of Hands in a Dead Sea Scroll'. *Israel Exploration Journal*, 7, 1957, 107.

Fontenrose, J.: *The Ritual Theory of Myth*. Berkeley, 1966.

Funk, R. W. and Hoover, R. W.: *Five Gospels, One Jesus. What did Jesus Really Say?* Sonoma, 1992.

Gadd, C. J.: 'Seals of Ancient Indian Style Found at Ur'. *Proceedings of the British Academy*. London, 1932, pp. 191–210.

Garbe, R.: *Die Samkhya-Philosophie*. Leipzig, 1894.

—: *Indien und das Christentum. Eine Untersuchung der religionsgeschichtlichen Zusammenhänge*. Tübingen, 1914.

Garcia-Martinez, F. and A. S. Van der Woude: 'A "Groningen" Hypothesis of Qumran Origins and Early History'. *Revue de Qumran*, 14, 1990, pp. 521–41.

Gerhardsson, B.: 'Illuminating the Kingdom: Narrative Meshalim in the Synoptic Gospels'. In: Wansbrough, H. (Ed.), *Jesus and the Oral Gospel Tradition*. Sheffield, 1991, pp. 266–309.

Goddard, D.: *Was Jesus Influenced by Buddhism?* Thetford, 1927.

Golb, N., Die Entdeckungen in der Wüste Judäas – neue Erklärungsversuche'. In: J. B. Bauer, J. Fink and H. D. Galter (Eds.), *Qumran. Ein Symposion*. Graz, 1993.

Golzio, K.-H.: *Der Tempel im alten Mesopotamien und seine Parallelen in Indien*. Leiden, 1983.

Grim, E.: *Die Ethik Jesu*. Leipzig, 1917.

Gruber, E. R.: *Tranceformation. Schamanismus und die Auflösung der Ordnung*. Basel, 1982.

—: *Traum, Trance und Tod*. Freiburg, 1985.

Haas, H.: 'Das Scherflein der Witwe' und seine Entsprechung im Tripitaka*. Leipzig, 1922.

Heine-Geldern, R. v.: 'Die Osterinselschrift'. *Anthropos*, 1938.

Hengel, M.: *The Charismatic Leader and His Followers*. New York, 1981.

Hilgenfeld, A.: *Die jüdische Apokalyptik*. Leipzig, 1857.

—: *Ketzergeschichte des Urchristenthums*. Leipzig, 1884.

Hjerl-Hansen, B.: 'Did Christ Know the Qumran Sect?' *Revue de Qumran*, 1, 1959, pp. 495–508.

Humbach, H.: 'Die aramäische Inschrift von Taxila'. *Akademie der Wissenschaften und Literatur, Mainz. Abhandlungen der geistes- und sozialwissenschaftlichen Klasse*, 1969, pp. 3–13.

Jackson, A. V. W.: *Zoroaster*. New York, 1898.

Jacolliot, L.: *La Bible dans l'Inde*. Paris, 1869.

Jaspers, K.: *Vom Ursprung und Ziel der Geschichte*. Munich, 1949.

Jouveau-Dubreil: *Dupleix ou l'Inde conquise*. Pondicherry, 1941.

Judge, E. A.: 'The Early Christians as a Scholastic Community'. *Journal of Religious History*, 1, 1960/61 pp. 4–15, pp. 57–65.

Kee, H. C.: *Jesus in History: An Approach to the Study of the Gospels*. New York, 1970.

Keenan, J. P.: *The Meaning of Christ: A Mahayana Theology*. Maryknoll, 1989.

Kelber, W. H.: *Written Gospel*. Philadelphia. 1983.

Kennedy, J.: 'Buddhist Gnosticism, the System of Basilides'. *Journal of the Royal Asiatic Society*, 1902, pp. 377–415.

—: The Early Commerce of Babylon with India, 700–300 B. C.' *Journal of the Royal Asiatic Society*. 1898, pp. 241–88.

Kern, H. (Trans.): *The Saddharm-Pundarika: or the Lotus of the True Law*. New York, 1963.

Kersten, H. and Gruber, E. R.: *The Jesus Conspiracy*. Shaftesbury, 1994. (2nd ed.).

Kersten, H.: *Jesus Lived in India*. Shaftesbury, 1994.

Klatt, N.: *Literarkritische Beiträge zum Problem christlich-buddhistischer Parallelen*. Cologne, 1982.

Klimkeit, H.-J.: 'Der Buddha Henoch: Qumran und Turfan'. *Zeitschrift für Religions- und Geistesgeschichte*, 32, 1980, pp. 367–75.

Klimkeit, H.-J.: Gottes- und Selbsterfahrung in der gnostisch-buddhistischen Religionsbegegnung Zentralasiens'. *Zeitschrift für Religions- und Geistesgeschichte*, 35, 1983, pp. 236–47.

—: 'Christian-Buddhist Encounter in Medieval Central Asia'. In: G. W. Houston (Ed.), *The Cross and the Lotus. Christianity and Buddhism in Dialogue*. Delhi, 1985, pp. 9–24.

Kloppenborg, J.: *The Formation of Q: Trajectories in Ancient Wisdom Collections*. Philadelphia, 1987.

Kloppenborg, J.: *Q Parallels: Synopsis, Critical Notes, and Concordance*. Sonoma, 1988.

Koch, K.: *Das Buch Daniel*. Darmstadt, 1980.

—: 'Buddhistisches in den apokryphen Evangelien'. In *Gurupujakaumudi*. Festgabe zum 50jährigen Doktorjubiläum Albrecht Webers. Leipzig, 1896.

Lassen, C.: *Indische Altertumskunde*. Bonn, Vol. I, 1847, Vol. II, 1849, Vol. III, 1858.

Lemberg-Karlovsky, C. C.: 'Trade Mechanisms in Indus-Mesopotamian Interrelations'. *Journal of the American Oriental Society*, 92, 1972, pp. 222–9.

—: 'Excavations at Tepe Yahya 1967–1969. *American School of Prehistoric Research Bulletin 27*, 1970.

Lévi, S.: 'Le bouddhisme et les Grecs'. *Revue de l'Histoire des Religions*, XXIII, Paris 1893, pp. 36–49.

Lidzbarski, M.: *Das Johannesbuch der Mandäer*. Giessen, 1915.

Lillie, A.: *Buddhism in Christendom or Jesus, the Essene*. (1887), Reprint New Delhi, 1984.

Lubac, H. de: 'Textes alexandrins et bouddhiques'. *Recherches de science religieuse*, 27, 1937, pp. 336–51.

Mack, B. L.: *The Myth of Innocence*. Philadelphia, 1987.

—: *The Lost Gospel. The Book of Q and Christian Origins*. Shaftesbury, 1993.

Maier, J. & Schubert, K.: *Die Qumran-Essener. Texte der Schriftrollen und Lebensbild*. Munich, 1991.

Mansel, H. L.: *Gnostic Heresies*. London, 1875.

McCrindle, J. W.: 'Anonymi [Arriani ut fertur] periplus maris ery-thraei'. *The Indian Antiquary*, 8, 1879, pp. 107–51.

McGregor Ross, H.: *The Gospel of Thomas*. Shaftesbury, 1991.

Meyer, B. F.: 'Some Consequences of Birger Gerhardsson's Account of the Origins of the Gospel Tradition?' In: Wansbrough, H. (Ed.), *Jesus and the Oral Gospel Tradition*. Sheffield, 1991, pp. 424–40.

Modi, J. J.: *Who were the Persian Magi, who Influenced the Jewish Sect of the Essenes?* Festschrift Moritz Winternitz, Leipzig 1933, pp. 208–11.

Monier-Williams, M.: *Sanskrit-English Dictionary*. Oxford, 1889. (Repr. Delhi, 1976).

Montfaucon, B. de: *Libre de Philon de la vie contemplative . . . avec observations, où l'on fait voir que les Thérapeutes dont il parle étoient Chrestiens*. Paris, 1709.

Mookerji, R. K.: *Indian Shipping: A History of the Sea-Borne Trade and Maritime Activity of the Indians from the Earliest Times*. Bombay, 1957 (2nd Ed.).

Mukherjee, B. N.: *The Rise and Fall of the Kushana Empire*. Calcutta, 1988.

Müller, M.: 'On the Migration of Fables'. *The Contemporary Review*. XIV, 1870, pp. 572–98.

Mus, P.: *Barabudur. Esquisse d'une histoire de bouddhisme fondée sur la critique archéologique des textes*. Hanoi, 1935.

Mylius, K.: *Geschichte der altindischen Literatur*. Berne, Munich, 1988.

Nestle, W.: *Krisis des Christentums*. Stuttgart, 1947.

Neumann, K. E.: *Die letzten Tage Gotamo Buddhos. Aus dem grossen Verhör über die Erlöschung Mahaparinibbanasuttam*. Munich, 1922.

Nguyen, Van-Töt P.: *Le Bouddha et le Christ. Parallèles et ressemblances dans la littérature canonique et apocryphe chrétienne*. Rome, 1987.

Oppenheim, A.L.: 'The Seafaring Merchants of Ur'. *Journal of the American Oriental Society*, 74, 1954, pp. 6–17.

Osborne, R. E.: 'The provenance of Matthew's gospel'. *Studies in Religion* 3, 1973/74, pp. 220–35.

Overbeck, F.: *Christentum und Kultur*. Basel, 1919.

Pagels, E.: *Versuchung durch Erkenntnis – Die gnostischen Evangelien*. Frankfurt, 1981.

Pattabiramin, M. P. Z.: *Les fouilles d'Arikamedu (Podouke)*. Pondicherry, Paris, 1946.

Philonenko, M.: 'Un écho de la prédication d'Ashoka dans l'épître de Jacques'. *Ex Orbe Religionum*, Studia Geo Widengren Oblata I. Leiden, 1972, pp. 254–65.

Pigott, S.: Notes on Certain Metal Pins and a Macehead in the Harap-pan Culture'. *Ancient India*, I, 1948, pp. 26–40.

Piper, R. A.: *Wisdom in the Q-Tradition: The Aphoristic Teaching of Jesus*. Cambridge, 1989.

Plange, Th. J.: *Christus – ein Inder?* Stuttgart, 1906 (4th Ed.).

Przyluski, M. J.: 'Les Trois hypostases dans l'Inde et à Alexandrie'. *Mélanges Franz Cumont*, 1937, pp. 925–33.

Radhakrishnan, S.: *Die Gemeinschaft des Geistes*. Darmstadt, Genf, 1952.

Rahn, O.: *Kreuzzug gegen den Gral*. Freiburg, 1933.

Raychaudhuri, H.: *Political History of Ancient India*. Calcutta, 1953.

Reese, W.: *Die griechischen Nachrichten über Indien bis zum Feldzuge Alexanders des Grossen*. Leipzig, 1914.

Rhys Davids, T. W.: *Buddhist Birth Stories*. Vol. 1, London, 1880.

—: 'The Sambodhi in Ashoka's Eighth Edict'. *The Journal of the Royal Asiatic Society*. 1898, pp. 619–22.

Rienecker, F.: *Das Evangelium des Markus*. Wuppertal, 1971.

Riesner, R.: *Jesus als Lehrer, eine Untersuchung zum Ursprung der Evangelien-Überlieferung*. Tübingen, 1988 (3rd Ed.).

Riesner, R.: 'Jesus as Preacher and Teacher'. In: Wansbrough, H. (Ed.), *Jesus and the Oral Gospel Tradition*. Sheffield, 1991, pp. 185–210.

Robertson, A.: *Die Ursprünge des Christentums*. Stuttgart, 1965.

Robinson, J. M. and Koester, H. (Ed.): *Trajectories Through Early Christianity*. Philadelphia, 1971.

Röhrborn, K. (Ed.): *Eine uigurische Totenmesse. Berliner Turfantexte II*. Berlin, 1971.

Roth, C.: *Geschichte der Juden*. Stuttgart, (n.d.)

—: *The Dead Sea Scrolls. A New Historical Approach*. Oxford, 1965.

Rückstuhl, E.: *Die Chronologie der Passion und des Letzten Mahles Jesu*. Einsiedeln, 1963.

Rudolph, K.: *Die Gnosis*. Göttingen, 1990 (3rd Ed.).

Salomon, R.: 'Epigraphic Remains of Indian Traders in Egypt'. *Journal of the American Oriental Society* 111, 1991, pp. 731–6.

Scheil, V. E.: 'Un nouveau sceau hindou pseudo-sumerien'. *Revue d'Assyrologie et d'Archeologie Orientale*, 22, 1925, pp. 55f.

Schiffman, L.: 'The New Halakhic Letter (4QMMT) and the Origins of the Dead Sea Sect'. *Biblical Archeologist*, 53, 1990, pp. 64–73.

Schlumberger, D.: L. Robert, A. Dupont-Sommer, E. Beneviste, 'Une bilingue gréco-araméenne d'Asoka'. *Journal Asiatique*, 1958, pp. 1–48.

Schmidt, I. J.: *Über die Verwandtschaft der Gnostisch-Theosophischen Lehren mit den Religionssystemen des Orients, vorzüglich dem Buddhismus*. Leipzig, 1828.

Schneider, C.: *Kulturgeschichte des Hellenismus*. Vol. 1. Munich, 1967, pp. 898–901.

Schomerus, H. W.: *Ist die Bibel von Indien abhängig?* Munich, 1932.

Schroeder, L. v.: *Pythagoras und die Inder. Eine Untersuchung über die Herkunft und Abstammung der Pythagoreischen Lehren*. Leipzig, 1884.

Schumann, H. W.: *Der historische Buddha. Leben und Lehre des Gotama*. Cologne, 1986.

—: *Mahayana-Buddhismus. Die zweite Drehung des Dharma-Rades.* Munich, 1990.

Schütze, A.: *Mithras: Mysterien und Urchristentum.* Stuttgart, 1972.

Schwarz, G.: *Jesus 'der Menschensohn'. Aramaistische Untersuchungen zu den synoptschen Menschensohnworten Jesu.* Stuttgart, 1986.

—: *Wenn die Worte nicht stimmen. Dreissig Evangelientexte wiederhergestellt.* Munich, 1990.

—: *Fehler in der Bibel?* Munich, 1990.

—: *Die Bergpredigt – eine Fälschung?* Munich, 1991.

Schwarz, G. and Schwarz, J.: *Das Jesus-Evangelium.* Munich, 1993.

Sedlar, J. W.: *India and the Greek World.* Totowa, 1980.

Seeberg, E.: 'Ammonios Sakas'. *Zeitschrift für Kirchengeschichte,* LX, 1941.

Seydel, R.: *Das Evangelium von Jesu in seinen Verhältnissen zu Buddha-Sage und Buddha-Lehre.* Leipzig, 1882.

—: *Die Buddha-Legende und das Leben Jesu nach den Evangelien. Emeute Prüfung ihres gegenseitigen Verhältnisses.* Leipzig, 1884.

Smith, R.: *The Religion of the Semites.* London, 1894.

Snelling, J.: *Buddhismus.* Munich, 1991.

Sternbach, L.: 'Indian Wisdom and its Spread Beyond India'. *Journal of the American Oriental Society,* 92, 1972, pp. 97–123.

Streeter, B. H.: *The Buddha and the Christ.* London, 1932.

Talmon, S.: 'Die Bedeutung der Qumranfunde für die jüdische Religionsgeschichte'. In: J. B. Bauer, J. Fink und H. D. Galter (Ed.), *Qumran. Ein Symposion.* Graz, 1993, pp. 117–72.

Teicher, J. L.: 'Die Schriftrollen vom Toten Meer – Dokumente der jüdisch christlichen Sekte der Ebioniten. *Zeitschrift für Religionswissenschaft und Geistesgeschichte,* 1951, pp. 153–209.

Thundy, Z. P.: *Buddha and Christ.* Leiden, 1993.

Vendryes, J.: *La religion des Celtes.* Paris, 1948.

Vermes, G.: 'The Etymology of "Essenes"'. *Revue de Qumran,* 2, 1960, pp. 427–44.

Volney, C. F. von: *Die Ruinen oder Betrachungen über die Revolutionen der Reiche.* Braunschweig, 1860 (11th Ed.)

Walhouse, M. J.: 'The Westward Spread of Some Indian Metaphors and Myths'. *The Indian Antiquary,* 8, 1879, pp. 162–4.

Wetering, J. van de: *Der leere Spiegel,* Munich, 1987.

Wheeler, M.: *The Indus Civilization.* Cambridge, 1968.

Winston, D.: 'The Iranian Component in the Bible, Apocrypha, and Qumran: A Review of the Evidence'. *History of Religions,* 1966, pp. 183–216.

Zürcher, E.: *The Buddhist Conquest of China.* Leiden, 1959.

Glossary

Where Indian terms are not designated Skt (Sanskrit) or Pali, they are the same in both languages.

Abhidhammapitaka (Pali): 'Basket of Dogma [Metaphysics]'. Third part of the Tripitaka with discourses on the foundations of philosophy.

Adi Budda (Skt): Universal 'primary buddha', personified *dharmakaya* body, eternal, transcendental principle of buddhahood.

Amitabha (Skt): Buddha of infinite light, heavenly *dhyani* buddha embodied on earth in the historical Gautama Buddha.

Anchorites (Greek): Third-century Christian ascetics who lived as desert hermits in Syria and Egypt.

Apocrypha (Greek): Religious writings not incorporated in the canon of sacred texts.

Arhat (Skt): Pali *arahant*. Holy man who attained enlightenment during his lifetime and thus entered directly upon Nirvana after death. The highest ideal in the Hinayana school (Theravada) as opposed to the Mahayana bodisattva.

Aryans (Indo-Aryans, Indo-Iranians): Indo-Germanic equestrian nomads who brought the vedic religion to India.

Atman (Skt): Pali *atta*. In Hinduism (Vedanta): the eternal self – part of the world-soul Brahman, like a drop of water in the ocean.

Avalokiteshvara (Skt): 'The compassionate Lord on high'. Guardian of the *Sukhavati* paradise and embodiment of compassion. Popular bodhisattva divinity in east Asian Buddhism.

Avesta (Old Persian): Collection of holy Parsee writings.

Bhikkhu (Pali): Skt *bhikshu* (female *bhikkuni/bhikshuni*). 'Mendicant'. Term for Buddhist monks.

Bodhi: 'Enlightenment, awakening'.

Bodhisattva (Skt): 'Enlightened being'. Enlightened holy man who renounces entering Nirvana out of compassion for suffering beings. The highest ideal in Mahayana (as opposed to the *arhat* in Hinayana).

Brahma (Skt): Hindu god. Creator of the world in the *Trimurti* trinity of Brahma-Vishnu-Shiva.

Brahman (Skt): In Hinduism (Vedanta) the absolute, the world-soul, the eternal primal ground of all being.

Brahmanas (Skt): Appendices to the Vedas, produced around 1000 BC. Prescriptions regarding sacrifices and rituals as well as theologi-

260

cal discourses with metaphysical speculation initiating the period of brahminism.

Brahmins: Highest class in Aryan caste society – priests and scholars.

Brahminism: Stage within the development of orthodox Hinduism (the schools of thought recognizing the revelations of the Veda and dominance of the brahmin priestly caste) where the many vedic gods were ordered in a philosophical system and the brahminic principle was developed, from around 600 BC to 400 AD.

Dhammapada (Pali): Skt *dharmapada*. A chapter from the *Suttapitaka Khuddakanikaya*. Elaborate literary collection of the Buddha's sayings in verse. Viewed as a kind of 'gospel' of early Buddhism and the Theravada.

Coromandel coast: Southern part of India's east coast in what is today the state of Tamil Nadu (Madras).

Dharma (Skt): Pali *dhamma*. The eternal, universal law which holds the cosmos together, manifesting itself among human beings as the moral law and religious teaching. In Buddhism a synonym for the Buddha's teaching.

Dharmachakra (Skt): Pali *dhammacakka*. The eight-spoked Wheel of Teaching. Symbol of the Buddha's teaching.

Dharmakaya (Skt): The Buddha's universal body containing the cosmos and all personal buddhas. See *Trikaya, Adi-Buddha*.

Dhyani bodhisattva (Skt): A bodhisattva who emerges as a spiritual reflection of a *dhyani Buddha*, e.g. Avalokiteshvara out of Amitabha.

Dhyani Buddha (Skt): The five heavenly buddhas of the Sambhogakaya body, to be experienced in meditation.

Diaspora (Greek): Jewish minorities outside Palestine, spread all over the world.

Dighanikaya: Part of the *Suttapitaka*.

Dipavasmsa: *Island History* – a chronicle of the island of Sri Lanka compiled around 400 AD. The *Mahavamsa* (*Great Chronicle*) – written by Mahanama, a monk, around 500 AD – is based on that.

Dravidians: Pre-Aryan population of India with a highly developed culture, forced southwards or declared to be low caste by the newcomers. Dravidian languages: Tamil, Telugu, Kannara, Malayalam, etc.

Eschatology: Teachings about the Last Things and the world's ultimate fate.

Gandhari Dharmapada: See *Dhammapada*.

Gymnosophists (Greek): Term used in the Greco-Roman world for Indian wise men.

Hinayana: The 'Little Vehicle'. The conservative school of early Buddhism that rejected the innovations of Mahayana. The only Hinayana school still in existence is Theravada.

Hitopadesa: A later working of the Pañcatantra collection of stories.

Indra (Skt): Early Indian god – the most important in the Vedic pantheon.

Jainism: Early Indian religion of redemption, organized as a monastic order by Parshva (eighth century BC) and Mahavira, a contemporary of the Buddha. Developed out of the anti-brahminic order of *sramanas* ascetics.

Jatakas: Early Buddhist collection of legends about the Buddha's previous incarnations.

Karma (Skt): Pali *kamma*. The law of the consequences of actions whereby every activity (including thinking and feeling) determines one's personal fate and lives to come.

Khuddakanikaya: Part of the *Suttapitaka* containing the *Dhammapada*.

Krishna (Skt): Popular god in modern Hinduism, particularly associated with *bhakti* devotional mysticism. A central figure in the *Bhagavad Gita*.

Kshatriya (Skt): Pali *khattiya*. After brahmins the second highest Aryan caste – aristocracy and warriors.

Lalitavistara (Skt): Legendary narrative of the Buddha's life, describing the Awakened One as a redeemer descended from heaven.

Lotus of the Good Law (*Lotus Sutra*): Skt *Saddharmapundarika*. First-century Mahayana sutra describing the historic Buddha as an eternal god and universal bringer of salvation.

Mahabharata (Skt): Indian heroic epic and Hinduism's most important religious document. Consists of eighteen books including the celebrated *Bhagavad Gita*.

Mahaparinibbanasutta (Pali): Part of the *Suttapitaka* (*Dighanikaya*), which describes the Buddha's last days and his death.

Mahaparinirvana (Skt): Pali *Mahaparinibbana*. Death as access to Nirvana.

Mahasanghika (Skt): 'Great Community'. Buddhist school. Precursor of Mahayana.

Mahavagga: First book of the Vinayapitaka, containing rules and commandments for the monastic life.

Mahavamsa: See *Dipavamasa*.

Mahayana: 'Great Vehicle', designating those Buddhist schools striving for the liberation of all suffering beings – as compared with Hinayana ('Little Vehicle') where teaching focuses on redemption of individuals.

Maitreya (Skt): Pali *metteyya*. The 'Loving One', the expected future Buddha.

Majjhimanikaya: Part of the *Suttapitaka*.

Malabar coast: Southern section of India's west coast in today's state of Kerala.

Manushi Buddha (Skt): 'Human Buddha' in the *nirmanakaya* body.

Mithras (Greek): Skt *Mitra*. God from the Indo-Iranian pantheon, who in the Roman Empire became the redeemer figure in a widespread syncretic cult existing alongside Christianity.

Mudra (Skt): Symbolic hand and finger positions of mystical significance.

Nidanakatha (Pali): Assumed to be the oldest coherent biography of the Buddha, written down in Pali during the fifth century AD by Buddhaghosa, a monk.

Nirmanakaya (Skt): Human body of an earthly buddha (e.g. Gautama). See *Trikaya*, *Manushi* Buddha.

Nirvana (Skt): Pali *Nibbana*. 'Dissolution, extinction'. Enlightenment in terms of complete elimination of greed, hatred and blindness.

Pali: Middle Indian dialect (Prakrit) in which the Theravada version of the *Tripitaka* is written.

Pali Canon: The Sri Lankan Pali version of the *Tripitaka* used by Theravada Buddhists.

Pancasila: The five (*panca*) fundamental ethical rules of Buddhism, which also apply to the laity, involving not killing, stealing, behaving unchastely, lying and taking intoxicating drinks.

Pañcatantra (Skt): Indian collection of stories from the first centuries AD, which had spread all over the known world by the eleventh century with more than 200 versions in over fifty languages.

Patimokkha (Pali): Skt *Pratimoksha*. Part of the *Vinayapitaka*. Monastic statues with over 200 prescriptions which monks recite every fortnight to confess their sins.

Prajna (Skt): Pali *panna*. 'Wisdom, knowledge, reason'. Study of the Buddha's teachings (see *Trishiksha*). In Mahayana active compassion as a way to wisdom and enlightenment.

Prakrit: Middle Indian languages derived from Sanskrit used for Theravada (Pali Canon) and Jain texts.

Puranas (Skt): Collection of mythical, philosophical and (pseudo-) historical narratives.

Pythagoreans: Adherents of the Indian-influenced teachings of Pythagoras, the sixth-century BC Greek philosopher.

Ramayana (Skt): After the Mahabharata India's second great national epic.

Rig-Veda (Skt): Oldest surviving Indian religious text and first part of the Veda. Hymns to the gods.

Samadhi (Skt): Contemplation, meditation, spiritual absorption.

Sambhogakaya (Skt): Body of a transcendent, heavenly *dhyani* buddha. Emanation from the universal *dharmakaya*.

Samkhya (Skt): 'Enumeration'. Pre-Buddhist Indian philosophy, presenting a cosmic opposition between spirit (*purusha*) and matter (*prakriti*).

Samsara (Skt): The suffering, transient world. The Wheel of Rebirths.

Sangha: The Buddhist monastic community. Triratna.

Sanskrit: Old Indian. The high language of ancient India, related to Latin and Greek. Still vital today as a scholarly language.

Shakyamuni: 'The wise man [from the lineage] of the Shakya'. Epithet of the historical Buddha.

Shiva (Skt): Hindu god, part of the *Trimurti* trinity – Brahma, Vishnu, Shiva.

Shulvasutra: Old Indian manual on setting up a sacrificial site.

Sibyl: Lat. Sibylla. In antiquity the name of a woman oracle.

Sila: Moral conduct as part of the Buddhist way towards enlightenment. See also *Trishiksha*.

Sramana (Skt): Pali *samana*. Wandering ascetic. Member of an anti-brahminic monastic order or representative of the ancient Indian tradition of asceticism.

Sthavira, Sthaviravada (Skt): See *Thera*, Theravada.

Stupa (Skt): Pali *thupa*. A dome (deriving from the ancient Indian cult of mountains) over relics of the Buddha or another saint. Symbolizing the universe in the oldest Buddhist sacred buildings.

Sukhavati (Skt): 'Pure Land'. The paradise established by the *amitabha* Buddha.

Sutra (Skt): Pali *sutta*. Buddhism: the teaching discourses attributed to the Buddha. Hinduism: religious and philosophical teaching works.

Suttapitaka (Pali): Skt *Sutrapitaka*. 'Basket of Teaching Discourses'. Second part of the *Tripitaka* with explanations of the Buddha's basic teachings. Consists of five main sections (*nikaya*).

Swastika (Skt): Ancient Indian symbol.

Syncretism: A conflation of various religious influences.

Synoptics, synoptic Gospels: The Gospels of Matthew, Mark and Luke.

Talmud (Hebrew): 'Teaching'. Collection of laws and religious traditions in post-biblical Jewry.

Tamils: Dravidian people in southern India whose language is among the world's oldest written forms.

Tanha (Pali): Skt *trishna*. 'Thirst'. Greed, desire, covetousness.

Thera (Pali): Skt *sthavira*. Older, experienced monk. Ranking in Theravada Buddhism.

Theravada (Pali): Skt *Sthaviravada*. 'The Teaching of the Elders'. Conservative – and sole surviving – school in the Hinayana 'Little Vehicle'. Spread throughout south-east Asia.

Torah (Hebrew): 'Teaching'. The five books of Moses – the Mosaic Law.

Trikaya (Skt): 'The threefold body'. Mahayana teaching on the Buddha's three bodies: *dharmakaya* (universal body), *sambhogakaya* (transcendental body) and *nirmanakaya* (earthly body).

Triptaka (Skt): Pali *Tipitaka*. 'Threefold Basket'. The tri-partite written canon (*Sutta-, Vinaya-, Abhidhammapitaka*) of classical Buddhism.

Triratna (Skt): The 'three jewels' – Buddha, Dharma, *sangha*.

Trishiksha (Skt): Buddhist monks' 'triple discipline' – *sila, samadhi, prajna*.

Upanishads (Skt): Post-vedic (*c*. 1000–500 BC) mystical and religious treatises whose speculation about *karma*, reincarnation and the unity of *brahman* and *atman* supplanted the previous ideology and established classic Indian philosophy.

Upasakas: Lay followers of Buddhism.

Varuna (Skt): Ancient Indian (vedic) god. Corresponds to Ahura Mazda in Persia and Zeus in Greece.

Veda (Skt): 'Knowledge'. The totality of the oldest Indian holy writings. Consists of the *Rig-Veda* (hymns to the gods), *Sama-Veda* (songs), *Yajur-Veda* (sacrificial sayings) and *Atharva-Veda* (magical songs).

Vedanta (Skt): Original designation for the Upanishads. In the Middle Ages became a collective term for a group of metaphysical systems including Shankara's eighth-century AD monistic *advaita* ('non-dualism').

Vihara: Buddhist monastery.

Vinayapitaka: 'Basket of Monastic Discipline'. First part of the *Tripitaka* with rules of the Buddhist order.

Vishnu (Skt): Hindu god, part of the *Trimurti* trinity – Brahma, Vishnu, Shiva. Monotheistic god in Vaishnava Hinduism where he is worshipped in his earthly manifestations as Rama and Krishna.

Yajur-Veda (Skt): Part of the Veda.

Yoga (Skt): Mystical way of practice originating in pre-Aryan times. Breathing practices, bodily postures, control of the senses and meditation in order to achieve liberation of the soul.

Zarathustra (Zoroaster): Persian prophet, founder of Parseeism. Probably at work around 600 BC in eastern Iran.

Zen (Japan.): From the Skt *dhyana* (Chinese: *ch'an*). 'Meditation'. Mahayana practice centring on meditation.

Index of Places

Index of People

Abraham 90, 180
Achaimenes 48
Aelius Gallus 71
Agatharchides of Knidos 46
Ajatashatru 16
Akbar 28
Alexander of Corinth 67
Alexander of Epirus 67
Alexander Polyhistor 54, 73
Alexander the Great 46, 53, 58–62
Ambhi 59
Ammonios Sakkas 232
Amore, R. C. 80, 123, 150
Amun 226
Ananda 16, 17, 21, 102, 236
Anaxagoras 51
Anaximander 52
Anthony of Egypt 226
Antigonus Gonatas 67, 201
Antiochos 61, 67, 199–200
Arada Kalama 13
Aristobulus 25, 201
Aristophanes 51
Aristotle 25, 57
Artaxerxes II 57–8
Asita 85–7, 157
Asoka 21, 63, 64–7, 69, 94, 171–3, 197
Athenaios 57
Augstein, R. 223
Augustus 73, 74

Bar-Kochba 210
Basil 226–7
Basilides 231
Baudhayana 46
Bauer, B. 3
Becket, Thomas à 148
Benedict of Nursia 226–7
Berosus 48
Bhandarkar, D. R. 174
Bhartrihari 25
Bimbisara 16, 19
Bindusara 61, 63, 187
Buddhaghosa 171
Bultmann, R. 9

Cantor, M. 56
Caracalla 74
Cassian 226–7
Celsus 6
Champollion, J. F. 172
Chandaka 12
Chandragupta 61, 62, 158
Claudius 5
Clement 54, 139, 232
Confucius 30
Constantine 230
Conze, E. 113
Curitus Rufus 58
Cyrus 49–50

Darius I 50, 57, 58
Darius II 50
David 43
Deimachos 187
Demetrius 72
Democritus 51, 53
Deutero-Isaiah 49, 204
Devadatta 16–17, 130
Dion Chrysostomos 177
Dionysios 67, 187
Dogen-zenji 140
Droysen, J. G. 68
Dupont-Sommer, A. 205–6
Dutthagamani 178

Elijah 91
Empedocles 51, 53, 223
Enoch 180, 183, 200

Flavius Josephus 5, 143–4, 195–6, 202, 207
Flavius Arrianos 58

Garbe, R. 29, 52, 86, 98
Garcia-Martinez, F. 211
Genghis Khan 28
Gordian 234
Grimm, E. 9
Gundofarr 239

Index of Subjects